The Heritage of Music

By Katherine B. Shippen

The Heritage
of Music

by Katherine B. Shippen & Anca Seidlova

Illustrated by Otto van Eersel

New York · The Viking Press

Library of Congress catalog card number: 63-18368

Fifth Printing July 1967

780.9 1. Composers
2. Music—History

PRINTED IN THE U.S.A. BY VAIL-BALLOU PRESS, INC.

"Music is the most worthy, courteous, pleasant and joyous and lovely of all knowledge; it makes a man gentlemanly in his demeanor . . . for it acts upon his feelings. Music encourages us to bear the heaviest afflictions, administers consolation in every difficulty, refreshes the broken spirit, removes headache, and cures crossness and melancholy."

The Venerable Bede
Tenth Century

For Ellen,

Frances,

and Charles

Bain Murray, musicologist and composer, a member of the Theory-Composition faculty of the Cleveland Music School Settlement, and President of the Cleveland Composers' Guild, has given kindly criticism and many constructive suggestions in the preparation of this book. The authors acknowledge his help with gratitude.

Contents

10   *Contents*

The Heritage of Music

CHAPTER ONE

From the Very Beginning

FROM the very beginning man has been surrounded by the primeval sounds of nature. Hunched in his shelter he heard the rhythmic beating of the rains, the rush of the winds; along the shore of the sea he heard the wash of the waves grow into fierce pounding as a storm approached—and in the forest birds sang their melodies to him. His own heart, throbbing with a steady rhythm, increased its tempo in times of stress.

For who knows how many thousands of years he may have

13

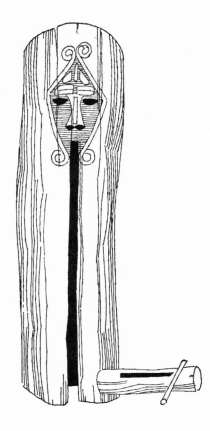

listened to these sounds before he tried to imitate the pounding rhythms and the mating calls and cries he heard. When at last he had succeeded in arranging a few sounds according to his own choice and capability, man was making music for the first time.

The first music that men made was probably crude though exhilarating. Very likely they clapped their hands and slapped their thighs and stamped their feet, and yelled and shouted. Gradually, then, they extended their efforts beyond their own bodies: they made rattles of hollow seashells or empty turtle shells; they made "scrapers" by rubbing sticks or notched bones together, and "stampers" of hollow wood that they could thump up and down in rhythm. A primitive instrument called a bull roarer, made by fastening a flat piece of wood or bone to the end of a string, produced a roaring noise when it was whirled around.

Later people cut reeds and young wood and began to make flutes. Sometimes the players blew the flutes with air from their nostrils; they believed that the soul was breathed out through the nose. These were men's first musical instruments.

Early men must surely have sung, too, but we have no way of knowing what their songs were like. Probably there were work songs and love songs, and dirges to mourn the dead. But they were never written down, so they have all disappeared.

Primitive music was probably made all round the world; it seems likely that it first developed into an art in the Far East. Legends say that gods gave music to the Hindus. From earliest times there were minstrels at the courts of the Indian princes, and music held an important place in all Hindu religious ceremonies. Indian orchestras with stringed instruments are known to have existed in very ancient times, and the ancient Hindu "ragas"—melodic themes which musicians used in composing new songs—were said to be presided over by special gods. Strict rules regulated how and when each raga might be played. Sometimes the Hindus sang Sanskrit words accompanied by instrumental music, believing that such singing would make them both energetic and heroic, and that it would bring them peaceful hearts.

The Chinese idea of music was very different from the Indian, but the Chinese people, too, believed that music influenced character. Good music, they said, guaranteed a well-ordered community; bad music endangered the state. The state must be brought into harmony with the universe, and the musical instruments which could accomplish this must be integrated with the cosmic forces—with the changing seasons, with wind, thunder, water and fire, with eternal space (north, south, east, and west), and with all matter. The times and conditions of the playing of their instruments, therefore, were regulated by these cosmic forces. The substances of which the instruments were made were the eight substances of which all matter was thought to be composed.

Each of these substances—stone, gourd, bamboo, wood, silk, clay, metal, and skin—could produce tones of a certain pitch or timbre. By listening to them men might perceive the life of the substance of which the instrument was made. Music to them was sounding matter.

"Singing stones," or stone chimes hung on a rack, were among the most prized instruments of the Chinese, and they loved bells whose deep, long throbbing tones told them of the life of the metal of which they were made. In both these instruments exactness of pitch was all important. According to legend an emperor of China once sent his minister all the way to the western mountains to get the correct pitch from the phoenix which lived there.

In both India and China, then, music as an art had a promising beginning. And though Western music cannot be said to owe very much to it, this music did contribute the pentatonic or five-tone scale which is used today in much of the folk music of Europe and America. This is the scale that corresponds to the sound of the five black keys on our pianos. After a time music in the Far East ceased to grow and develop, but this was not true in the Western world. The music that began in the countries at the eastern end of the Mediterranean Sea changed and grew as the centuries went by until it encompassed all the music that we know—the religious chants and the love songs, the dance music and the martial airs, the oratorios and operas and symphonies. All these grew from the small seeds of music planted long ago at the eastern end of the Mediterranean.

Perhaps it began in Sumer in the Mesopotamian Valley. There was music in Sumer more than six thousand years ago. A harp inlaid with gold and mother-of-pearl has been found in the tomb of the ancient Queen Shub-ad.

There was music in Egypt from very early times, too. The paintings on the walls of tombs and the hieroglyphic records bear testimony to this. In the huge temples—so vast that six hundred players were needed for the temple orchestras—the performers were arrayed in splendid robes, and played harps, lyres, lutes, flutes, and bell rattles called sistrums. Presumably the Egyptians marked time by clapping their hands, for there is no evidence that they had drums. They used neither trumpets nor tambourines in the temples; these were reserved for the army.

The first musicians who were paid to play appear to have been those who attended the bearded Assyrian kings. A stone slab carved in bas-relief shows them playing ensemble, and the accompanying inscription indicates that they used harmonic combinations much like those of later times.

In Palestine the Hebrews' great enjoyment was not in instrumental music, though they used "timbrels," or little drums, to beat out the rhythm for their singing and dancing, and they played the "kinnor," or harp, at times when they felt happy and serene. They also had small flutes called "ugabs," and blew the "shofar," or ram's horn, to call the people to repentance. But instrumental music was not half so important to the Hebrew people as was their singing. "I, *even* I, will sing unto the Lord," Deborah the prophetess cried, and all the people joined her in her desire.

Samuel, the last of the Judges, built a school of prophecy and music, and David, who has been called the Great Musician, studied there as a boy. The music of the Psalms of David has been lost, but as poems they have been an inspiration to generations of men. David, too, is believed to have conceived the ritual, with its antiphonal chants, which was practiced in Solomon's temple nearly a thousand years before Christ. That ritual is still used in the Jewish synagogues today.

The ancient music in all those places must have been sturdy and strong and filled with spirit and beauty. But the last echoes died away so long ago that our ears will never hear the sounds. It was the Greeks who laid the foundations for music as we know it.

CHAPTER TWO

The Greeks and Their Divine Discovery

T HE GREEKS were the first people who tried to study and understand music. And, having studied it, they came to the conclusion that its power was so great that it was beyond man's comprehension. They called music a "divine discovery."

It was probably Pythagoras in the sixth century B.C. who first found out that the pitch of musical notes depended on the speed of vibrations. Some people believe that the Greeks knew this before Pythagoras' time. At any rate, it was Pythagoras who first made a monochord to measure the vibrations.

Pythagoras took a board, and stretched along it a string of a certain length, fastened at both ends with nails. The device which he thus created was a monochord. He plucked the string to make it vibrate and listened to the sound it produced. Then he pressed his finger just halfway up the string and found that the shortened length vibrated faster and made a higher note. When he placed his finger farther down, so that the vibrating section of the string was longer, it vibrated more slowly, and the note was lower. Soon he was creating various notes at will and working out a definite relationship between the length of the plucked string and the sound it produced. "All things are numbers," he said, and music, too, was a matter of mathematics.

Gradually, after that, other Greeks became interested in the tones the monochord produced, and they divided them into whole tones and semitones. They arranged the tones in series of four notes called tetrachords, and combining two of these tetrachords they made a scale or mode. The tones of the scale ascended or descended in pitch according to a specified scheme of intervals.

The various scales or modes which the Greeks contrived in this way seemed to them to reflect various moods or states of mind. One expressed anxiety and suspense, another ecstasy, and still another courage. And just as they named their various styles of architecture after the regions in which they had originated, now they named their scales or modes after the various provinces of the Greek world—the Lydian mode, the Phrygian, the Dorian, the Aeolian, and so on.

The state established very strict rules for all music making in those days. Each separate kind of music had to be written in the appropriate mode—military marches in one mode, "paeans," or hymns of praise, in another, dirges in still another. The rise and fall of the melody, moreover, had to correspond to the rise and fall of the speaking voice, and the instruments had to be made according to exact regulation. Only two kinds of instruments might be used, the "kithara," or lyre of four strings, and the flutes, or Pan pipes.

Once the musician Terpander quelled a civil war in Greece by organizing a singing contest between the two opposing sides; the Greeks were very grateful to him. However, when he dared to increase the number of strings on his kithara from four to seven, he was severely punished and forbidden to play it for a year.

The Greeks must have made great music with their well regulated scales and modes, their kitharas and flutes; every state occasion was graced with triumphant music. They made lovely songs, too, and they were the first people in Europe to write these down. Above the words of their songs they wrote symbols to indicate the notes and the time. But fewer than a dozen of these songs remain. One of them is typically Greek in its spirit—its words, "Be happy always, as long as you live," were borrowed by the early Christians and made into the hymn, "Hosanna to the Son of David."

Almost all the Greek melodies have disappeared, like the sound of the waves that beat against the Aegean shore or the wind that rustled through the olive trees so many centuries ago. But the principles of music that the Greeks "discovered" are the basis of our music today.

The truth they recognized, that music has power beyond our understanding, has remained, too. Truths have often been preserved in the form of legends, and this one about the power of music is embodied in the well-known legend of Orpheus.

Orpheus lived in the forests of Thrace, that wild, mountainous country that lay north of Greece. He played the lyre so beautifully that the listening forest creatures were charmed by his music. The shy ones came out of their hiding places and sat down before him; the wild ones were tamed.

In time Orpheus fell in love with the nymph Eurydice, and

when she died he was stricken with grief. He went up and down through the forest playing music of such sadness that all who heard it wept.

At last his wandering took him to the border of Hades, and he entered the shadowy world, still playing his lyre. Then Pluto, the King of Hades, heard him, took pity on him, and agreed to let him have Eurydice again. He might lead her up to the world, and she might follow him, but he must not look back at her until they had left Hades behind them.

Joyfully the pair started—he leading and she following—and he played his lyre as they went. But when they had almost finished their journey, when they came to the boundary that divides the earth from Hades, Orpheus felt a misgiving lest Eurydice might not be there. Quickly he glanced over his shoulder and saw her snatched back into the shadows again.

Then Orpheus wandered through the world, mad with sorrow, and he paid no heed to anyone or anything. The women of Thrace, angered because he made no more music, set upon him and tore him to pieces.

The story of Orpheus has been told and retold and set to music. More operas have been written on its theme than on any other. And since the days of the ancient Greeks no better way has been found of telling of the incomprehensible power that music holds over the lives of men.

CHAPTER THREE

Hymns and Plain Song

CENTURIES passed, and there was little new development in music, for the Greeks were conquered by the Romans, and the Romans were concerned with other affairs. Greek slaves were employed to perform at the Roman banquets, and occasionally some Roman dilettante gave a concert. It is said that the Roman Emperor Nero traveled from place to place performing before audiences and took a claque of young men with him to be sure of applause.

In the first and second centuries the Christians hid under the city of Rome in the catacombs, or burial caves, where they were forced to take refuge from their persecutors. There they partook of the feast that commemorated the Last Supper and sang their hymns of praise with muted voices lest they be heard in the street above. Little is known of the songs they sang, for these songs were secret and never written down. Tradition has it, however, that *"Lux Beator"* ("O Blessed Light"), the oldest of the Christian hymns, comes down from those far distant times.

The names of those who worshiped in the secret darkness of the catacombs have almost all been forgotten. There is indeed only one that we can identify. This was Cecilia, a patrician who was killed by the Roman soldiers. She was canonized later as St. Cecilia, the patron saint of music.

In 325 A.D. the Emperor Constantine himself became a Christian, and it was no longer necessary for Christ's followers to hide in the catacombs. Their worship was now held above ground and openly.

Christianity spread fast in the Roman Empire, and people of many different races and languages became Christians. But now there was chaos in the Empire and in the Church, for the Goths, Vandals, Lombards, and other tribes were filtering in over the northern borders. These invaders took up Christianity enthusiastically, but they were still half pagan. So the intelligent and scholarly Church Fathers, who laid the foundations of the Christian church, had a difficult task. Each separate group of people wanted to worship in its own way and in its own language.

Ambrose, Bishop of Milan, was one of the most influential of the early Church Fathers. His statue, carved in stone, stands at the east portal of the cathedral of Chartres near Paris and shows him with a thin, aristocratic face, and wearing a bishop's miter. But, of course, it cannot show that he was a poet and a lover of music.

Ambrose was the son of a long line of Roman senators and was a man gifted in administration. He traveled through the Roman Empire, visiting churches in various parts of the country. He heard the hymns which were in one place Egyptian, Persian, or Greek, while in another they were based on Roman street songs or pagan German tunes, and he decided that he would change all this. He would bring uniformity into the church music and make a liturgy or order of service that would be the same wherever it was sung. This he believed would give the Church a sense of unity and strength.

In order to do this he collected prayers, psalms, and canticles from every part of the Empire and translated them all into Latin. He did not employ a secretary but wrote everything out with his own hand. When he had finished his translations he set them to melodies that seemed suitable, using four of the ancient Greek modes. No instruments were to be used in the churches; all the music was to be sung. The human voice was more "natural," he said, than instrumental music. He admired the music of the Eastern churches and used a great many of their melodies, saying they would "buoy up the spirits" of those who sang them.

In Constantinople the music Ambrose admired particularly was the antiphonal chant which the Christians there had borrowed from the Jewish temples. The congregation was divided into two parts which alternated in singing the Psalms. At first the men sang one part, the women the other. Later, when women were forbidden to take part in the church services, the priest chanted the first line and the men responded with the second. The lines were intoned on one note until the end of the sentence; then the melody moved up to a higher note, keeping always within the range of the particular Greek mode which Ambrose had chosen. The Ambrosian chants, which were somber and unadorned, are still sung in some churches in Milan.

Ambrose was filled with exuberance as he worked, and he composed many original hymns. "A hymn," he said simply, "is a song in praise of the Lord." There is a tradition that a Te Deum, which is still used today, was composed jointly by Ambrose and another of the Church Fathers, Augustine.

It is said, though some have doubted it, that when Ambrose was baptizing Augustine he was so filled with emotion that he burst forth spontaneously, "We praise Thee, O Lord!"

Augustine responded, "We acknowledge Thee to be the Lord!" Then the two continued their joyful responses, until the beautiful song of praise was complete.

So Ambrose began to unify the Christian Church through its music, and this beginning was added to two centuries later by another Church Father, Gregory the Great.

Gregory the Great was hot-tempered, vigorous, steeped in Roman traditions, with restless eyes and great intelligence. He became a Roman senator in the sixth century, wore a purple robe, and drove a handsome chariot with four white horses. But, having reached the pinnacle of his ambition, he decided to set worldly matters aside and join the Benedictine order of monks. At the monastery he used his great intellectual powers in building up the Church. He was the first monk ever to be named pope. That was in about the year 590.

Gregory's work for the Church took many years to complete. Tradition has it that he assembled all the Ambrosian hymns and added more to them, and all these he had copied into a thick volume called the Antiphonary. This volume, leather-bound and beautifully copied on vellum, was fastened with a chain of gold to the altar of St. Peter's Church in Rome. Bishops, priests, and monks traveled from every corner of the kingdom to see and study it, and precious handwritten copies were sent to monasteries and churches in many different places.

More important than the Antiphonary, however, were the chants or plain song which Gregory originated. These chants were sung in a spirit of deep reverence and dignity, for they were based on passages from the Book of Psalms. Their music was based on old Greek modes, and singing them took much skill and practice, so that the congregation was not permitted to take part. They were sung by special choirs trained in singing schools. The most celebrated of these was the *Schola Cantorum* in Rome.

The choir sang the Gregorian chant in unison, sometimes using only four or five different notes. The music had great solemnity and beauty, and the Biblical prose gave it richness and dignity. In time the chanting developed into a flowing song with broad embellishments, especially on such words as "Alleluia" and "Amen."

Gregorian chants are still sung in modern churches, and it has been estimated that there are twenty-five hundred Gregorian melodies. However, no one knows which of them have come down from Gregory's time and which were added later. They have been a great inspiration to later composers. The concluding fugue of Mozart's *Jupiter Symphony* is based on a Gregorian melody; one of the themes of Berlioz' *Symphonie Fantastique*, on another; and many other composers have borrowed fragments of the old plain song.

Now it seemed that the Church had music worthy of it. Ambrose and Gregory had done their work well, for the muted voices of the catacombs had flowered into glorious, rich song. But that music, so beautifully and grandly conceived, was difficult to sing, for the free rhythm was very subtle and an infinite variation of modes was used. It took years of practice and memorizing to bring the singing of chants to perfection.

In about 600 A.D. organs were made, and they were tried in some churches. But they were clumsy contraptions, and churchmen generally disapproved of them. A trained choir was considered to be the only proper way of praising God, and the choirmasters struggled on with their teaching.

Gradually a system of notation was worked out so that the music of the chants could be written down precisely and read by the singers. When Gregory had the Antiphonary copied he had had little marks placed above the words to show whether the voice should move up or down in singing them. The Greeks had made similar marks to indicate the rise and fall of the voice. These marks were called "neumes."

Dots, dashes, and other symbols were gradually added to these neumes, but the signs were all so vague that Hucbald, a Flemish monk of the late ninth century, said, "The first tone is easy to sing, but when it comes to the second, lower sign, you do not know whether to go down one tone, two, or three, if you have not heard it sung before."

Guido d'Arezzo, choirmaster in the monastery at Pomposa in Italy, impatient with the tedium of teaching the chant, made more innovations. He claimed that by his method a monk could learn in five months what had formerly taken him nine years.

What Guido did was to increase the number of lines drawn across the manuscript from two to four, to five, six, or seven. Sometimes he made the number as many as eleven, for the lines of the staff were not fixed as they are today.

Now Guido arranged symbols either on the lines or in the spaces between the lines, and was thus able to show with some exactness how the chant should be sung. He made black marks to replace the neumes, and these were now called notes. They were little squares made by dipping the end of his stylus in ink and pressing it down on the paper.

To help further in the execution of the music Guido d'Arezzo drew a red line across a page of music he was copying. The neumes marked above that line were to be sung higher than the present tone F, those below it lower. Later he drew an additional line, a yellow one, that represented the present tone C, and he drew a green line when B Flat was needed. With these lines the choir was able to hold fairly well to the chant as it was indicated by the neumes.

The members of the choir did not have individual copies of the words and the melody. Originally they had had to memorize both, but after a time the practice was introduced of copying words and music onto big placards to be held up before the choir, and this made their singing easier and more accurate.

Another improvement which Guido d'Arezzo made was to give names to the notes. For this purpose he chose the first syllables of the lines of an old hymn to John the Baptist. The words of the hymn were:

> Ut *queant laxis*
> Resonare *fibris*
> Mira *gestorum*
> Famuli *tuorum*
> Solve *polluti*
> Labia *reatum.*

This has been translated:

> Grant that the unworthy lips of thy servant
> May be gifted with due harmony.
> Let the tones of my voice
> Sing the praises of thy wonders.

The choirs were now singing, "*Ut, re, mi, fa, so, la*," but in time the syllable "*ut*" was changed to "*do*," because that was easier to sing. And "*si*" was added to complete the scale. The letters *s* and *i* were taken from the initial letters of *Sancte Ioannes* (St. John) to whom the hymn was written.

Guido d'Arezzo had small thanks for all his pains. The Church did not like innovations. He was thrown into prison and stayed there a year until Pope John XIX released him. Then he collected into a book all the improvements he had made in musical notation, and this book was used by choirmasters in many places to make the teaching of Gregorian chants easier.

As time passed the Church grew more and more proud of the music of its choirs and thought indeed that music was so powerful it could influence all men's lives. In the tenth century the Venerable Bede in England wrote:

> Music is the most worthy, courteous, pleasant and joyous and lovely of all knowledge; it makes a man gentlemanly in his demeanor . . . for it acts upon his feelings. Music encourages us to bear the heaviest afflictions, administers consolation in every difficulty, refreshes the broken spirit, removes headache, and cures crossness and melancholy.

LATE XIV CENTURY MUSIC SHEET

CHAPTER FOUR

Webs of Woven Melodies

I N T H E twelfth and thirteenth centuries the walls and spires
of new cathedrals were rising everywhere in Europe. In sheds
near the sites of the new buildings hundreds of craftsmen worked.

30

Woodworkers carved figures to decorate pulpits or choir stalls; stonecutters hacked out gargoyles for gutter spouts; sculptors carved the images of saints; goldsmiths fashioned monstrances and communion cups of wonderful, intricate beauty; and weavers made bright tapestries picturing the stories of the Old and New Testaments, so that those who could not read might learn. In time the great buildings were ready, the priests began to chant the Mass, and men and women came and went, lighting their candles and saying their prayers.

The men and boys who sang in the cathedral choirs took as much pride in their work as any of the craftsmen. For many years they had sung their chants in unison, but now they wanted to ornament their music as the woodcarvers or stonecutters ornamented their work. Experiments began to be made in two-part singing.

Exactly when the change from unison to two-part singing occurred is not known. Perhaps it began accidentally as many changes do. Perhaps while choirs still sang in unison, a singer unable to reach the higher notes of his plain song would let his voice fall a few notes below the other voices. Instinctively then he might sing a melody which was a kind of companion to the original plain song. This may have come to be accepted as perfectly proper. But however two-part singing first began, it became quite customary during the early twelfth century for the plain songs to be sung in two parts.

At first the second part was improvised and only the most talented choristers were allowed to sing it. After a time strict rules were made for it. The upper or principal voice was called the "tenor," because the Latin verb *tenere* means "to hold," and the tenor held the melody. The lower voice was called the "organum." This term was taken from a phrase in St. Jerome's translation of the Bible which means "to glorify the Lord." Sometimes the term organum was used also for the style of singing in two parts. Two-part singing was an exciting discovery. Musicians now realized that certain notes sound well when they are sung together, and this realization is the basis of our modern harmony.

Gradually there were more discoveries. The singers found that the part which had been sung below the tenor could also be sung above it and that the two voices did not have to move at an even rate—the added part could be sung with a different rhythm and could blossom into beautiful decorative passages which they called "melismas."

Then, before long, a third part was added to the other two, and soon there were more voices that echoed one another or sang independent melodies simultaneously. This became known as polyphonic "many-voiced" music, or counterpoint.

Gradually the old way of singing in notes of even length was abandoned altogether. The notes became shorter and shorter, and sometimes short notes were mingled with long ones.

Now a new way of writing music for this kind of singing had to be found. The old notes which Guido d'Arezzo had devised could not begin to show how it should be done. A number of men tried to work out a better system of notation. In the eleventh century, a monk named Franco succeeded. He lived in the German city of Cologne.

Franco found a way to show on his parchment not only what the various tones were, but how long they should be held. He made a square note with a tail, ◼▐ , to indicate a long sound, and a square note without a tail, ◼ , for a "breve," or short sound. Then he made a lozenge-shaped mark, ◆ , for a still shorter note, a "semibreve." The breve was the unit of measure. After about a century Franco's marks were replaced by the rounded black and white symbols that we use today.

Franco's improved way of writing music made it possible for the choirs to sing much more accurately than they had before, and composers now threw themselves with great enthusiasm into writing complicated polyphonic music. They tried to write as many melodies as possible to be sung at the same time. The voices sang against each other, crossing back and forth, echoing each other and overlapping, while throughout it all the tenor maintained the basic plain song or sacred chant. This was called the *cantus firmus,* and it gave unity to the whole.

In Paris in the twelfth century two great masters worked on problems of musical notation much as Franco had done. They were Leoninus and Perotinus, who laid the foundations of three- and four-voice counterpoint.

Later, in the famous choir school at Notre Dame in Paris, where polyphonic singing was developed to a high degree, the singers used not only different melodies but also different words in their singing. While the tenor sang his chant, using the words of a plain song or an old Latin hymn, a second voice sang a melody with entirely different words (perhaps it was some folk song or a popular tune; it might even be in a different language), while other voices echoed and imitated each other. The French called this kind of singing a "motet," from the French word *mot* meaning *word.* We still use that term for a polyphonic composition on a sacred text.

The composers of these intricate and sometimes beautiful compositions were generally anonymous. No one knew who had composed the music the choir sang any more than they knew who had designed the choir stalls or the patterns woven into the tapestries. Craftsmen in those days seldom signed their work, and there are hardly any names in the history of European music until the fourteenth century. Then Guillaume de Machaut wrote his name beneath his compositions.

Machaut was in the service of King John of Bohemia, for by that time it had become the custom for kings to take an interest in music. They displayed their wealth and power by building royal chapels and employing musicians to write music for them.

Machaut, King John's chapel master, was a jolly, worldly gentleman. He wrote the first book about musical instruments, describing each instrument and telling how it was made and how it was played. He said the organ was the "king" of them all.

He was a poet as well as a composer—one of the best poets of the fourteenth century. He wrote gentle, melancholy love songs, long lyric poems, rondos, and ballades, and set all these to music that had great rhythmic richness and artistry. He is said to have been the first composer to use syncopation.

He was also the first to write a unified musical Mass. Formerly, separate, unrelated pieces had been played while the priest chanted each part of the Mass. But Machaut had the idea of relating the five parts, somewhat as the parts of a symphony are related now. One of his Masses is said to have been played at the coronation of Charles V. In writing his unified Masses Machaut set a precedent which many composers were to follow. Johann Sebastian Bach's B Minor Mass is an example of this.

As time passed, other names appeared, and music was identified with definite composers. There was Jean Okeghem, a Fleming renowned as a great teacher and famous for his skill and ingenuity in counterpoint. One of the motets he wrote had thirty-six different voices. And there was Guillaume Dufay, who composed a famous Mass with a popular song for its *cantus firmus*. The song was called *"L'Homme Armé"* and many composers imitated it. The words of this song have been translated:

> Oh! the man, the man at arms
> Fills the folk with dread alarms.
> Everywhere I hear them wail,
> "Find, if you would breast the gale,
> A good stout coat of mail."
>
> Oh! the man, the man at arms
> Fills the folk with dread alarms.

Besides Dufay and Okeghem there was Josquin Desprès. "He is the master of his notes," his friend Martin Luther wrote enthusiastically. "They have to do as he bids them; other composers have to do as the notes will."

Josquin's music was deeply emotional, but still he enjoyed working out his compositions as if they were mathematical problems, and he used an astonishing number of different voices, blending them together in the web of his music in Masses, motets, and chansons.

In Italy, in France, and in the Netherlands the voices of the choirs were weaving themselves into ever-changing, kaleidoscopic patterns. By the end of the fifteenth century the prosperous burghers of the Netherlands established chapels that vied with the papal chapel in Rome in their luxury and searched all Europe for boys to sing in their choirs. And they employed distinguished chapel masters who were well paid and much respected. Men and women in brocades and velvets crowded the chapels to hear the music they composed. And that music, ornate and often beautiful, set the style for church music throughout Europe.

The men who composed this music were the first group to constitute a "school" of music. This group was known as the Northern or Franco-Flemish School, and they came from northern France, Flanders, Belgium, and Germany. The music they wrote was extraordinarily intricate. But that is not surprising—it was the fashion of the day. The notation for this music grew increasingly difficult to decipher; someone has said that reading it was like solving a crossword puzzle.

The Masses now were often accompanied by noisy blaring instruments, and the *cantus firmus* was generally some popular song or folk tune that stemmed from the people. These melodies, alive and vital, rough hewn, angular and aggressive, often chronicled some past event and were martial and irrepressible.

Late in the fifteenth century, when Ottaviano dei Petrucci of Venice brought the printing of music to perfection, this complicated ornate music spread throughout Europe. And by the sixteenth century choirs were no longer singing to glorify God as they had done three hundred years before, but were performing technical feats of skill and ingenuity.

The Northern School had in the past produced rich and beautiful music, but such extreme and seemingly irreverent music as they were now producing could not be tolerated by the devout leaders of the Church.

Blasts were issued against it by church leaders. One wrote:

Their voices are incessantly running to and fro, intoxicating the ear, not soothing it, while the men themselves endeavor to convey by gestures the sentiments of the music they utter. As a consequence of all this, devotion, the true end of all worship, is little thought of, and wantonness, which ought to be eschewed, increases.

What could be done about it? Should polyphonic singing be done away with altogether? If it was, what would take its place?

CHAPTER FIVE

Palestrina and Orlando di Lasso:
Great Figures of the Sixteenth Century

I N T H E year 1545 a great meeting of learned men and church officials came together in the city of Trent, which lies on the boundary between the German-speaking and Italian-speaking peoples. There bishops and archbishops, cardinals, abbots, and patriarchs met to deliberate on the state of the Roman Catholic Church. They announced that they intended to "effect a reformation, both in head and body," and their discussion lasted intermittently for the better part of eighteen years and was to influence to some extent Giovanni Pierluigi da Palestrina who had been born earlier in Palestrina, Italy, in the Sabine Hills not far from Rome.

As a boy Palestrina had such a clear, sweet voice that someone sent him to Rome to have his voice trained. He joined the choir of the Church of Santa Maria Maggiore, and later became choirmaster and organist in his own home town. He was made director of the choir in connection with St. Peter's and then a chorister in the papal chapel by Pope Julius III, formerly Bishop of Palestrina.

A fable has long been carried down that when Pope Marcellus II, who followed Julius, urged the papal choir to sing in a less careless and routine way and to display some reverence, some clarity of enunciation, Palestrina was troubled by his words. A deeply religious man, he was determined that somehow he would

manage to purify the music that his choir sang. Polyphonic singing could be beautiful and reverent, he knew. He would try with
all his power and all his knowledge to make it so. He would write
a new Mass, to show what could be done.

It is said he threw himself into the work of composition with
the utmost dedication. This was to be no ordinary piece of music;
he would put into it all the fervor, all the mystical beauty of
which he was capable.

When at last it was finished, when the voices of the choir began
to sing, he listened while the "heavenly harmonies" filled the
chapel. Had he succeeded? he must have wondered. Surely he
knew that he had!

When Palestrina invited Pope Marcellus to hear his Mass,
tradition says that the pope was completely won over by the
music, for the choir sang with wonderful grace and delicacy, and
the exquisite strains seemed to be cleansed of all worldly artificiality as they soared to the heights of spiritual ecstasy.

Actually, the Mass was probably composed in Marcellus'
memory and performed much later, for Marcellus died after three
weeks as pope. Palestrina was dismissed from the chapel choir
and held several positions and composed many works before
being reappointed as choirmaster at St. Peter's years later.

Meanwhile, the Council of Trent had continued to meet, and
many and varied were the topics which it discussed—the position of the pope, the continued use of Latin in the liturgy, the importance of the sacraments. One subject which seemed to them
of greatest importance was the music of the church service. They
all agreed that the music of their time had become irreverent
and lacking in the spirit of devotion, that composers and choirs
were more interested in demonstrating their ingenuity than in
praising God, that Masses based on vulgar popular airs were to be
heard everywhere. If music of this kind continued, they agreed,
there could be no true worship. Ought they to forbid polyphonic
singing by the church choirs? Ought the Church to return to the

ancient plain song of Gregory's time? Ought the elaborate and intricate music that the Netherlanders had created to be done away with?

Martin Luther had already faced that question and had abolished polyphonic singing by choirs in the Protestant churches. He thought that the congregations ought to sing. He had collected a large number of simple hymns in what was to be the first hymnal. They were stately, slow, and dignified, and the people joined in singing them with hearty faith and enthusiasm. "A Mighty Fortress Is Our God" was one of them.

Yet the churchmen at the Council of Trent did not want congregational singing. They wanted somehow to purify the singing of their choirs. They agreed to forbid all church music based on secular tunes, but this was not sufficient. Some way must be found to bring reverence back into the services, and no one at the church council could find out exactly how this could be done, for it was a matter of the spirit rather than of technique.

Palestrina's music had this spirit, and he produced Masses one after another, and, despite the objections of the Council of Trent, some of them were based on secular music—one on the melody of *"L'Homme Armé"*!

In Palestrina's Masses the music was subtle and transparent. It contained a consonant harmony and an even rhythm; when one part stopped at a cadence another part began, and this resulted in the continuous flow that is now recognized to be characteristic of Palestrina's music. He continued to compose until he was a very old man, and much of the music he produced was as beautiful as the *Marcellus Mass*.

There is a legend of a bright day in Palestrina's life, his fiftieth birthday, when the people of his native town came to Rome to do him honor. Fifteen hundred of them crowded the road to Rome and formed a tremendous procession when they reached the city. The priests marched first; behind them came the laymen; and women and children brought up the rear. They made

Palestrina walk at their head, as they marched, singing his music, through the streets of Rome.

Palestrina died in 1594. When he knew that his end was near he sent for his only living son, Iginio. "I leave behind me many works that are unpublished," he said. "But I leave with them enough money to have them printed."

Iginio promised to see that they were published, but he could not have been very diligent, for every few years, still, unpublished works by Palestrina are found. And the Church and the world are still grateful to Palestrina on whose tomb in St. Peter's in Rome are written the words: *"Musicae Princeps."*

So Palestrina succeeded in bringing new life to the music that the church choirs sang. That music flowered forth now, fresher, more delicate, more graceful and spirited than it had ever been.

One after another new composers followed. Their work was not like Palestrina's, for each man had his own individuality. But, like him, they put aside worldly and elaborate feats of skill and composed with grace and sincerity.

One of the men who was inspired by Palestrina was the Spanish priest, Tomás Luis de Victoria. A deeply religious man and a mystic, he said that his aim in creating music was to raise men's minds to the contemplation of divine truth, and he dedicated his book of psalms and motets not to any earthly prince but to "The Blessed Virgin Mother of God and to all the Saints. . . ." His music combined Spanish gravity and asceticism with Italian grace and gentleness, for he had studied in Italy as did so many musicians of his day.

More brilliant and original than any other composer of this time, however, was the Belgian-born Orlando di Lasso, the outstanding figure of the Northern School. He directed the choir of the Duke of Bavaria with such genius that, according to a contemporary, "like warriors taking courage at the sound of the trumpet, the expert singers needed no other orders than the expression of that powerful and vigorous countenance."

Orlando himself seemed to overflow with music, and motets and Masses and settings for psalms came pouring from him. He wrote *Seven Penitential Psalms,* filled with emotional auguish, which the Duke of Bavaria considered so fine that he had them specially bound. Orlando visited the French king, Charles IX, and presented him with a new book of songs. The king was so pleased that he offered him the position of court musician, but the composer decided to remain in Munich.

Orlando also wrote a motet for Corpus Christi Day that was miraculously beautiful. Legend has it that the first time it was performed the sun came piercing through the clouds and a threatening thunderstorm suddenly disappeared. In memory of this event Orlando's "Motet for Corpus Christi Day" was performed in Munich for many years after that on Corpus Christi Day itself, the Thursday after Trinity Sunday.

Orlando did not confine himself to church music. He was a man of the world who had traveled in many countries and heard music of many kinds. His secular music is as distinguished as are his Masses. There is great variety in it. Sometimes he wrote compositions for strings alone, sometimes for voices. And he liked to accompany the voices with wind and brass instruments.

By the time he was in his middle sixties he had composed enough music to fill sixty volumes. Perhaps he was tired out after that, for he produced little in the last years of his life. But he had done enough. He was a very great figure; except for Palestrina he was the greatest musician and composer of his time.

GERMAN MINSTRELS

CHAPTER SIX

It Was Not All Church Music

WHILE the monks in their choir schools were struggling to follow the neumes and to read those first musical notes which Guido d'Arezzo had evolved, there was an older and livelier music in Europe that had nothing to do with the Church. These were the vigorous and earthy songs and dance tunes of the people that later found their way into the rhythms of Josquin, Dufay, and Okeghem. No one knows who first composed them.

Some of them may perhaps have been sung before the dawn of history when people worshiped trees and stones and running brooks. As they passed down from one generation to another, no singing schools were needed to teach them.

The Church adapted a few of these old melodies, but generally disapproved of them. They were too lively, the Church maintained; some of them even made people want to dance. But the people continued to sing the old songs in spite of the disapproval of the clergy. There were spinning songs and lullabies, battle songs and stories of brave deeds, wedding songs so gay they made the singers stamp their feet, harvest songs and drinking songs. Toward the end of the eighth century, the Emperor Charlemagne ordered a big collection of them made.

At that time each separate locality had its own special style of singing. The music of the Scandinavians was different from that of the Welsh and Irish; the music of the Spanish was different from that of the French. But these were not to continue distinct and separate. In time the composers would influence one another.

After the break-up of the Roman Empire, with its accompanying wars and dissensions, there were a great many homeless people in Europe, as there are after every war. In the ninth and tenth centuries thousands of these people took to the roads. Among them were bands of mimes or actors who had played in the cities of the Roman Empire, but there were many other homeless wanderers besides these actors. Some of them were artisans who had no work to do, some were servants whose masters had been killed, some were unemployed workers or vagabond monks who found the discipline of the monasteries too harsh, and some, of course, were merely adventurers who wanted to find out what life was like beyond their own farms and villages.

Having left home, these people had to earn a living somehow, and this they did by amusing people with songs. Sometimes they added acrobatic stunts to their music. Sometimes they took trained bears or monkeys with them.

These "minstrels" stopped to perform wherever they could find an audience—in the courtyards of taverns and at country fairs, along the roads where pilgrims were journeying toward the shrines of saints, in the great halls of noblemen's castles. They were generally welcome in the castles, for life there was dull, and the wandering minstrel brought not only entertainment but also news from the outside world.

Sometimes when a minstrel played before the lord of a castle he flattered him by relating in verse the deeds of the lord's noble ancestors and the heroic feats they had performed. Such songs were the *"chansons de geste"* which told of the brave deeds of heroes such as Roland or Charlemagne. Sometimes they sang romantic tales in verse—for example, that of the lovers Aucassin and Nicolette. For the most part, however, they sang songs they had picked up here and there along the road.

Because they were poor but quick-witted, the minstrels often helped themselves to what they wanted, and this gave them a bad reputation. People loved to hear them perform but were afraid to have them around. Officials of both State and Church declared that they were "lawless fellows." For that reason they were required to wear special costumes so that they would be easy to identify. Here they must go in green and yellow stripes; there, in checked suits of red and blue. At one time they were required to wear their hair long; then sometimes, with a saucy gaiety, they twined peacock feathers in it.

Although the minstrels' reputations were not always the best, some of them managed to make themselves so indispensable to the lords in the castles that they were permanently attached to the servant staffs. Then they were brilliantly attired, with jingling bells on their caps and scepters in their hands. "Lords of Misrule," they were called.

Up to the beginning of the twelfth century it had been the custom in Europe for pious folk to visit the Holy Land, for such a pilgrimage meant that a man's sins would be forgiven. But in the twelfth century the Mohammedan Turks captured Jerusalem and blocked the roads the pilgrims took. Then a great cry went up in Europe; the holy places must be recovered from the infidel Turks. The wars between Christians and Moslems began, and the Crusaders rode toward the East, their fluttering banners bearing the device of the Cross.

The knights who rode off on the Crusades generally took their minstrels with them to lighten the tedium of their journeys. And those who finally succeeded in reaching home again, having stood the rigors of long hard travel over land and sea, the fighting and the epidemics that raged among soldiers and civilians alike, had strange stories to tell.

They had looked on fine cities with mosques, libraries, and hospitals; they had heard talk of new discoveries in astronomy, mathematics, and medicine; they had seen beautiful objects made with delicate craftsmanship such as Europeans had never imagined.

Often the Crusaders brought back musical instruments from the Near East for their curious friends to see and try to play. Among these were lutes and mandolins, guitars, and several kinds of drums. And there were also "rebecs," instruments which were to develop later into the French *vielles* and which the English were to call "fiddles."

The minstrels performed on these instruments, for the knights apparently thought it beneath their dignity to try to play them. When the minstrels rode out in company with their lords, they generally carried one or another instrument slung across their shoulders. Gradually all the minstrels learned to play, whether they were attached to knights or not. Generally they taught each other or learned by experiment, but before long a school for learning to play musical instruments was opened in Paris. Then, during the season of Lent, when the Church forbade minstrels to perform in public, large numbers of minstrels studied there.

At first the player followed the melody of the song he sang on his lute or rebec. Then gradually he tried little flourishes or embellishments, and sometimes short preludes before the song.

The knights, though they left the singing and playing to the minstrels, were soon creating new music of their own, for among the returning Crusaders there were a number of gifted poets who had been inspired by the melodies and rhythms of the Moslem countries to write new songs and set them to music.

They wanted to revive the melodies they had heard in the East and to make new ones that told of spring, of love, of homecoming. They had found joy, they said. The French word for "to find" is *trouver*. Therefore, they were called "troubadours" in the language of Provence in southern France, and later *"trouvères"* in the provinces farther to the north.

Most of these troubadours and *trouvères* were kings and princes, counts, dukes, and knights. Guillaume de Poitiers was the first one we know of. Here is the translation of one of his songs:

> Behold the meads are green again.
> The orchard bloom is seen again,
> Of sky and stream the mien again
> Is mild, is bright!
> Now should each heart, that loves, obtain
> Its own delight.

Peire Vidal was another troubadour. Called by his contemporaries "the sweetest singer of them all," he loved the cadences of the soft Provençal speech.

> Whenever I hear the good speech of it
> I listen a-laughing and straightaway
> Demand for each word a hundred more
> So fair to me is the hearing.

Another, Bertran de Born, found joy in battles:

> And it pleaseth me when I see through the meadows
> The tents and pavilions set up, and great joy have I
> When I see on the campana knights armed and horses arrayed.

All these singers were alike in the freshness of their songs.

Styles in music are not necessarily contained by geographical boundaries. Before long joyous new music like that of the troubadours was being made in Germany, where Wolfram von Eschenbach and Walther von der Vogelweide were delighting the German people with their songs. The Germans called their singers "minnesingers"—"*minne*" was the old German word for "love." As time passed the songs of the minnesingers took on a religious tinge—the lady whom they addressed was the Virgin Mary. "These songs bring us to the courts of Paradise," one writer said. "But the atmosphere is still that of the courts of Love."

In Italy the knightly singers were called "*trovatori*," but their music never equaled the music of the French troubadours or the German minnesingers. The Italian songs were called "*laudi*" and they were first sung by the followers of St. Francis of Assisi, whom people sometimes called "God's Troubadour."

In the thirteenth century plagues swept through town and city in Italy, and the fields and vineyards of the countryside were ruined by devastating wars. The frightened people thought they must have sinned greatly to be afflicted by such misfortunes, and long processions of them marched up and down the twisting white roads, scourging themselves with whips and crying out to God to save them. Then in the hill town of Assisi, St. Francis, who had cast aside all his worldly possessions and who called Poverty his "Sister," joined the bands of penitents and taught his followers to sing even in the midst of their affliction. Of all these laudi only one remains, "The Canticle of the Sun." An old manuscript shows the words of this canticle beautifully written, with lines ruled for the notation of the melody. But these lines are blank. No one knows the music of "The Canticle of the Sun."

As the strains of minstrels, troubadours, minnesingers, and penitents spread across Europe, the people, especially of England, had found a new musical enjoyment. They were singing "canons" or "rounds."

The rounds were polyphonic, like the motets of the Church, but they were not religious. Probably the first ones were sung in Wales, but they soon spread across the British Isles, and people loved to sing them. In these rounds the voices joined in the singing at different points, all singing the same tune. One familiar round of this kind is "Scotland's Burning"; another, "Three Blind Mice." Perhaps the most beautiful of them all is "Sumer Is Icumen In," a round for six men's voices, the bottom part being a bagpipe drone. John of Fornsete, a monk, is said to have written it down about 1240, and ever since then, fresh and joyous, this greeting to summer has been sung over and over through the centuries.

Vocal music was much more highly developed than instrumental music during this period, but gradually people became interested in making instrumental accompaniments for the voices that sang the rounds. Then the rounds were supplanted by "madrigals," secular compositions for two or more voices, which had originally been brought from Italy, but which were extremely popular in England in Queen Elizabeth's day. Soon madrigals were not confined solely to secular music; there were also sacred madrigals performed by choir and instruments in the churches.

So eventually music in Europe broke away from the rigid old rules that had bound it. Hitherto music had been a matter of strict precepts, songs that took nine years to learn. The stately melodies of the Gregorian Chant had moved in even tones within the confines of the few intervals prescribed by the ancient church modes. Now new music could be freshly created.

Because this new music was built on poetry, it had a whole host of new rhythms. Where there had been dignified periods, now there were new refrains, new meters, melodies that lent themselves to dancing. Where there had been solemn restraint, now there was the expression of personal emotion. Love, courage, penitence, adoration, were the motives.

There were no bounds and restraints now. Old hymns, folk tunes, melodies from Islam—all were intermingled and sung to the accompaniment of the beautiful new instruments brought home from the Crusades.

CHAPTER SEVEN

The Elizabethans
and That Meteor, Henry Purcell

EVERYWHERE in Europe by the time the sixteenth century came there was a new freedom in music, and nowhere was this truer than in Queen Elizabeth's England. There men of every degree seemed to take joy in song. The milkmaid sang as she leaned her head against the cow's warm flanks; the sailor sang as he pulled at the ropes of the little vessel plunging across rough seas; there was singing on the village green at May Day, and there were carols when the halls were decked with green boughs at Christmastime. In the streets of London vendors of fruits and vegetables advertised their wares with songs, while the chimney sweep, the bellows mender, and even the tooth puller had special songs of their own.

England had a magnificent musical tradition. Beginning in the Middle Ages and all through the Renaissance she had built innumerable singing societies and church choirs. These reached a peak in Queen Elizabeth's time.

In the parlors of the well-to-do, the ladies and gentlemen loved to entertain themselves by singing madrigals, motets, and airs. All educated people had some musical training. An English writer of the time tells how in one great house, when the music books were brought out after dinner so that the company might sing, one gentleman confessed that he could not sing at sight, and "everyone began to wonder, yea, some whispered to others, demanding how he had been brought up."

England's madrigals were considered among her greatest treasures by those who sang them, and soon the singers began to take delight in experimenting. Then soprano, alto, tenor, and bass echoed and imitated each other in happy fa-la-las. Before long they became used to listening not to separate voices, but to blended voices.

Because so many madrigals were sung there was constant need for new ones, and a great many composers wrote vocal music in this style. Among them were William Byrd, Thomas Morley, John Bull, and Orlando Gibbons. The most celebrated of these was William Byrd.

"Master Byrd," as he was called, was organist in Queen Elizabeth's Chapel Royal. But he was versatile; he could write secular music as well as Masses, and his madrigals are counted among the very finest pieces of English music.

With all this singing and songwriting in England, more and more songbooks were needed. Music printing had been invented in Italy nearly a century before, but paper was scarce in England, and songbooks were therefore expensive and hard to get. For this reason the queen gave a license to William Byrd and to Thomas Tallis, another gifted composer, to manufacture them. Soon English songbooks were being passed around in many households— *Madrigals and Pastorals, The Muses' Garden of Delight,* and *Songs of Sundry Natures.* There were many others like these—their title pages beautifully engraved, their words and music carefully set down, and all bearing the names of William Byrd and Thomas Tallis.

But music in that golden time was not confined to singing; instrumental music was very popular too. In barber shops a customer waiting to be shaved was often given a "cittern" to play upon. This instrument was like a lute and was played with a small piece of ivory or metal. The patrons at the country inns were provided with flutes while they waited for their beef and ale. Many a man was accustomed to carrying a flute in his pocket; you could hear flute music warbling and shrilling in the gardens on every moonlight night.

During family sings after dinner, if a guest played a recorder, he would be asked to play one of the parts of a madrigal while the family sang the rest. Vocal and instrumental music were interchangeable. Viols were used as frequently as recorders.

In those days princes, counts, dukes, and other rich men were accustomed to investing a part of their fortunes in collections of musical instruments, in whose beauty they took much delight. The graceful lines of these instruments, the harmony of their proportions, and the fresh gleam of their varnished surfaces gave their owners pleasure. They contended that the instruments not only gave much delight to the ear and animated the spirit but also "greatly pleased the eye." Often these treasures were fashioned from rare woods and inlaid with ivory, tortoise shell, and mother-of-pearl.

Although the great collections of wind and string instruments belonged to the nobility, every music-loving family possessed a modest share of them. The various kinds of instruments were made in families or "consorts" at this time. There might be a consort of recorders in varying sizes, for example, or a consort of oboes, or of trombones or viols. The wind instruments on the whole were as popular as those with strings.

The sizes of the instruments in each consort were graduated from the very small, high-pitched ones to the very large, deep-toned ones, so that when they were played together they could cover a much wider range of tone than could instruments all of one size.

The sound of a consort of viols and flutes was delicate and pleasant, but not very loud. This music was suitable for family living rooms rather than for palace halls, and people called it, therefore, "chamber music."

Sometimes the flutes or viols played what were called "variations on a ground." Then the lowest pitched instrument began by playing some "fol," song or dance tune, over and over in solemn fashion. Meanwhile the higher pitched instruments took up this tune and played variations which mingled with the lower tones of the original player's ground bass.

When the playing was over, the precious instruments were carefully put away. They were kept in large chests which were covered with leather and lined with bright cloth. Such a "chest" of instruments was treasured by the family that owned it and passed down from one generation to another.

These wind and string instruments were not the only ones that well-to-do families of the sixteenth century enjoyed. There were also keyboard instruments of three different kinds: regals, clavichords, and harpsichords.

The regals were little organs, whose tone one writer said was "good and lovable." A regal organ had a graduated series of hollow reeds, like whistles, through which air was blown by bellows when the keys were pressed down. The bellows were so small that when the instrument was folded up it looked like a good-sized Bible. For this reason it was often called a "Bible regal."

The clavichord was small, too. It looked like a wooden box with strings drawn across it, and it was generally set on a table. When one of its keys was pressed, a little hammer was released which struck against a string and produced a thin, metallic sound. The strings were all the same length, and the tone varied according to what part of the string was struck.

The harpsichord was the third keyboard instrument. This, also, was a wooden box, and it was usually delicately carved and inlaid. Often the lid was beautifully painted by some first-rate artist. One harpsichord, made in 1560, bears the inscription: "I give pleasure at once to the eyes and to the heart."

The harpsichord was not square like the clavichord; it was shaped more like a harp and it lay flat on a table or on a stand especially built for it. Its strings were of graduated lengths, and it was played not by hammers striking against the strings but by plucking with quills. When one of the keys was pressed it released a jack or little upright piece of wood to which a quill was attached. The string made a twanging noise when it was plucked by the quill. This noise was not very loud, so harpsichords were sometimes played in pairs to increase the volume of the sound.

Sometimes harpsichords were called "virginals" and sometimes "spinets" or "*clavecins,*" and there were variations in their size and shape. But the principle on which they were played was the same.

The fancies, dance suites, themes and variations these early keyboard instruments played were not at all like a Chopin prelude or a Liszt rhapsody. Still, they gave pleasure to the Elizabethans who played them. The queen herself spent many hours practicing on her virginal though it was said she lost her temper if anyone was listening.

It must not be thought that all the music in Elizabethan times was produced at home. For many years singing societies and church choirs had been gradually developing in England and this long vocal tradition came into full flower in Elizabeth's time.

Music reached a peak in the Elizabethan and Restoration periods which has not been equaled since, at least in quality.

Elizabeth's was not only an age of music but also one of poetry. Sir Philip Sydney and Edmund Spenser were at the height of their powers then, and Thomas Campion was writing lovely lyrics, while Shakespeare and Ben Jonson were lightening their plays with poetry. Soon a way was found to combine such poetry with music, and this combination resulted in the English masques.

A masque was a kind of play in which both instrumental and vocal music was used. Sometimes it was performed by artisans and craftsmen at festivals on the village greens, and sometimes by prominent members of the various guilds in the guild halls. Or again, noblemen took part, and the masques were performed in the great halls of the castles. Queen Elizabeth herself liked to perform in masques, and much beautiful music was written for her court.

Queen Elizabeth died in 1603, and for a long time no music was created in England—or none at least of any consequence. Across the English Channel in the mid-seventeenth century, however, Jean Baptiste Lully, a former pastry cook, was cleverly composing music for the court of Louis XIV. He wrote ballets in which the ladies of the court took part and dance music, for the king liked to dance. He also wrote and produced a number of operas and organized the king's orchestra with its famous "twenty-four violins." For this orchestra he created a new form of orchestral overture with three separate parts, the first slow, the second fast, and the third slow.

Lully's work gave French music a widespread fame, but back in England the musical scene was dreary after Elizabeth's death. The Puritans under Oliver Cromwell were inclined to think that all things enjoyable must be wicked. True, there were many talented musicians; the blind poet John Milton was one of them. Nevertheless, the Puritans frowned on the singing of madrigals and the playing of chamber music. They destroyed the hymn books in the churches and dispersed the choirs and so discouraged pageants and masques that few of these were to be seen.

When James II came to the English throne, he must have felt the lack of music in his kingdom, and he wanted to do something about it. He had lived in France and had been enchanted by the music of the French court, so he decided to bring French musicians to his own court in England.

His effort was not very successful. He did not pay his musicians enough to live on after they reached England. It is said that one of them, a harpist, actually died of starvation. And employing foreign musicians did nothing to help the cause of English music.

It was just at this point that Henry Purcell appeared, and, though he was influenced by French music, his was truly an English genius.

Henry Purcell sang in the choir of the Chapel Royal in London until he was about fourteen and later became its organist. He was also "keeper of the king's instruments," and copyist of the royal music manuscripts. In all these ways he gained a wide experience in music. By the time he was twenty-one he was producing distinguished music of his own.

His music for strings heralded the early symphonic and string quartet *sounds,* although he did not herald these *forms.* His vocal music is vital, rhythmic, and full of bold harmonies with cross relations. He composed for both instruments and voices. He called his instrumental works "sonatas" (music to be "sounded"), distinguishing them by this word from "cantatas" which were meant to be sung. He directed that his sonatas be played by two violins and a bass viol. Violins had only recently been developed, and though many musicians disapproved of them, Purcell liked them.

Purcell wrote music for the organ and the harpsichord, and he composed many distinguished choral compositions. He was one of the first English musicians to mark the tempo and expression of his music by using Italian terms such as *allegro, largo, adagio,* and so on.

He also composed dramatic pieces, the best known of which is *Dido and Aeneas,* an opera he composed for the "Young Ladies of Dr. Josiah Priest's Academy for Young Gentlewomen."

This opera tells the story of Aeneas who, returning home from the Trojan wars, stopped at Carthage and was welcomed there by Dido, Queen of Carthage, who listened to the recital of his exploits and fell deeply in love with him. The months passed by, and Aeneas lingered on at Carthage until at last Jupiter sent him a message reminding him of his high destiny. Then Aeneas raised sail and started back toward Rome. When Dido saw that he had gone, she ordered a great pyre built on the shore, climbed to the top of it and stabbed herself.

The story is filled with drama, and Purcell made the most of it. He was one of the first composers to put strong dramatic emotion into music; certainly he was the first English composer to do so. The power and passion of the music of this opera, and the tragedy of Dido's lament, are not soon forgotten.

Before long the young musician, who was growing in popularity, became a kind of laureate. Whenever king or prince came home from a visit, when a new arrival was expected in the royal family, when a birthday was to be celebrated, or the coronation of the king, and at many other times besides, the laureate was invited to compose a song of welcome, and these "welcome songs" flowed from him, incredibly rich and melodious.

He was only thirty-six when he died, an age when many men are just beginning their lives. Only slowly did Englishmen realize what they had lost. It took time for them to understand that Henry Purcell had lifted English music out of its doldrums to its highest pinnacle. In time he came to be considered the foremost composer of his age. One writer said, "He blazed like a meteor across the English sky."

CHAPTER EIGHT

Monteverdi
and His Operas

IN A dark palace on the narrow street called the Via dei Bardi
in Florence in the sixteenth century, a group who called themselves the "Camerata" met together to talk of music. They were
all familiar with the motets and the madrigals of their day, and

with the musical instruments that were becoming so popular, but they were not all musicians. Their host, Count Giovanni Bardi, was a poet and scholar, and there were among them singers and musicians as well as the astronomer Vincenzo Galilei whose son was to become the great Galileo. There was at least one woman, also a poet, Laura Guidiccioni.

The room in which these friends met was a sumptuous but gloomy one; yet this fact did not dampen their spirits. They were dazzled by what they were trying to do. They wanted to revive the glories of the ancient Greek music.

The year of the Camerata's first meeting was about 1580. Everyone in Florence then, and indeed throughout Italy, was stirred with excitement at the thought of reviving the ancient civilizations whose importance they had just begun to realize. Benvenuto Cellini, apprentice to a goldsmith, spent his holidays searching in the rubble of old buildings for fragments of Greek and Roman sculpture; Raphael, the painter, was bewailing the destruction of ancient temples which the pope was tearing down to build new Christian churches. Many rich men were proud of the collections of antique vases, Roman glass, and the old coins and jewelry they could display in their houses.

The members of the Camerata, too, were moved by this admiration for the ancient world. Could they revive the music of the Greeks? they asked each other.

All they had to go by were the words of old Greek dramas and their choruses, which they believed had once been sung, some fragments of lyric poetry whose music now was lost, and statements about music such as those the philosopher Plato made in *The Republic*. With these they tried to reconstruct what they believed had been the music that for more than a thousand years had been still.

Each member of the group had his own idea of how to do it, but the first true discovery was Galilei's. He pointed out that a single voice declaring the singer's love or bewailing his fate or giving vent to some other emotion was very much more effective than several voices announcing the same thing together in madrigal style. He believed the Greeks must have sung solos. He wrote a scene from Dante's *Inferno* in which he tried introducing solos sung with the accompaniment of an instrument. At first the instrument was a viola da gamba or a violoncello, but later other instruments were tried. Galilei's experiment was the kernel from which the arias of later times were to spring.

One of the members, Jacopo Peri, on the other hand, was trying a new kind of musical narrative called *"stile rappresentativo."* It was something that was "intermediate" between singing and speaking. He said, "Therefore, abandoning every style of vocal writing known hitherto, I gave myself wholly to [a] sort of imitation [of speech]." This was to become the recitative which has been used in opera ever since.

The new ideas of solo singing and recitative having been explored, the Camerata now tried a third experiment. They combined various instruments into a little orchestra. They knew well how to blend voices together into madrigals, but here there were only instruments playing together. They used a harpsichord, a lute provided with bass strings, a viola da gamba or violoncello, and a *"liuto grosso,"* or large lute. The result could hardly have been Greek, but it was a milestone in the development of orchestral music.

So gradually, one after another, they tried out new musical ideas, and each of the Camerata believed that he had made a great discovery. It was Peri who thought of putting all these ideas together. In 1597 he composed music for a play which Ottavio Rinuccini, one of the members, wrote. Its story was based on the Greek legend of Daphne, the nymph who was taught by the god Pan to play the flute, and who was changed into a laurel tree when she was pursued by Apollo.

It was in *Dafne* that the Camerata first conceived the idea of dressing the singers in costume, and using a painted scene on the stage behind them. *Dafne* was a "truly princely spectacle and delightful beyond all others," one of the Camerata wrote.

There were arias in *Dafne,* and recitatives, and there was an orchestra, as well as costumes and scenery, but no one could say there was anything very Greek about it. Still, the audience was impressed. Before long everyone in Florence who had any claim to culture was talking of the new work the Camerata had done.

Gradually the reputation of the Camerata spread. In 1600, King Henry IV of France married Maria de' Medici, and Peri and Rinuccini were invited to write an opera to celebrate the royal wedding. So their *Euridice* was performed with great pomp and style in the Pitti Palace, and several noblemen took part in it. This was the first true opera.

The orchestra for *Euridice* was an ambitious one. One man played a harpsichord, three others played large guitars called *"chitarrones,"* and there were also a viola da gamba, a theorbo or double lute, and three flutes. The score of *Euridice* was written in "figured bass." That is, the chords meant to accompany the melody were indicated by means of bass notes with figures written above them. Bach and Handel used this figured bass for their later compositions, as did many other eighteenth-century composers. It is a form of musical shorthand.

With all their experiments, the Camerata never recovered the music of ancient Greece, of course, but they made their own discoveries. Claudio Monteverdi, the true founder of Italian opera, built on their work.

Monteverdi was born of an aristocratic family in Cremona. That was the village in which the Amati family had already begun to make their violins and where the Guarnieri and Stradivari families were to carry on the great tradition of violin-making.

Monteverdi began his musical career early. By the time he was sixteen he had published his first book of madrigals, and as he continued writing madrigals the critics began to condemn him. One of his critics, the monk Giovanni Artusi, was especially harsh in his comments, for he thought the madrigals were filled with dissonances that "offended the ear." Monteverdi's work was careless and radical, Artusi said. Musicians should have nothing to do with it. The young Monteverdi was not disturbed by Artusi's disapproval.

"I do not write things by accident," he answered, explaining that all he had done, he had done on purpose. "And be assured that the modern composer builds his works on the basis of truth," he said.

The Duke of Mantua at that time was Vincenzo Gonzaga. He was a great patron of the arts and was devoted to displays, fetes, plays, balls, and ballets. He had a little orchestra and he asked Monteverdi, then twenty-three, to be his singer and viola player. Monteverdi accepted the post, and the duke began demanding music for his establishment on such short notice and in such great quantity that the composer soon protested.

"I do most humbly beseech your Serene Highness, for the love of God, no longer to put so much work upon me; and to give me more time; for my chief desire is to serve you, and this excess of fatigue will not fail to shorten my life," he wrote his master.

Still he had compensations. The duke provided him with a handsome house, and with both men and women servants, and he had a coach and four. When the duke went traveling he took Monteverdi with him, and he even took him along in 1595 when he went to fight against the Turks. Then Monteverdi spent his days with his master on the battlefield, but at night, in the privacy of his tent, he worked on his compositions.

When the war was over, master and servant went on a journey to Flanders, and they stopped off in France, where they heard the light, gay music of the French court. Monteverdi was charmed by it. He began writing in a new style under its influence. He called his new music "heart music."

They returned to Italy, and in 1607 the duke, no doubt envious of the successful performances of the Camerata, ordered Monteverdi to write an opera for him. So *Orfeo* was written, and it proved a great success when it first was performed in Mantua, on February 24, 1607. It could not have been created without the work of the Camerata, but it was far greater than anything they had done.

Monteverdi employed forty pieces in the orchestra of his first opera. Experimenting with this grand collection of instruments, he soon found out which combinations sounded best, and he also discovered that certain instruments could express certain moods. For instance, the trombones and cornets could produce an eerie, weird atmosphere which suited scenes in the mythical underworld. Trumpets and drums, of course, were good for battle scenes, but flutes and oboes could create idyllic moods. The voice of the bassoon was ideal in comical situations, but no instrument did so well in passages dealing with love as the viol, while harps, lutes, and regals seemed suitable for creating the atmosphere of heaven.

Perhaps because *Orfeo* was such a success, the duke demanded another opera the following year, and Monteverdi composed *Arianna*. This opera tells the story of Ariadne, daughter of the King of Crete, who was in love with Theseus and helped him find his way out of the labyrinth where a dreadful beast, the Minotaur, was kept.

Arianna was performed to celebrate the wedding of the duke's son. The poet Rinuccini composed its libretto, and the famous architect Antonio Maria Viani built an immense theater for it in the duke's castle. Its success was even greater than that of *Orfeo;* six thousand people came to see it that day it was performed in 1608.

Only one fragment of *Arianna* remains. This is the "Lament of Arianna," who, deserted by Theseus on a rocky island, cries, "Let me die! Let me die!" The "Lament" is part of the repertoire of many singers today.

The Duke of Mantua died in 1612, and Monteverdi became

chapel master of St. Mark's Cathedral in Venice. The pageantry
and grandeur of life in Venice, the gold mosaics of her churches,
the luxury of her palaces, the color and vivid life of her canals
and narrow streets—all these were fresh inspiration to him. Some
of his best work was done in Venice.

He became a priest in 1633. Then he wrote religious music, but
still he continued with his dramatic work. One form he used was
called a *cantata da camera.* In this form he wrote *Il Combatti-
mento di Tancredi e Clorinda,* based on a poem by the Italian
poet Torquato Tasso. One dramatic scene in it portrays a duel
on horseback. The two actors ride at each other flourishing their
swords and announcing their intentions in *stile rappresentativo.*

Monteverdi himself directed the orchestra in his opera, and at
one point where the action grew more and more exciting, he
ordered the viol players to strike quick, repeated notes on the
strings, for he wanted to produce in the hearers a feeling of excitement and fluttering restlessness. He called this style of playing *"agitato."* The members of the orchestra were horrified at it,
and threatened to put down their instruments and go home. Only
with the greatest effort could the conductor persuade them to
go on playing.

Operas with lavish scenery and costumes, with singers who
had to be paid high fees and musicians who also had to be paid,
were extremely expensive. Kings, dukes, and princes could commission them for wedding celebrations or occasional festivals, but
they could not afford them very often. However, operas were now
so popular that it was obvious that with the right management
they might be turned into successful commercial ventures. The
coins collected at the door, if the audience was large enough,
would soon amount to as large a sum as any prince could pay.

So the impresarios, or business agents, began to build opera
houses. The first public opera house in the world, the Teatro San di
Cassiano, was opened in Venice in 1637. It was larger than the
chambers of the royal palaces, for the financial success of the per-

formance depended on the size of the audience. Well-paid singers and musicians were brought to it from every corner of Italy, and famed artists and architects were employed to design the scenery. The costumes of the performers were of velvet, satin, and rich brocade, which glittered and shone with golden jewelry. Venice, with her tradition of sumptuousness and luxury, surpassed herself now.

In former days, the performances had been held in the daylight hours, but now the managers decided that it would add to the glamour of the opera if it was given at night. The stage was therefore lighted up with torches and candelabra. But though the stage was brightly lighted the business management had no idea of spending money on candles for the house itself. Therefore, when the patrons paid admission at the door and were sold their librettos, they were also sold small candles so that they could find their way to their seats.

Though the lighting was poor and the ventilation very bad, the audience, when they were finally seated, could feast their eyes on marvelous stage architecture with all sorts of waterfalls, flying scenes, and quick transformations.

L'Incoronazione di Poppaea (*The Coronation of Poppaea*), Monteverdi's last and greatest opera, was performed in this opera house. It was the crowning work of his career.

Poppaea was not composed on a mythological theme, as most of the earlier operas had been. It was about the Emperor Nero and Imperial Rome, and the Venetians, who loved splendor and intrigue, thrilled to the music as they watched and listened. The music of *Poppaea* has aria-like sections which seem to pave the way for the Italian manner of singing called *bel canto*. And in this, his last opera, Monteverdi used dramatic characterization and symbolic musical expression that seem to foreshadow Wagner's "leitmotivs," or leading motives. Monteverdi was seventy-four when he wrote *Poppaea*. He died two years later.

And now men came traveling to Venice in ever increasing

numbers to see and listen to his great operas and to learn from them. Soon opera houses were built in Rome and Naples, and great schools of opera flourished in both those Italian towns. Heinrich Schütz, the German composer, traveled twice to Venice, heard Monteverdi's work and returned to Germany to write brilliant choral works of his own. Austria was soon producing operas too, and France was not behind the other countries. In France the performances grew into the most elaborate and lavish spectacles. Voltaire the philosopher described one of them when he wrote:

The opera is a spectacle as outlandish as it is magnificent, where the eye and ear are more satisfied than the mind, where the fact that everything has to be set to music causes the most ridiculous situations, where they sing while a town is being destroyed, and dance around a tomb, where one sees the palaces of Pluto and the Sun, gods, demons, magicians, marvels, monsters and palaces rising before one and destroyed in the twinkling of an eye. One suffers, nay, enjoys these extravagances, because this is fairyland; and so long as there is some display, good dances, beautiful music, and a few interesting scenes, one is pleased enough.

Though Voltaire laughed at it, as he laughed at most things, opera continued to flourish, and enthusiastic audiences heard it everywhere. This was a new kind of music—it was not the solemn polyphony of the church choirs, or the music made for capricious aristocrats and kings. It was the music of the emotions; it gave expression to people's feelings as no music theretofore had done, and it was Monteverdi who had first created it.

GEORG FRIEDRICH HANDEL

CHAPTER NINE

The King Stood Up

BEHIND a creaking coach that lumbered along the road between Halle and Saxe-Weissenfels in Germany, a small sturdy boy of seven was running and crying as he ran. The year was 1692. Inside the coach, the boy's father, a plump barber-surgeon, set his jaw and waited for the boy to tire himself out and go home. But the boy kept on running. After a while the barber-surgeon shouted to the driver to stop, and took his son into the coach. They had come too far for him to be sent home again. The boy was Georg Friedrich Händel, and his father, who had been forced against his will to take him on this journey, was on his way to visit his stepson, who was *valet-de-chambre* to the Duke of Saxe-Weissenfels.

At the castle of the duke the boy, his face washed and the dust brushed from his clothes, was made much of by the duke's staff who were the friends of the *valet-de-chambre*. Soon he was telling them that he could play the organ. Some time before a friend had brought a little portable organ to the house where he lived and he had smuggled it up to the attic. There he had learned to play it secretly, for his father would never have allowed him to spend his time on it.

The duke's retainers were delighted. There was an organ in the duke's chapel; they would take him there so he could play. The organ bench was a high one, so they lifted him up to it, and soon music was filling the chapel.

"He must play for the duke," the listeners said to each other And a little recital was arranged. Georg was helped up to the organ seat again, and the duke sat listening.

The Duke of Saxe-Weissenfels was tremendously impressed with Georg's playing; he insisted that the boy must have a musical education. The father grumbled, for he wanted his son to study law. But how could a barber-surgeon disagree with a duke? A compromise was made. Georg might study music, but he must study law as well.

So when they returned home the young Händel was given music lessons by Friedrich Wilhelm Zachau, the organist at the *Liebfrauenkirche* in Halle. He learned to play the keyboard instruments, and also the oboe and the violin. By the time he was eleven he had written six trios for two oboes and a bass viol.

"I wrote like the devil in those days, and chiefly for the oboe, which was my favorite instrument," he said when he looked at the trios many years later.

Händel's father died and Händel entered the law school, as his father had wished. He studied law for three years, but all the time he knew that the legal profession was not for him.

He went to Hamburg, where the best German opera of the day was being performed, and there he joined an orchestra. By the time he was twenty he had written two operas, *Almira* and *Nero*, and people began to say that he had promise.

If you were to become a composer of operas, Händel knew, you must go to Italy, so he set off on the long journey by stage coach across the Alps. The Italians liked him, calling him "the dear Saxon," and he was soon composing new operas, but he also attracted much attention by his harpsichord playing.

Once, masked, at a fancy dress ball, he sat down to play the harpsichord, and people drew around him, marveling and wondering who it could possibly be who played so well. Then Domenico Scarlatti, the great harpsichord virtuoso, drew near and listened. "It is either the famous Saxon, or the devil himself," Scarlatti said.

That may be only a legend. It is a fact, however, that a contest between Händel and Domenico Scarlatti was held at Cardinal Pietro Ottobuoni's palace in Rome. There the two musicians, both of whom were twenty-five years old, competed in improvising on the harpsichord and the organ. Though they were rivals, they were good friends, and it is said that they undertook short musical journeys together.

Scarlatti, who later settled in Spain, bequeathed us a priceless treasure of more than five hundred and fifty sonatas, some of which he called *Esercizi* (*Exercises*). These are not sonatas in the later classical form. They are short, elegant, and witty compositions, often suggesting orchestral effects, the strumming of castanets, or the calling of trumpets. They sparkle with original keyboard devices such as the crossing of hands, or daring skips.

Händel was still twenty-five when he returned to Germany and accepted the post of musical director for the Elector George of Hanover. But still his mind was filled with plans for operas. In 1711 he wrote *Rinaldo* (it took him just two weeks) and managed to have it produced at the Queen's Theater in the Haymarket in London. The duke gave him a leave of absence so he could go to the opening.

England was very warm in the reception of his work. The next year he went back there again on another leave of absence from the duke—and stayed in London for the rest of his life. The year was 1712, and he was twenty-seven years old. His name thenceforth was not Georg Friedrich Händel, but George Frederick Handel.

Producing these operas was a strenuous proceeding. The texts were all in Italian, and Handel kept quarreling with the librettists because they did not write them fast enough. He was composing the music at a tremendous rate of speed. At rehearsals, there were more difficulties. He insisted on employing Italian singers since he maintained that no English singers could do his work justice. And he rehearsed them in the most exacting way, losing his temper when they did not follow his directions exactly. Nevertheless, the operas were a great success. The audiences came crowding to the Haymarket.

During the next few years Handel found time to write much music. His former employer, the Elector of Hanover, had been crowned George I of England, and after a little awkwardness (for Handel had never been given permission to leave his employ) he began writing orchestral music for the royal fetes and festivals. In 1717 some of the *Water Music*, with its lovely combination of strings and brasses, was played at a water carnival on the Thames. The king attended it in his royal barge. The *Fireworks Music*, with its brilliant effects of light and shade, was also intended to be played outdoors.

For about three years Handel lived with the Duke of Chandos, one of the richest men in England. Then he wrote Te Deums and anthems to be sung in the duke's chapel, and his fame spread throughout England. Often in his compositions he borrowed melodic ideas or whole tunes from other composers and by some magic transformed them. Songs of street urchins, folk tunes, melodies Purcell had first conceived, and themes from his own earlier work—he took them all, altered them in color and form, made them his own. The "grand old robber" people have since called him, but in Handel's time plagiarism was a frequent and accepted thing in the arts.

In 1719 he managed an opera company in London—the Royal Academy of Music. Now he had a fine opportunity to produce the new operas with which his mind was filled.

For all the time opera was what he cared for most. He always returned to opera. One after another, new productions appeared at the Haymarket. He worked so fast that one of his librettists said, "Mr. Handel barely allowed me time to compose my verses." Altogether he produced forty-three operas.

The public is fickle and easily led. At first they crowded his theater and were loud in his praises. Then his jealous rivals, eager to discredit him, began to make trouble. One of them, an Italian composer named Giovanni Buononcini, was great competition for a while. Also, one of his chief subscribers set up a rival theater and succeeded in drawing the audience away from Handel's opera house. But Handel was a giant in more than physical stature. With colossal energy he tried to revive the waning popularity of his productions. He traveled down to Italy to engage new singers. He moved his opera to Lincoln's Inn Fields and then to Covent Garden, where he hired a finer theater. He continued to write and produce new operas.

Meantime other troubles beset him. His mother, to whom he was devoted, died, and as the audiences of the theater fell off he was more and more deeply in debt. At one time his creditors threatened to have him committed to debtors' prison.

Still he tried to extricate himself from his difficulties. He gave promissory notes to his most pressing creditors, not knowing how he would meet them when they came due.

And now, added to all these things, a stroke of paralysis affected his whole left side. He went to Aix-la-Chapelle to seek a cure. When he returned cured, his friends miraculously came to his rescue. They patronized a benefit concert for him which brought him 1000 pounds sterling, or about $5000. Not long after that they collected funds by popular subscription to have his statue set up in the fashionable Vauxhall Gardens. The French sculptor Louis François Roubillac was commissioned to make it, and nightly concerts of Handel's music were held at its base.

So in the warm glow of public approval Handel's health continued to improve. He began working again. Now he wrote *Serse*, one of whose arias, *"Ombra mai fu"* ("Never was there a shadow") is familiar to us now as Handel's stately "Largo." And he wrote *Deidamia*. But neither of these operas had much success.

Deidamia, produced in 1741, was Handel's last opera. It appeared to him shortly before this that "Italian opera" had run its course in England. He resolved to devote himself to another musical form.

He had always had a special gift for writing choral music, and he decided that he would write dramatic music that depended largely on choruses with a few solos interspersed among them with an orchestral accompaniment. These are called oratorios.

When the oratorio *Saul* was produced it was a failure. Even the solemn "Dead March," which has stirred hundreds of listeners since that time, fell on unresponsive ears. At the second performance the producers tried putting operatic songs between the choruses, but this did not help; after the third performance the oratorio was discontinued. Then followed *Israel in Egypt*, the dramatic story of the Exodus. The music was exalted, but this, too, failed.

Still Handel continued to compose his oratorios, with their

swelling choruses and tremendous crescendos. Not dependent in any way on scenery and costumes, and putting only slight emphasis on the virtuosos' powers, they revealed the words of great poetry with new emphasis.

Gradually now, though they paid no heed at first, people began to listen. His setting of Dryden's *Ode for St. Cecilia's Day* was followed by *L'Allegro, il Penseroso, ed il Moderato* based on Milton's "L'Allegro" and "Il Penseroso." By this time Handel began to retire more and more into himself. He seldom went out and never appeared at the concert hall, but still the music flowed on.

In 1741 he came out of his retirement. He was invited by the Duke of Devonshire, who was Lord-Lieutenant of Ireland, to visit "that generous and polite nation." He went in November and was so warmly received that he lingered there until spring.

In March it was announced that there was to be a benefit performance for a charitable institution in Dublin. Would Handel write some music for it?

Handel had music ready for it. He had brought the score of the oratorio *The Messiah* with him in his traveling bag. It had been composed in London in August and September 1741.

The Messiah, with its brilliant choruses, was performed on April 13, 1742, and it was a tremendous success. Audiences listened and marveled. The hall where it was sung was filled to overflowing. Soon the management was issuing special regulations for the sedan chairs which crowded the streets outside the concert hall and asking the ladies of the audience to come without their hoops —the hall would hold seven hundred people if they did not wear hoops, only five hundred if they did. Every penny of the money taken in for *The Messiah* the composer gave to the Foundling Hospital in Dublin.

It must have been pleasant staying in Ireland and listening to the reverberations of his great *Messiah,* but Handel returned to London the following year. He had been born in Germany, but, though he never learned to speak any but broken English, he had become a British subject.

In London on March 23, 1743, *The Messiah* was given again, and King George II was in the audience. It is said that when the singers had reached the great chorus which begins "For the Lord God Omnipotent Reigneth," with its glorious weaving of hallelujahs, the king started to his feet. In England, when the king stands, those with him must stand also. So the entire audience rose while the hallelujahs resounded triumphantly around them. Those who have listened to *The Messiah* since that time have always remained standing while the "Hallelujah" chorus is sung.

One oratorio after another followed now, with amazing speed. Among them were *Judas Maccabaeus, Joshua,* and *Solomon. Theodora* and *The Choice of Hercules* were both written in 1750, and there were others.

As he worked Handel's sight grew dimmer, and the gray film of cataracts spread across his vision. Three times he tried operations, but they were unsuccessful. A time came when he could scarcely see.

Still, he could play without seeing, and he was present to direct from his seat at the organ when his oratorios were produced. It is said that there were tears in the eyes of the audience as they watched the towering, nearly blind man led to his place at the organ.

Year after year Handel continued to conduct performances of *The Messiah*. And all the proceeds he received from them he turned over to the Foundling Hospital in London, for he had now become its chief benefactor.

On April 6, 1759, he attended *The Messiah* at Covent Garden for the last time. He died on the Saturday of Easter week, April 14, 1759, and was buried with England's great, in the south transept of Westminster Abbey.

Before he died, Handel had brought the art of choral singing to a grand climax. And his oratorios, those dramatizations of heroic narratives which he struggled to produce, still echo unsurpassed in their vitality and monumental grandeur. These oratorios, which, according to his biographer Friedrich Chrysander, relate the whole Biblical history of the Jewish people, are towering achievements. In them Handel brought together all the vocal and instrumental techniques which he had learned in his long life of travel and study. Here were sonorous, tight-fisted chords and fast-moving contrapuntal lines—all the color, scope, and vitality of a master artist.

Handel had acquired the limpid vocal line of his melodies in Italy. They are free flowing, long-limbed, pulsating. In Italy, too, he had learned the older forms of composition: the motet, the Venetian double chorus, antiphonal singing, the madrigals, and the *aria da capo* which had been developed by Alessandro Scarlatti.

But the tremendous choral tradition of England inspired his choral composing. As he worked, his choruses grew mightier, and gradually he began to use the chorus, even in recitative, as a kind of collective narrator, to paint vivid scenes and violent emotions.

The oratorios reflect Handel's deep concern with all mankind. "Why do the nations so furiously rage together?" he asks in solemn, troubled tones in *The Messiah*. And again, marveling, "The people that walked in darkness have seen a great light."

But he is interested in nature as well as in men. There are echoes across fields and valleys, the hum of woodlands, the hunter's horn, even the chirp of insects. All these effects he achieved by a highly original use of instruments and voices.

Interspersed among the choruses are solo arias in florid style, often of such deep and affecting simplicity that they remain unsurpassed even today.

Handel's orchestra was large and sonorous for his time. It has been said that he "wished for a cannon" to add to its volume. He raised the *concerto grosso*, an Italian form, to its highest pinnacle. This is a succession of movements, played by two or more solo instruments and accompanied by a full or stringed orchestra. Six of his *concerti grossi* are for woodwinds, twelve for strings. Besides these he wrote many concertos for organ and other solo instruments. He taught King George II's granddaughters for some time and wrote two books of suites for them which he called *Pièces pour le clavecin* (the French word for harpsichord). The air and variations known as the "Harmonious Blacksmith" are from the fifth suite of the little English princesses' first book.

Straightforwardness and vigor mark all Handel's work. It is so free from puzzling digression and mysticism that he is easily accessible and easily understood even by those who know little of music. That is why he not only was an idol in his own time, but is still popular and well beloved today. And audiences listening still rise to their feet when they hear the "Hallelujah" chorus as did King George II when he heard it more than two centuries ago.

JOHANN SEBASTIAN BACH

CHAPTER TEN

"Be Proud of Him . . ."

IT HAS been said that the music of Johann Sebastian Bach was like a mighty river whose tributaries drained a whole continent. All music seemed to be absorbed and combined in him—the little rivulets, the broad, smooth-flowing streams, the strong currents of great rivers—all came together, losing separate identities, emerging only as the mighty music of a great master.

For Bach had heard and absorbed the magnificent strains of

the organs of North Germany as they were played by the Scandinavian Dietrich Buxtehude and the Germans, Johann Reinken and Johann Pachelbel. But he knew also the exquisite music of the French court as Lully played it and as François Couperin and Jean Philippe Rameau wrote it for the *clavecin*. Besides these he had studied the famous *Treatise on Harmony* by Rameau, and the work of such Italians as Antonio Vivaldi, the great violin composer, and he had learned much from that of Girolamo Frescobaldi, the great Italian organist.

He had studied, copied, arranged, and combined the styles of all these composers and gradually incorporated many of their techniques into his own compositions. The Buxtehude influence appeared in the dark chromatic harmonies and in the toccata of his organ pieces, and Vivaldi and Arcangelo Corelli perhaps suggested the long, warm, melodic lines of his string writing, while the French influence is seen in the mannered ornamentation of the suites and the overtures.

But he did not confine himself to instrumental music. He knew the polyphonic singing of the Catholic Church, and the strong, simple Lutheran chorales. These last appear in his cantatas and are echoed through his Passion music.

To all the different kinds of music that he knew, as varied and as different as they were, Bach brought the genius of a master mind, so that they were no longer separate and varied, but were combined into a magnificent musical texture. Hearers now listen with awe to the work of this supreme master. One of them has written, "Bach is of the company with whom every age and every individual must arrive at a new understanding; and still his greatness has not been appraised, nor ever can be."

Who was this man in whom all music was thus blended and recreated? He was a simple, plain, hard-working German organist with an irascible temper, who never left Germany, nor indeed traveled more than three hundred miles from his home. Many have wondered whence his great power came; no one has been able to find out.

For who can tell what is the soil where genius grows? Many different elements must compose it. Perhaps Bach's musical genius was an accumulation that reached its peak after it had been passed on through many generations of musicians. Perhaps it was generated in the spiritual climate of Germany after the suffering of the Thirty Years War, for suffering strengthens moral fiber. Perhaps Bach's genius was developed through his own personal experience, through the severity of his upbringing, his orphaned childhood, his isolation from the main current of the world of men as he worked at organ playing and choir practicing, his need to make a living for his large family.

Whatever made that genius, there it was—a thing for which the world could be thankful.

Bach's family lived in Thuringia, a region of central Germany, and many of his ancestors were talented musicians. Records of them go back about three hundred years before Bach's time. One of them, Veit Bach, was a baker and is said to have taken his guitar with him when he went to the mill to have his corn ground into meal. He played it, so they say, while the mill wheel turned, regardless of the din around him. Veit Bach had many descendants, and they were nearly all musical in one way or another.

Some members of the family played organs in little Thuringian churches, others were violinists at ducal courts, and still others were town pipers. They had a great attachment for each other, and though as time passed the family spread over all Upper and Lower Saxony and Thuringia, they used to come to Erfurt once every year. Then fathers, sons and grandsons, uncles and cousins met for a lively family reunion. They usually began by singing a chorale, or simple hymn, for they were all religious. After that they sang anything they pleased, sometimes joining in comic songs, singing whatever else came into their heads. This made a queer kind of harmony that caused them all to laugh. They called it a *"quodlibet"* (whatever pleases).

It probably did not appear to any of these vigorous musicians that there was anything extraordinary about the new member of their clan who was born at Eisenach and baptized in the old church there in late March 1685.

Johann Sebastian's father taught the boy to play the violin when he was just big enough to manage the bow, but then both his parents died, and he was sent to live in the village of Ohrdruf where his older brother was organist in the Protestant church. There Johann Sebastian began to play the organ.

In the brother's house was a cabinet filled with the work of some of the great composers of the time, Johann Jacob Froberger, Johann Pachelbel, and Dietrich Buxtehude. Johann Sebastian wanted to open it and to study its contents, but his brother kept putting off the day when he would unlock it. Johann was not yet old enough, he said.

But Johann Sebastian could not wait. Secretly he managed to pull out the music sheets through the cabinet's grille. And secretly, at night by moonlight, he copied the treasured music. It was a useless effort, for his brother discovered him and took the copied sheets away.

When he was fifteen, Johann Sebastian left his brother's house to become a chorister in the School of St. Michael at Lüneberg. When his voice broke, he played the violin in the church orchestra. There was a good music library at Lüneberg and he was free to study there. Whenever he had a holiday he went on little expeditions to neighboring towns to hear some organist play or some choir sing. He had no money, so these expeditions had to be made on foot, but he was strong and did not care. Once he walked all the way to Hamburg, about thirty miles, to hear the famed organist Reinken. It seemed to him as if the whole world of music was waiting for him to explore.

At eighteen he was violinist for a time in the private orchestra of the Duke of Saxe-Weimar. But after a few months he heard that the people of Arnstadt had bought a fine new organ, so he went to see it, tried playing it, and was fascinated, for most of the organs he had played before had been old and broken down. This one was new, beautifully made, wonderful in its tone. His feet and hands moved nimbly over the pedals and the keyboard. The people of Arnstadt heard him, and invited him to be their organist.

So the young Bach went to Arnstadt, and there his true career began. Now he composed cantatas for the Arnstadt choir and wonderful organ preludes and fugues. The fugues were contrapuntal, written for several voices. The musical patterns of one part were imitated by the other parts at regular intervals in echo fashion. For a fugue is something like a verbal relay race—a group of actors all debating the same topic, each commanding attention for a few minutes and then retreating into the background.

The young organist's compositions were never dated, so no one can be sure which ones were written at Arnstadt and which later. There is one, however, whose date we know. It is a light piece of music, a caprice, which he called the *Cappricio on the Departure of a Beloved Brother*. It was written when Bach's brother, John Jacob, went to join the Swedish guard of Charles XII. The music describes his departure, and the various parts of it are labeled. One is "A general lamentation by friends"; another, "Friends coming in to take leave"; still another is "A fugue on a post-horn tune as the coach departs."

This kind of music which describes an event or a scene has since been called "program music," and it was to be very popular in the nineteenth century. But it apparently did not interest Bach very much, for this *Cappricio* is the only piece of program music he ever wrote. He greatly preferred "absolute music" which did not depend on external events or scenes.

While Bach was acting as organist at Arnstadt, he continued to make expeditions to neighboring towns where he could hear the performances of other musicians. Once he persuaded the consistory, or governing body of his church, to give him a month's leave of absence so that he could go to Lübeck, two hundred and twenty-five miles away. He wanted to hear the renowned organist Dietrich Buxtehude play.

Buxtehude not only played the organ at the regular church services, but also gave recitals on the afternoons of the five Sundays before Christmas between four and five o'clock. They were called *"Abendmusicken,"* and the public was invited to attend them. Bach was fascinated by these concerts and by Buxtehude's playing. He lingered on in Lübeck until the month which had been allowed him stretched out to four.

When he finally got back to Arnstadt, the consistory was very angry. They did not think much of his music anyway, they said. They considered his chorale variations too "surprising" and said that he bewildered the congregation with "many strange sounds." His organ preludes seemed to them too long, and when he altered them they were too short. He was so busy composing that he did not hold a sufficient number of choir rehearsals. They accused him of visiting the wine shops during the sermons and said he had a "strange maiden" in the choir loft making music with the choir. Johann Sebastian Bach had better find another place to go.

The new place turned out to be Mühlhausen, where Bach was engaged as organist at St. Blasius Church. The "maiden" was his cousin, Maria Barbara Bach. He returned to Arnstadt to marry her, and she went with him to Mühlhausen. They were very poor, for they received less than the equivalent of fifty dollars a year, but to this were added each year a few measures of corn, two cords of firewood, some brush, and three pounds of fish.

In Mühlhausen, in addition to his work as organist and choirmaster, Bach managed to go on with his composition. He wrote the *"Rathwechsel Cantata,"* which was a vocal composition to be sung before the town council met. And he also composed the beautiful *"Gott ist mein König,"* with its combination of instruments and voices. The funeral cantata, *"Aus der Tiefe rufe ich,*

Herr, zu dir," was also written at this time. The chorale is the unifying theme in these cantatas. They are composed with peerless skill and imagination.

But Johann Sebastian and Maria Barbara could not live on what was paid them at Mühlhausen. In 1708 when Duke William of Saxe-Weimar offered Bach the position of director of the court orchestra, he accepted it.

At the duke's court Bach played both the violin and clavier, and had an opportunity to study both French and Italian music and to experiment with suites and fugues. Here he wrote the well known Toccata in D Minor for Organ and some of his famous violin concertos, and in 1714 was promoted to concert master. But here, too, the composer was treated as a servant at the beck and call of his master. On feast days he was required to dress up in Hungarian costume and wait on the table.

By 1717 Bach decided that he had had enough of this. He wrote his master a letter of resignation; he had been invited to join the entourage of the Prince of Anhalt-Cöthen.

When the duke read Bach's letter, he was enraged. He hated the Prince of Anhalt-Cöthen and said that Bach had no right to leave his service anyway. So he threw his musician into prison from the sixth of November till the second of December. When the duke released him, he found that Bach was as eager as ever to leave his employ. He had his way at last. The duke allowed him to go, but "ungraciously," and the Bachs lost no time in packing up and moving to Cöthen.

There was no organ at Cöthen, and heretofore Bach's chief interest had been in organ music. But the prince had a small orchestra, so Bach turned to composing instrumental music.

The orchestra which he directed was not like the great symphony orchestras of the present day. It was what might be called a "chamber orchestra," consisting for the most part of large and small instruments of the violin family. Added to these "strings" there were flutes, oboes, and sometimes a bassoon for "woodwind" instruments, a trumpet and a horn or two for the "brasses," sometimes a kettledrum, and a harpsichord to fill out the harmony. Bach himself generally sat at the harpsichord to conduct, indicating the tempo with a nod of the head, a change of pace with a gesture of the hand.

The music which this orchestra produced was complex, highly organized, and full of infinite variation. Some movements of the orchestral suites and concert are very dramatic, loud, and virile, but even when the music was quiet it was strong.

Among these works were the six famous Brandenburg Concertos, each of which employs a different combination of instruments. They were dedicated to Christian Ludwig, Margrave of Brandenburg, who never had them performed.

Bach used a great many old dance forms called "suites" in his composing, but he filled these old forms with vivid, sparkling life. No one had ever written such suites as his, and no one has done so since his time. He used dance forms from many countries. Among them were stately dances like the "sarabande," lively "gavottes," bright "minuets," thoughtful "allemandes," and quick-running "courantes" and "gigues." Besides these suites he wrote concertos for solo instruments and orchestra, and *concerti grossi* that combined different groups of instruments. All these were the ancestors of the yet undreamed-of symphony and concerto of the present day.

Bach had not been very long with the Prince of Anhalt-Cöthen when Maria Barbara died of a fever. She had been a good companion to him and had borne him seven children. He was desolate without her, for he was essentially a domestic man, and his home and children meant much to him.

In about a year, therefore, he married again. His new wife was Anna Magdalena Wülken, the daughter of the town trumpeter. And now his family increased again until the number of his children was thirteen from this second marriage. Some of them did not live to maturity.

Anna Magdalena was more than a good housekeeper; she was much interested in music. She copied Bach's music for him in a clear style that gradually became so much like his own that it was hard to tell them apart.

And Bach, on his side, spent many happy hours teaching her to play the clavichord. He worked out a new fingering technique which he taught her, curving her hand over the keys in such a way as to use the thumb and little finger. Generally, up to that time, players had used only the three middle fingers, although some masters in France and Italy had begun to use all five.

In teaching his wife to play, Bach wrote a series of practice pieces for her called *Ein Kleines Clavier-Büchlein für Anna Magdalena Bach*. Some of the short pieces in this book were assembled later into suites, among them the well-known "French Suite" and the "English Suite."

Anna Magdalena was not Bach's only pupil; he took the musical education of his children very seriously. Two of his eldest sons, Wilhelm Friedemann and Karl Philipp Emanuel, appeared to be especially gifted. In teaching them he adopted a new way of tuning the clavier.

Before Bach's time keyboard instruments were tuned in such a way that if some of the major and minor keys were in tune, others had to be violently out of tune. Therefore when compositions in harmonically distant keys were played on the same program, it was necessary to stop and retune the whole keyboard. Many musicians were troubled by these interruptions to their programs, and many instrument-makers tried to find a better way of tuning.

Bach's contemporary Andreas Werckmeister is said to have found the solution to the problem. He lowered some of the notes slightly and raised others. And so by altering their mathematical relationship he established the division of an octave. This octave he divided into twelve equal semitones. The new method of tuning made it possible to have a continuous performance, and it also brought a new freedom of modulation, a possibility of changing tonalities, within the same composition.

Bach was delighted by Werckmeister's new system of tuning. He wrote a superb collection of twenty-four preludes and twenty-four fugues for his pupils and called this collection *Das Wohltemperirte Clavier* (*The Well-Tempered Clavier*). Here he adopted not only the tuning system which has remained in use ever since, but also the term "well-tempered," which Werckmeister had coined.

Bach might have stayed on at Cöthen composing fugues and suites and enjoying his happy life with Anna Magdalena and their growing family, but unfortunately the prince married. His new wife was not much interested in music, so the prince lost interest in it, too. Anyway Bach was ambitious to have his children well educated, and there was not much opportunity for schooling at Cöthen. At Leipzig, however, there was a famous university.

So Bach decided to give up his pleasant life as director of music at the prince's court. He applied for the position of singing master at St. Thomas's School in Leipzig, and was successful in obtaining it after he had passed a rigid examination on his religious beliefs.

The new position was not an easy one. Bach had to teach the boys of the school not only singing but also Latin, and he was required to supply music for weddings and funerals in all four of the great churches of Leipzig. The boys were often from poor families, ill-disciplined, and often sick. They had to remain in the unheated church for three or four hours at a time and walk through the streets, singing and begging, in all kinds of weather, besides singing in frequent processions on holy days.

The new choirmaster often lost his temper with the unruly boys, and he was very poorly paid, though an occasional funeral added a few coins to his stipend. One year he complained that the air of Leipzig was so good that not many people died.

Yet out of this difficult situation came the music that was to crown Bach's whole career. For while he was scolding the choirboys and shivering in the cold church, his magnificent cantatas were taking form. Every Sunday morning a new cantata was produced till at last he had composed over two hundred and fifty of them. They were an expression of his strong Lutheran faith. Each one was different from the others for they did not adhere to any set form. In them he used arias, recitative, chorale, fugue, and many other forms. No one thought them worth printing, and many of the manuscripts have been lost or destroyed. About two hundred remain, and it has been said that "there is nothing in modern music that is not contained in them." Among them is the *Magnificat*, with its many arias and a double chorus, which has been called a Protestant homage to the Virgin Mary.

At this time, too, Bach wrote his Passion music, intended to accompany the words of the Scriptures as they tell of Christ's suffering and death. He may have composed four Passions for the four Gospels, though only two of them remain. They are the *Passion According to St. John* and the *St. Matthew Passion*.

The *St. Matthew* Passion had been called "the greatest offering to Christ ever created by man." It lasts four hours and employs two orchestras, two choruses, and soloists. Bach had only thirty-four performers including orchestra, soloists, and choir to produce it, whereas nowadays when it is performed more than a hundred are employed.

Into this music Bach poured all his deep religious feeling and brought together all his musical techniques, marking little prayers such as "Jesus help me" in the margin of the score. He treated the words of Christ with special reverence, reserving for them his most melodious music as he made the high voices of the violins weave over them.

Beautiful as is the music of the *St. Matthew Passion*, it was not very well received. One of Bach's pupils described its first performance in this way:

Some high officials and well-born ladies in one of the galleries began to sing the first chorale with great devotion to their books. But as the theatrical music proceeded they were thrown into the greatest wonderment, saying to each other, "What does it all mean?" While one old lady, a widow, exclaimed, "God help us! 'Tis surely an opera comedy!"

The opinion of this old lady did not greatly matter to Bach; what troubled him very much more was the attitude of the city council toward his music. The council, according to the German custom of the time, was in charge of all the music of the city, and its members did not like Bach's music. He had run into trouble with them in almost his first days at Leipzig. They had already written him letters expressing dissatisfaction with his work and reprimanding him for negligence of official duties and insubordination. At one time he was so troubled and dissatisfied that he wrote to an influential friend asking his help in finding another post. "My masters are strange folk," he wrote, "with very little care of music in them." But he received no encouragement.

At last, in despair, he resolved to appeal to Frederick August, King of Saxony and Poland, whose residence was in Dresden, the capital of Saxony. Bach's eldest son, Wilhelm Friedemann, had become organist at the *Sophienkirche* in Dresden. Bach sent to the king two sections of a new Mass he was composing, the "Kyrie" and the "Gloria." The Mass was the great B Minor Mass.

The king, however, put off hearing his music. In Leipzig, for three years Bach waited and continued to work on his Mass. The B Minor Mass is one of the mightiest of all choral works. It was too gigantic to be performed as a church ceremonial, but parts of it were often given in Lutheran churches, and it is still performed for large audiences at more or less regular intervals throughout the world.

Perhaps Bach did not need the approval of men to do his best work. He continued to compose whether people liked what he wrote or not. He wrote the *Christmas Oratorio,* which has one part for each day between Christmas and the Epiphany. And he wrote the beautiful *Goldberg Variations.* This is a long composition for harpsichord and was commissioned by Baron Kaiserling to be played to him at night when he had difficulty in sleeping. They were named after Johann Gottlieb Goldberg, one of Bach's pupils who performed them.

So the years passed, and Bach grew old. His eyesight failed, but Anna Magdalena helped him, and he continued to teach, to conduct, and to compose. But even with age and failing eyesight his work lost none of its freshness. All the time people thought of him simply as a craftsman, like his forebears, the Bachs of Thuringia, and as a hard-working music teacher and choirmaster. That, in fact, was how he thought of himself.

One last episode must be told of those final years. He had been working at that great composition called *The Art of the Fugue,* when he received a summons from King Frederick the Great of Prussia to come to the royal court at Potsdam. An invitation from the king is a command, so, although he was not well, and the journey by stagecoach was a hard one, Bach obeyed. He took his son, Wilhelm Friedemann, with him.

When they reached the court, King Frederick, who was himself a good musician, was playing a flute concerto with his orchestra. When he heard that Bach and his son had arrived he put down his instrument.

"Gentlemen, old Bach is here!" he announced to the musicians.

Then he welcomed Bach, who was wearing his dusty traveling suit though he had brought his neat black outfit with him to wear at court, and led him through the rooms of the palace, letting him try several pianos, which were new instruments in that day. Bach never liked pianos, and most other musicians of his time agreed with him.

So the king brought him back to the clavier, gave him a theme, and asked him to improvise a fugue.

"No one can play like Bach," the monarch kept repeating as he listened.

Bach returned to Leipzig soon after that and wrote a musical memento of the occasion which he sent to the king. He called it

Das Musikalisches Opfer (*The Musical Offering*). It consists of thirteen pieces in various contrapuntal forms in which he embodied all forms of canon in a masterly way.

Toward the end of his life Bach's eyes troubled him more and more. For years he had strained them with copying music, beginning with those early days when he had copied his brother's music by moonlight. At last it became necessary to have an operation, and the same English surgeon who had operated on Handel was summoned. The operation was not successful; Bach became totally blind. He suffered a stroke not long after that, died on June 28, 1750, and was buried near the Church of St. John in Leipzig.

"Be proud of him," his biographer, Johann Forkel, was to write later. "Be proud of him, O Fatherland, but also worthy of him."

But that was not written until 1802, long after he had died, long after the pages of his manuscripts had been scattered, and Anna Magdalena, who tried to copy and arrange them, had been forced by poverty to take refuge in an almshouse.

So Bach remained neglected, his works unappreciated, unfashionable, conservative, and backward-looking to his contemporaries. For at the emperors' and princes' courts another style had come into fashion, a light, gay music with airy accompaniment in a style called "galant." And Bach's own sons, whom he had trained so carefully, turned away from his music toward this new, worldly style.

It was not until a full century after his death that the German composer Felix Mendelssohn discovered the manuscript of the *St. Matthew Passion* and performed it, and the world began to appreciate the genius of Johann Sebastian Bach.

CHAPTER ELEVEN

Gluck Attains a Grand Simplicity

BACH never wrote an opera. It has been said that every note he wrote was dedicated to God, and every piece of music he composed was an expression of his deep faith. There was no place in his work for the worldliness of opera.

Yet opera in the seventeenth and eighteenth centuries was extremely popular. From Venice, Naples, and Rome, it had been carried to the royal and ducal courts of the rest of Europe, where it had become fashionable. Operas then were gala occasions, the very high points of the social season. Grandees attended them arrayed in a glitter of jewels and brocades. They sat in their loges sipping beverages and playing cards or throwing dice while they discussed politics or argued about the merits of the various singers.

The performances themselves had changed greatly in the century and a half since Monteverdi wrote his operas. Now in the period which historians call the "baroque," custom demanded that the composer of opera follow many hampering conventions.

First of all he must comply with the personal whims of his patron, for if he failed to do this there would be no opportunity for his opera to be heard at all.

Second he must please the one or two singers who were the stars of the performance; they maintained a kind of tyranny over the operas in which they performed. The arias they sang had to be written in such a way as to give each singer an opportunity to demonstrate his special abilities. Sometimes, therefore, the composer was permitted to indicate only the barest outline of his aria so that the singer could add his own embellishments with roulades, trills, and turns to suit his own special aptitude. Some of the famous singers at that time had artificial voices that spanned the whole range of the female tones but surpassed any woman's voice in volume. Their flexibility seems to us now extraordinary. Normal tenors, baritones, and basses cannot sing the music that was written for these counter tenors or *castrati,* so we cannot judge what it was like nor can we reproduce it.

Besides the problem of pleasing both patrons and singers, the composer had other difficulties. He had to observe a whole host of arbitrary regulations that had grown up around opera. The orthodox number of "persons" in the cast had to be six—no more, no less. Music for artificial voices was preferred. Moreover the character of the arias was rigidly set; some arias had to be dramatic; others, express pathos; others, demonstrate the extreme agility of the singer's voice. Often there was a demand for an aria of imitation, generally with *flute obbligato.* This was studded with attempts to imitate birdcalls, or trumpets, or there might be echo effects.

Not only were the kinds of arias prescribed, but also their place in the opera was strictly regulated. Every scene must end with an aria, and the most important arias must come at the end of the first and second acts. This might not be at all in accord with the logic of the narrative or the dramatic sense of the composition. But that did not matter: the rule must be obeyed.

Because of these restrictions the Florentine *dramma per la musica* had shriveled by the seventeenth century into a sorry state. Opera had become little more than a collection of show pieces intended to exhibit the singers' virtuosity. The recitatives between the stilted arias did little to help. They were not meant to advance the plot, but merely served as resting spaces for the acrobatic singers.

It must not be thought that those who cared for music were

content with this state of things, for that was far from the case. Although the royalty and audiences generally liked it as it was, there were many of taste and culture who objected to the condition into which the opera had fallen, and many who raised their voices against it. But the tyranny of patrons and singers and the hold of operatic convention were all so strong that it appeared unlikely that anything could be done about it. And then Christoph Willibald von Gluck appeared.

Gluck did not come full-armored to do battle with the old conventions. For a long time no one realized that he was to try to reform the opera; perhaps he did not know it himself. He was a German, born July 2, 1714, the son of a gamekeeper in the employ of Prince Lobkowitz of Bohemia. The boy was given music lessons at a Jesuit school near the prince's estate. When he was eighteen, he showed musical promise, and his father sent him to Prague, one of the great musical centers at that time. The gamekeeper had not enough money to support his son in Prague, however, so the youth managed for himself by playing at village fairs and dances. In time, Prince Lobkowitz called him to go from Prague to Vienna, and there Prince Melzi befriended him. Prince Melzi took him to Milan, where he studied under the renowned teacher G. B. Sammartini. And at that time he became interested in classic Greece, an interest which led him to choose Greek legends for his themes.

The promise that the forester's son had shown in Bohemia was coming to fruition; he was developing into a fluent composer. Between 1741 and 1745 he produced nine operas, all well received by the fashionable world. They followed the conventions and were skillfully composed, but his aim in writing them was purely commercial.

Still, the young Gluck was making a name for himself. In 1745 he was invited to London to compose two operas and a *"pasticcio"* for the famous Haymarket Theater. The word *pasticcio* is Italian for pastry. This was a medley of many popular melodies. While he was working on these compositions he entertained the Londoners by playing musical glasses. That is, he made music by rubbing a moistened finger on the rims of twenty-six glasses tuned by filling them with different quantities of water.

When the two operas were finally performed, they were failures. Handel, who was in London at that time, said, "Gluck knows no more of counterpoint than my cook." He did not add that the cook was an excellent and well-trained singer. Other knowledgeable English musicians agreed with Handel in his scorn, and Gluck, no doubt angered by their comments, returned to Vienna.

Now the Empress Maria Theresa appointed Gluck her court chapel master and the pope conferred on him the Order of the Golden Spur. This was the same order that he was later to confer on Mozart, but, though Mozart made light of the honor, Gluck was impressed by it and always signed his name thereafter "Ritter von Gluck."

It looked as if Gluck would live out his life composing conventional operas for the fashionable world. But then he began to experiment with ballet music. His friend, the dancer Jean Georges Noverre, was an advocate of simplicity and naturalness in interpreting the emotions of human beings through the dance. The dramatic ballet based on Molière's *Don Juan,* which Gluck wrote for him, was a great artistic success. But he did not keep on with ballet music, either, for he met Raniero da Calzabigi, an Italian poet, and their friendship changed not only Gluck's own work but the whole course of opera.

Calzabigi hated the conventions that had bound opera so long, and he hated especially the writer Pietro Metastasio, whose librettos dominated the operatic stage. He and Gluck were soon talking of a new kind of opera on the classic theme of Orpheus and Eurydice.

Orfeo ed Euridice was produced in Vienna, October 5, 1762. It was coldly received at first, but in two years the popular opinion of it changed, and it was enthusiastically acclaimed. It was performed on the occasion of the Archduke Joseph's coronation as Holy Roman Emperor at Frankfort, and there the young poet Goethe heard and admired it. Later it was given in a French version in Paris, and when the French philosopher Jean Jacques Rousseau heard it he ridiculed it. But later, when he heard it for the second time, he said, "Since one can have such keen pleasure for two hours, I imagine life may be good for something."

Orfeo could indeed give its listeners keen pleasure, but it did much more than this; it revolutionized the whole course of operatic music. Formerly, operas had been preceded by an instrumental piece in three movements which had no organic relationship to the opera that was to follow. Now Gluck created an overture that was truly an introduction. It set the mood and dramatic pace for the whole work.

Furthermore, he did away with the complicated plot that had been meant to provide the right number of arias for the customary six singers. Instead he told the classic story simply, centering all his music on the emotions that the myth stirred. *Orfeo* has only three characters besides the chorus, but the chorus plays a different role in each scene. Its members are mourners in the first act, lamenting with Orpheus at Eurydice's tomb. Again they are Furies trying to bar his way to Eurydice until they are banished by the strains of his harp. Later they are Elysian shades, and finally they are a human crowd rejoicing, for Eurydice has come back to life.

All the bombast, all the artificiality that had been associated with opera were set aside in *Orfeo*. Poetry and music were blended here in an atmosphere whose severe simplicity intensified its poignant emotion and created a dramatic continuity. Here the arias were no mere show pieces for versatile singers. The recitatives were not of the static kind that audiences had been used to; they were poetry accompanied by an instrumental obbligato.

Gluck had to support himself and could not be sure that his new style would suit his audiences, so he now produced more con-

ventional and less original work. In 1767, however, he and Calzabigi produced another opera on a larger scale, *Alceste*. This is the
story of a devoted wife who offers her life to save her husband,
and it contains her famous plea to the forces of the underworld,
"*Divinités du Styx.*"

Gluck dedicated *Alceste* to Duke Leopold of Tuscany and explained in his dedication:

> I have tried to reduce music to its real function, that of seconding
> poetry by intensifying the expression of sentiments and the interests
> of situations without interrupting the action by needless ornament.
> . . . I have accordingly taken care not to interrupt the singer in the
> heat of the dialogue, to wait for a tedious *ritornel,* nor do I allow him
> to stop on a sonorous vowel in the middle of a phrase to show the
> nimbleness of a beautiful voice in a long cadenza. . . . I also thought
> that my chief endeavor should be to attain a grand simplicity. . . .

Again he talked of simplicity in a letter to the editor of the
French newspaper *Mercure de France,* saying that he had tried
to make his music "as simple and natural as I can possibly make
it. . . . For this reason I do not employ those shakes, passages,
and cadenzas which Italians use so lavishly."

Gluck's idealism, however, did not gain him much popularity
in Vienna, and he was disappointed and dissatisfied with the reception of his new work there. So he went to Paris, no doubt hope-
ful of finding more success there. His former pupil, Marie An-
toinette, had married the "dauphin," or future king, of France,
and he was assured that she would help him. Several of his works
appeared there, and then the magnificent *Iphigénie en Tauride*
was produced in Paris in 1779, and it made him an idol there. But
unfortunately he became the center of an artistic controversy,
and eventually, disgusted, he returned to Vienna.

Gluck was one of the few dramatic composers before Mozart.
He invented sublime melodies, and, though he was not the first
to show that the timbre of the instruments could invoke emo-

tional response, he produced great musical effects by the most simple means.

Gluck wrote over thirty operas, though only seven of these were in his new style. His ideas were so revolutionary that they stirred controversy wherever his work was performed. He generally enjoyed this controversy, for he was a man of strong convictions. It has been said that he was the *crossest* conductor of his time.

He lived out a long, dignified, and prosperous life in a suburb of Vienna. Boastful and self-assured, he was flattered and made much of by a large circle of admirers. An English visitor spent a day with him and said that he was dressed magnificently in a gray suit embroidered with silver and that he carried a heavy gold-headed cane. His impatience and quick temper seemed to increase as the years passed, and his gray eyes flashed fire when the very name of one of his musical rivals or critics was spoken. But surely these things may be forgiven in the man who created *Orfeo ed Euridice.*

CHAPTER TWELVE

Haydn Creates an Orchestra

H A N D E L had already turned from his operas to writing oratorios, and Bach, at Leipzig, was working on the Masses that were to crown his career, when Franz Joseph Haydn was born in 1732 in the village of Rohrau, Austria. Joseph Haydn was to carry forward the tradition of European music. By experiment and trial, he was to develop an orchestra that was the ancestor of the great symphonic orchestras of the present day. And he was to show that folk tunes could give music vitality and richness. Austrian, Hungarian, Croatian, and gypsy folk music resound through all his work and give it substance. Many great composers since his time have followed his example in using folk-inspired tunes in their work, for the music that springs from the common people reflects life and strength.

What kind of man was this "Papa" Haydn, as the members of his orchestra liked to call him? What forces molded him? He had none of what men call advantages at first. His father was a wheelwright, his mother a cook for a local family of the nobility. They were very poor.

Nevertheless, his father owned a harp. In the evenings he would sit by the fire and play it, and he and little Joseph, who had a very high, sweet, singing voice, would sing together. They called the boy "Sepperl."

When Sepperl was about five years old his uncle, Johann Frankh, heard him sing and persuaded his father that he ought to have a musical education.

Johann Frankh was a school teacher and a registrar for the church, and he rang the bell for fires in his town. He took Sepperl home with him to Heinberg on the Danube where the boy could help him with these tasks and get some training in the church choir. When Sepperl was only six he was taking part in singing the Mass. Years later he wrote: "Our Almighty Father endowed me with so much facility that I stood up like a man and sang Masses in the church choir, and I would play a little on the clavier and violin."

It was not very long before Sepperl learned to beat the drum. The villagers laughed when they saw the sturdy little boy marching along the street in a procession while he hammered away at a kettledrum that was set on the shoulders of a hunchback.

Aside from his music Sepperl led a miserable life. His aunt made a drudge of him and neglected him. "I looked like a ragamuffin," he was heard to say. And his uncle beat him—"I had more beatings than food." Yet he withstood all these hardships without self-pity. Judging from his music he preserved to the end of his days an exuberant joy and a healthy acceptance of life.

And still he sang with his light, clear voice. When Karl Georg Reutter, the choirmaster of St. Stephen's Church in Vienna, came to Heinberg looking for choristers, he heard the eight-year-old Sepperl sing and offered him a place in his choir.

It was exciting for Sepperl to be in the historic St. Stephen's Church with its high tower from which he could look out across the Hungarian plain to the east and see the Moravian fields to the north and the woods and foothills of the Alps on the other two sides. And the new choirboy learned much from Reutter. But there was even less to eat here than there had been at his uncle's house, though sometimes the choirboys got "refreshments" when they sang at a reception.

When Sepperl's voice broke, he stayed on with the choir, playing the violin. He was a very lively boy who loved practical jokes, and this was his undoing. For once, on a sudden impulse, he came

up behind one of the older members of the choir and pulled off
his wig. Then Reutter beat him and turned him out.

He wandered penniless through the Vienna streets, his sole
possessions three ragged shirts and a worn coat. Hungry, he lay
down on a park bench and slept, and in the morning an acquaintance named Spangler came by. Spangler was a singer, and he was
poor, too. He took Haydn home with him to the garret where he
lived with his wife and baby.

Haydn joined a band of serenading musicians in order to earn
money for food. It was the custom in Vienna then for people to
hire musicians to play under the window of a lady on her birthday or of a gentleman on his name day, or to play at weddings or
other festive occasions. So Haydn made music in the streets of
Vienna and mingled with all sorts of people and learned songs
from them which he never forgot, but used later in his own
musical compositions.

After a time Haydn left the Spanglers, for he found a place to
live in a building called the Michaelerhaus. Here he had a cold
little room under the roof and acted as cook and stoked fires for
the richer occupants of the lower floors. When he had finished his
work, he lighted his candle and studied the music of the composers he admired. One night he discovered the sonatas of one
of Bach's gifted sons, Karl Philipp Emanuel. He played the sonatas
over and over on his clavier, "for instruction and for my own delight, especially when I felt oppressed and discouraged by worries, and always left the instrument gay and in high spirits."

The sonatas of Karl Philipp Emanuel Bach which Haydn
discovered with such joy were inventive musical essays in three
sections. Their form had unfolded gradually in the hands of Alessandro Scarlatti, of Johann Sebastian Bach, and now in the work
of Bach's son. Haydn himself was to develop and elaborate them
—but that was to come later. Now he was playing them for his
own "instruction" and "delight."

It happened that the famous librettist Metastasio lived at the

Michaelerhaus, and Haydn struck up a friendship with him. Metastasio was a gentleman and knew all the fine points of etiquette, so Haydn learned them, too, and these he found useful later in his dealings with the nobility. He also made the acquaintance of Nicola Porpora, the famous singing teacher, and soon was employed as his accompanist. They went together to fashionable "watering places" every season, and met all sorts of important musical people. One of these was Christoph Willibald von Gluck, who was then making a great stir in Europe by "reforming" the opera.

Several years later Haydn was invited to join the orchestra of Ferdinand Maximilian Morzin, who had a castle and a large estate at Lukaveč near Pilsen in Bohemia. There he composed his first symphony, perhaps not knowing the importance of what he had created.

This first symphony, which was written in 1759, used four wind instruments (two oboes and two horns) to increase the sonority of the full orchestra. Probably a harpsichord was used to fill out the occasional gaps between the melody and the bass.

Prince Paul Esterházy, a young man of twenty-five, was in the audience when that symphony was played. He lost no time in asking Haydn, who had recently married, to come to his castle at Eisenstadt to direct his orchestra, and Haydn agreed to go.

The Esterházys were the richest and most powerful of all the Hungarian nobility. They owned twenty-nine manors, twenty-one castles, sixty-six market towns and four hundred and fourteen villages. Besides these they had estates in lower Austria and a whole county in Bavaria. Prince Paul Esterházy had built himself a castle at Eisenstadt which had a chapel, a library, a picture gallery, and an opera house that accommodated four hundred people. The castle was surrounded by an artificial lake with forests, streams, and waterfalls. He also had a large and beautiful collection of musical instruments, and Haydn was to have the use of these, and to be in charge of the prince's orchestra.

Being in charge of the prince's orchestra was no small task, for
Prince Paul wanted concerts every day, and he wanted Haydn

to compose all the music for them. So Haydn had to work late at his compositions every night, and rehearse his orchestra every morning. In addition to this he acted as music librarian and saw that the instruments were in repair. And he was expected to act as a sort of counselor and look after the manners, morals, and dress of the musicians. Fortunately this last was not hard, for the musicians loved their generous, good-hearted leader. Haydn was happy in his work, though much of it was drudgery. He stayed on at Eisenstadt for nearly a quarter of a century, occupying three rooms in the servants' wing. Though Prince Paul died, his brother Nicolaus had the same love for music, and Haydn continued his work.

He had ideal working conditions for a composer of any age. He was called upon to produce new music continuously, and had an orchestra to try out his new works, making changes in them if he was not satisfied with the results.

"My prince was always satisfied with my works," he wrote later. "I not only had the encouragement of constant approval, but as conductor of an orchestra I could make experiments, observe what produced an effect and what weakened it, and was thus in a position to improve, alter, make additions or omissions, and be as bold as I pleased; I was cut off from the world, there was no one to confuse or torment me, and I was forced to become *original*."

So, making "additions or omissions" and being as "bold" as he pleased, he developed two different kinds of instrumental music. There was the music that was suitable for small informal rooms —the trios, quartets and quintets, and the compositions for solo instruments with orchestra. But there was also the music suitable to be played in great halls by large orchestras—the symphonies, overtures, and concertos. Here was the first distinction between chamber music and symphonic music, each one so beautiful in its own way.

In his chamber music Haydn himself considered the string

quartet, with its first and second violins, viola and violoncello, the most satisfactory form. No other combination of instruments, he thought, gave such purity of sound, such conciseness of volume, such exquisite restraint. He wrote a great many string quartets, and as quartet players could easily carry their instruments about with them and play them almost anywhere, Haydn's name was soon known not only in the great houses like that of the Esterházys, but also in more modest homes. He was known in Vienna, Paris, London, and Madrid.

The prince made a new summer residence called Esterház near Süttor with two theaters on the estate, and it was here that Haydn composed the greater part of his work.

Beautiful though Haydn's chamber music was, however, it was to the symphonic orchestra that he gave his greatest contribution. Experimenting with his orchestra, he found out how to use the individual tone color of each instrument, discovered the charm of muted strings, tried groups of instruments in varying combinations. He used flutes, oboes, bassoons, trumpets, horns, and sometimes kettledrums. He used violins, which were louder than the old viols. He also tried introducing a clarinet, an instrument which Handel and Rameau had used in the 1740s and which captivated Mozart in Mannheim in 1777.

Up to Haydn's time orchestras had been limited in the number of performers they employed, but Haydn could use as many as he wished, for his master, Prince Esterházy, was vastly rich.

Although Monteverdi was the first to prescribe the exact instrumentation for an orchestra, it was Haydn who created the forerunner of the modern symphony orchestra. On his foundation Beethoven, Wagner, Berlioz, Mahler, Stravinsky, and all the other composers of orchestral music were to build. His compositions, of course, were very different from theirs. Haydn's orchestral works were the essence of classicism: formal and restrained, graceful and elegant in their proportions.

One thing about Haydn's music that was very winning was its humor. His symphonies sparkled with earthy good humor, and this was so infectious that it suggested nicknames for them like *The Chicken,* or *The Bee.* People called one of his symphonies *The Miracle;* the ceiling fell when it was performed for the first time, but no one was injured.

Haydn put his keen sense of humor to good use when he noticed that occasionally some member of his audience dozed. He wrote what was called the *Surprise Symphony.* It had a crashing chord in the midst of the gentle andante. And wanting to suggest that the players of the orchestra needed a vacation, he produced the *Farewell Symphony,* in which each player, as he finished his part, rose, blew out the candle on his music stand, and tiptoed out of the room, until, at the end of the last movement, the conductor was left standing alone. It is said that the prince took the hint; the players had their vacation.

Prince Nicolaus died in 1790, and Haydn, now fifty-eight, moved to Vienna. His fame had spread across Europe, and that year a concert impresario named Johan Peter Salomon traveled to Vienna to urge him to come to England to conduct a series of concerts for which he was to compose twelve symphonies. Symphonies in those days were not as long as they are now, so although the undertaking was a gigantic one, Haydn agreed to try it.

Some time before, Haydn had made friends with Mozart, and, though Mozart was much younger than he, the two men were extremely fond of each other. Haydn often expressed the greatest admiration for Mozart's genius. Now, before going to London, Haydn stopped to see Mozart.

"Don't go, Papa," Mozart is reported to have said then. "It is so far and you know so few languages."

"But my language is universal," the cheerful Haydn is said to have answered.

So he set off for London. He was overwhelmed by the size

of that city, and walked through its parks with an English grammar in his hand and had a hard time understanding his English friends.

He was crushed when the news of Mozart's death was brought him. "I was for some time quite beside myself about his death," he wrote a friend. And even several years later he burst into tears at the mention of Mozart's name. "Forgive me," he said, "I must ever weep when I hear the name of my Mozart."

But life must go on. And Haydn had what the French essayist, Joseph Joubert, has called "the most beautiful of all courages, the courage to be happy."

Not only did he continue to live happily, but he worked extremely hard. For now he was reaching the very pinnacle of his symphonic creation. Inspired by the memory of his friend Mozart and freed from the fetters of a patron, he wrote for Salomon's orchestra.

His opening concert was held on March 11, 1791, at the Hanover Square Rooms, where he played his Symphony in D Major (op. 93). The orchestra consisted of forty excellent players. Salomon, the leader, played a Stradivarius violin, and Haydn conducted from the harpsichord. Dr. Charles Burney, the English musical historian, who was present, said the music had an "electrical effect on all present." Electricity had only recently been discovered, and its properties were much talked of then.

Haydn wrote twelve "Salomon" symphonies during his two visits to England, and each one was a triumph. One of them, *The Oxford Symphony*, commemorates the occasion on which the degree of master of music was given him, an honor he cherished all his life.

He soon had many friends in England and was often invited to Buckingham Palace, yet he missed Vienna and wanted to live in a little house there which he had recently bought. He returned to Vienna, gave Beethoven lessons, and then made his second visit to London. Prince Anton, Nicolaus' successor, did not want him to go and died shortly. Haydn's second visit to London was extremely successful, but after a year and a half he returned to Vienna.

When Haydn was in London he had heard an unforgettable concert of music composed by Handel. *The Messiah* had moved him deeply. Now he decided that he himself would write an oratorio. The subject was to be a grand one—the creation of the world. The text was based in part on the Book of Genesis in the Old Testament and partially on Milton's *Paradise Lost*.

The years he spent composing *The Creation* were perhaps the happiest of his life. He worked very slowly and in a deeply religious mood. "Never was I so devout as when I was composing *The Creation*," he wrote. "I knelt down every day and prayed to God to strengthen me for my work." And again, "I spent much time over it, because I intended it to last a long time."

The Creation was finally performed at the Schwarzenberg Palace in Vienna, April 29 and 30, 1798. It was intended to be heard only by invited guests, but crowds stood outside the palace, and the stalls of the market in front of the palace were removed to admit still more people, while eighteen mounted police guarded the entrance to the building. Inside, the cream of society, the most distinguished members of the artistic and literary world, listened in profound religious silence. Haydn himself conducted. It was a magnificent achievement, but with the happiness it brought him came complete exhaustion, and Haydn was forced, on his return to his own house, to take to his bed.

"Oh, God!" he wrote later. "How much yet remains to be done in this splendid art, even by a man like myself! . . . No one can believe the strain and effort it costs to produce them [his works]. For days afterwards I am incapable of formulating one rough idea, till at last my heart is revived by Providence and I seat myself at the piano and begin once more to hammer away on it."

So the last years came. He wrote two great Masses and a vocal arrangement for the "Seven Last Words," besides some of his best string quartets, three piano trios, and the Austrian national hymn. In those years he rose at six-thirty in the morning, taught, composed, played the piano, entertained his friends. He liked particularly to show his visitors the various medals he had received. Once a year he gave a party for his relatives at a little country inn and to this he invited his friends and also his servants, who loved him and stayed with him for years.

Finally, however, the day came when he did not leave his bed. Napoleon was besieging Vienna that spring, and on the twelfth of May a cannonball fell outside Haydn's house, rocking it as if there had been an earthquake.

"Children, don't be frightened," the old man called to his staff. "Where Haydn is, nothing can happen to you."

When Napoleon finally took Vienna he placed a guard of honor at Haydn's door.

Haydn died on May 31, 1809. His servants gathered round his bed when the end was near, and old Nännerl, the cook, held his hand. There could not be much of a funeral, for Austria was involved in a fierce struggle. But he lay peacefully on his catafalque with medals that he had received from Paris, Russia, Sweden, and Vienna around him. Here also was his favorite token of honor, an ivory tablet with his name upon it—his pass to the London concerts.

The friendly, sociable "Papa" Haydn had loved many people in the course of his long life, but of them all he loved the young Mozart best. "My Mozart," he called him. It was fitting, therefore, that the music sung at Haydn's funeral was the Requiem Mass by Mozart—the young genuis whose friendship had meant so much to Papa Haydn.

CHAPTER THIRTEEN

Mozart: Poverty and Genius

"ON THE evening of January 27 at eight o'clock my wife was happily delivered of a boy," wrote Leopold Mozart in his journal. So, simply, did the under chapel master of the Archbishop of Salzburg record the birth of his son, that genius Wolfgang Amadeus Mozart. The year was 1756.

There had been many eminent composers in Europe in the seventeenth and eighteenth centuries. Handel had composed his great oratorios; Haydn had created the string quartet and had composed his symphonic and sacred music; Gluck had revitalized the opera; but Mozart's was a universal talent, and he was supreme in all types of music.

His life was not an easy one. Heretofore musicians had earned their livings either in the employment of a church or in the service of some rich man. But Mozart, when he came of age, asserted that a musician should be able to support himself. He would serve no master. And, if for this reason he had a hard struggle with poverty, still he produced music of serene, transparent beauty and technical perfection beyond that of any that had gone before him.

His childhood was an exceptionally happy one, for he was reared within the small circle of an affectionate family. His father was intelligent and well educated, a music teacher who was the author of an excellent book of instructions for playing the violin. He is said never to have punished the boy, but to have guided his unfolding genius with great skill and tenderness.

Mozart's father realized very early that his son had genius. The child had hardly learned to walk when he climbed up to the bench before the clavier and amused himself by striking thirds with great delight. By the time he was four and a half, before he had learned to read, he was composing little pieces which he played to his father, who proudly wrote them down.

It was not hard for the child to learn to play the violin either, for he had a very sensitive ear. He could remember the difference of a quarter of a tone several hours after he had heard it. But he hated loud noises; the sound of a trumpet made him very unhappy.

One day his father and three friends were playing a quartet in the garden when the little boy joined them and played the second violin part without a mistake. Afterward they played it over again, and this time Wolfgang played the difficult third part equally well.

Gifts like Wolfgang's must not be hidden, his parents decided. He must travel and display his talent to the world. He must meet the eminent musicians of his day and perform in the houses of the great. His sister, little "Nännerl," who was also musically gifted, must go with him.

Therefore, when Wolfgang was six and Nännerl eleven their father borrowed some money from his friend and landlord, Lorenz Hagenauer, and organized a tour for the children. He had a little handbill printed which described the boy's accomplishments. Wolfgang could "play concertos on the piano," the handbill announced, "and the most difficult pieces of the great masters. . . . [He could] play a concerto on the violin, accompany on the clavier in symphonies, and with the keys covered with a cloth will play as if he had the keyboard under his eyes. Further, from a distance he will name exactly any note that may be sounded separately or in chords on the clavier, or on any other instrument, or on bells, glasses, clocks, and so on. Finally, he will improvise as long as he is desired to, not only on the clavier but on the organ, and in any key, even the most difficult, that may be stipulated. . . ." Armed with the announcement, the father and his prodigies set off.

They went to Munich first, and the townspeople went wild over the children. Then they sailed down the Danube, stopping off to play at various noblemen's houses. Wolfgang astonished the monks in a monastery along their way by playing the organ, and in one place he played the violin to the customs officials so sweetly that they did not charge any toll.

All up and down the Danube people were soon talking of the gifted children, and invitations came pouring in for them to play at the palaces of dukes and counts. At length an invitation came from the Empress Maria Theresa, and they performed at the court of Schönbrunn.

They returned home for a short while and then went to Paris and played for Madame de Pompadour; they were royally feasted in the great hall of Versailles; they crossed the English Channel and played for the King and Queen of England. They continued to travel and give concerts though they had various illnesses. The boy wrote his first symphony in England, his first light opera in Vienna, his first Mass in Salzburg.

And then in 1769, because Leopold was convinced that Italy was the very fountainhead of music, he took the boy across the Alps. Wolfgang loved the journey. He wrote his mother on the way, "My heart is completely ravished from sheer joy because the journey is so jolly, because it is so warm in the coach, and our coachman is a splendid fellow who when the road permits goes like the wind." In the end they made not one Italian journey but three, and they were triumphal tours.

In Italy the pope conferred the Order of the Golden Spur on Mozart, and the Accademia Filarmonica at Bologna set aside its age requirements and admitted him to membership. There too he received instruction and help from Padre Giovanni Battista Martini, who was a great musician and teacher and who had a music library of some seventeen thousand volumes. In Milan an opera the young Mozart wrote was performed with enormous success at the famous opera house, La Scala; in Naples he played the pianoforte so brilliantly that the audience thought there must be magic in the ring he wore. He took off the ring and played again, but the magic was still there.

So the years passed, and Mozart was leaving his boyhood behind him and beginning to grow up. His father realized that he was no longer a child prodigy, that he must somehow find a patron; at that time this was the only way a distinguished musician could exist. Such a position would give Mozart an opportunity to compose, for nearly all music then was commissioned for special occasions.

Before long Mozart was given a minor position in the archbishop's orchestra in Salzburg. But his father dreamed of greater things than this for him. He felt that his son needed to be in a bigger city and in a more cosmopolitan court.

In 1777, Wolfgang set out again, this time in search of some duke or prince who would employ him. His mother went with him, for the archbishop refused to give his father leave.

They traveled to Munich, and to Augsburg, and then to Mannheim, and in that latter city he heard the famous Mannheim Orchestra. The Czech Johann Stamitz had founded it, and it was said to be the best in continental Europe. "Their forte is a thunder," one writer said of the players in this orchestra, "their diminuendo a crystal streamlet bubbling away into the far distance."

After many months of waiting and hoping at the ducal court in Mannheim, Mozart was unable to secure an appointment, and he decided to go to Paris. But he could not find a patron there either. Gluck was the rage in Paris at that time, and it was hard for a newcomer, no matter how talented, to attract any notice. There were, besides, the usual intrigues and jealousies.

To add to the youth's misfortunes, his mother died in Paris and, greatly saddened, he decided to return to Mannheim. For in Mannheim lived the pretty Aloysia Weber, the daughter of the prompter of the opera, and he had fallen in love with her. He called upon her with black buttons sewed to his coat as a sign of mourning for his mother, but she would not have him, and before long he went back to Salzburg.

All this time he was producing music. In Paris he had written his Symphony in D, which was played by a famous French orchestra. And there also he had composed a concerto for flute and harp, accompanied by orchestra. This was commissioned by a French aristocrat who never paid for it. He was trying new ideas now, new combinations of instruments, new tonal shadings. He composed in a dozen different styles, writing little symphonies, sonatas, and even whole oratorios and operas. The exquisite *Eine Kleine Nachtmusik* with its utter clarity, its melodic flow, and transparency of texture belongs to this period.

Though he wrote so much distinguished music, nevertheless Mozart could find no patron, and he returned to Salzburg. In 1781 the grand opera for the carnival in Munich was put in his hands. After he finished, he received a summons from the new archbishop, and returned to Vienna. Hieronymus von Colloredo, who had succeeded the old archbishop, criticized Mozart for composing secular music and insisted that he sit at table with his valets, cooks, and confectioners.

"I don't want to talk about it," he wrote his father. "I don't even want to think about it."

The archbishop left Vienna, but Mozart stayed, determined to support himself as best he could without a patron. In Vienna he gave music lessons and arranged little concerts of chamber music in his room to which he charged admission.

He was one of the first to compose for the piano, and to have a piano in his room. His playing was miraculous, not for its technique, but for its exquisite clarity and wonderful, singing tone. He despised exaggerated speed in playing and improvised little flourishes and cadenzas that were gems of spontaneous creation. He crystallized the form of the piano concerto and achieved a perfect balance between the piano solo and the symphonic orchestra. He wrote twenty-odd piano concertos, and all of them are beautiful. Some of these he played or had friends or pupils perform in private houses, but for some he hired an orchestra and rented a concert hall. The task of getting subscribers for these latter concerts bore heavily on him. "Viennese people are not much interested in serious music," he wrote in one of his letters. Eventually he gave them up.

Mozart had been struggling along for some time when he received a commission to write an opera for the National Singspiel Theater in Vienna. He had already written a good many operas, beginning with *Bastien and Bastienne* when he was still a boy. None of them had been a great success, yet composing for the National Singspiel Theater appealed to him strongly. For in this opera house, which the Emperor Joseph II had founded, the operas were to be given not in Italian or French, but in German, and the costumes were to be the modern ones of that time. Here was an opportunity for sincerity and a fresh approach, and he was enthusiastic as he wrote *Die Entführung aus dem Serail* (*The Abduction from the Harem*). It was lighthearted, romantic, gay, and it was in German. It had lovely arias and lusty comic scenes, and the audience loved it. Buoyed up by his success, Mozart decided that he would write more operas.

Two weeks after *Die Entführung* was performed, he married Constanze, who was Aloysia Weber's younger sister. But, according to the custom of the time, the composer received no royalty for *Die Entführung*, except for its first performance, so he received very little money from it. He needed money desperately and tried to earn it by composing countless sonatas, concertos, and serenades. Still, poverty haunted him. Once some friends came to see the couple and found them dancing together to keep warm; they had no firewood.

No one in Vienna seemed to think anything of Mozart's music now. Gluck had come there from Paris, and the Italian composer Antonio Salieri was performing to great audiences. Still Mozart's expenses kept mounting. Constanze was sick and needed very expensive medicines.

After mixed good and bad times, Mozart was given the libretto for *Le Nozze di Figaro* (*The Marriage of Figaro*). It was written by Lorenzo da Ponte after a play by the French writer Pierre Augustin Beaumarchais, and it dealt with the relations between aristocrats and common people—a very combustible subject in those days just before the French Revolution. Mozart was immediately inspired by it. In six weeks he composed the magnificent opera with its exquisite melodies and wonderful human characterization.

The Marriage of Figaro has been called the ideal "*opera buffa*," or comic opera. Mozart had heard Gluck's *Iphigénie en Tauride*, but he was not influenced by Gluck's intellectual approach. Instinctively he seemed to blend dramatic truth with the supreme magic of his music.

The Marriage of Figaro is witty, yet it is tender and filled with elusive charm. When it was performed in 1786 it was greeted enthusiastically. Its reception must have helped Mozart's spirit, but it did not help his finances much. "I am still obliged to give lessons to earn a trifle," he wrote. It was not long before *Figaro* was dropped from the Vienna repertory.

That year he was invited by some amateurs to visit Prague. And in Prague he, who had been so neglected in Vienna, was feasted and dined and made much of. In Prague people talked of nothing but *Figaro*. They were whistling snatches of it in the streets—not only the cultured people, but the kitchen maids and the café singers loved it; it was heard everywhere.

As a result of the success of *Figaro*, Da Ponte was asked for another libretto, and he wrote the text of *Don Giovanni*. This opera, too, was quickly composed. The overture was written in a single night just before the performance in Prague, while Constanze kept Mozart awake by talking to him and bringing him glasses of punch.

When the night of *Don Giovanni's* opening arrived, October 29, 1787, there had been no time to rehearse the overture, and the audience waited nearly an hour for Mozart to appear on the podium, where he was to conduct. But when the opera finally began they were overwhelmed by the lovely flow of its music, by the combination of light and serious moods, of popular and symphonic music.

Don Giovanni in some respects heralded romantic opera. Its hero was wicked yet charming, in the style of the romantic heroes of the nineteenth century. The opera tells the story of a man freed from all restraints who fashions his life according to his own ideas. He is at odds with the laws of morality, of religion, of the state. He is a philanderer and a villain who combines rollicking humor and haughty tragedy. The music that describes him throbs with a sense of grandeur, and seems somehow to be a reflection of life itself.

After the performance, when Mozart turned to face his audience, he was greeted by a triple flourish of trumpets. *Don Giovanni* was a rapturous success.

Even *Don Giovanni* brought him hardly any money, however, and he returned to Vienna and went on with his composing. Within six weeks he wrote three of his finest symphonies: the E Flat Major, the G Minor, and the Symphony in C Major, which has been called the *Jupiter Symphony*.

The grand and dignified *Jupiter* was the last symphony he wrote, and he composed it in fifteen days, setting down its last note August 10, 1788. In it he incorporated a fugue in the sonata form of a symphony. The music is as spontaneous and lovely as any he ever wrote. It seemed to pour out of him effortlessly. And though it appeared deceptively simple, it was actually subtle and complex.

Alfred Einstein, the eminent musicologist, writes in *A Short History of Music:*

What distinguishes him [Mozart] from Haydn is a greater wealth of half-shades and transitions, a sensitiveness to sound that had remained altogether unique and was never again to be attained, and above all an entirely different sphere of emotion, at once sensuous and non-sensuous, hovering between grace and melancholy, indeed often changing color with a lightning-like abruptness. Mozart draws from a deeper well than the more earthy Haydn, a well at the bottom of which romantic lights begin to gleam.

Mozart in 1791 still needed money, and he turned now to another opera. He thought perhaps a fairy opera, based on the ideas of the Masonic order which he had lately joined, might bring him out of his financial trouble. So he wrote *Die Zauberflöte* (*The Magic Flute*). The libretto was by Emmanuel Schikaneder.

Die Zauberflöte tells the story of Prince Tamino who set out in search of high ideals. With him he took Papageno, a robust fellow who wanted the plain things of life—a glass of wine, a pretty girl, rough fun, and lots of children. The music is a fusion of simple folk songs, brilliant arias, and choral fantasies.

Mozart started to work at *Die Zauberflöte* feverishly and was in the midst of the composition when a somberly clad man with an obsequious manner entered the room. He did not say who he was, but it turned out later that he was the servant of a certain Count Walsegg. The count wanted a Requiem Mass to commemorate the death of his wife.

Mozart put aside *Die Zauberflöte* and started to work on the Requiem. His feverish imagination was haunted by the idea that this man was a messenger from the Beyond who had come to make him write his own funeral music. Now he worked at *Die Zauberflöte* and the Requiem alternately. When the opera was finally finished in September 1791, he was very ill. He never completed the Requiem.

Three months later, when Mozart was dying, a group of four friends gathered at his bedside and sang the parts of the Requiem that he had finished. It contains some of the most sublime church music that has ever been written.

Mozart's friends paid for his funeral. Constanze was too overcome to attend it. There was a blinding snowstorm that day, and one after another the people dropped away from the little procession that went to the cemetery. No one who knew him was present at the burial. When Constanze came a few days later and asked where he had been buried, the workmen at the cemetery could not tell her. He had been put with a number of paupers in a common grave. All that was left of Mozart was his immortal music.

After his death the immense treasure of Mozart's music was scattered. He did not have time in his short life to arrange and give opus numbers to his compositions. Only in the mid-nineteenth century did the Austrian Ludwig von Köchel collect and number Mozart's works. He numbered them in the order in which he presumed they had been written.

Mozart's life was short; he lived only thirty-five years. He had begun it gaily, had tasted success and discouragement, had asserted his independence like a true child of his age. For the world was changing in Mozart's time. In America and in France revolutions were seething. The happiness and freedom of individual men were now becoming more important than the wealth and power of kings. And musicians were no longer hidden behind the music they composed. With Mozart they began to put themselves into their music—their pain and grief, their mirth and joy. Beethoven, who was to follow him, did this to an even greater extent than Mozart had done.

CHAPTER FOURTEEN

Beethoven

HOW IS it that a boy grows into a great composer? Whence does his music come? How is it nurtured? No one knows. There was certainly nothing in the surroundings of the boy Ludwig van Beethoven to suggest that he would have a brilliant career. The boy's grandfather was indeed a good musician. He was of Dutch-Flemish origin and Beethoven was always proud of this and careful to keep the *van* before his name. But his father was a bad-tempered, irresponsible drunkard, who had a minor position as tenor singer in the court of the Archbishop-Elector of Cologne. His mother was a maidservant and later, like Haydn's mother, a cook. The boy was born on December 16, 1770, in a miserable attic in Bonn. What was there in all this to lead anyone to suppose that he would be a giant among composers? Or that he would reach out to all humanity as a prophet of universal love for all mankind?

The stormy political horizon of his young years must have had a great influence on him. When he was only six years old the United States of America was created through revolution. And a few years later revolution toppled the French monarchy and shook every throne in Europe with its cry of "Liberty, Equality, Fraternity." These were the things that must have echoed through the consciousness of the stubborn boy who was trying to make a place for himself in the world.

Even when Ludwig Beethoven was a very little boy, his father was continually trying to get him to make money. He thought he might turn him into a child prodigy like Mozart, but this effort failed, for Beethoven had none of the childish charm of the young Mozart, nor was he so precocious. When Ludwig was eleven he was made to play in a theater orchestra; when he was thirteen he was set to work helping the organist of the court chapel. That was how he came under the influence of Christian Gottlob Neefe, who was in charge of both secular and sacred music at the archbishop's court.

Neefe was the first to be really impressed with Beethoven's ability. He wrote that the boy was "playing with force and finish, reading at sight . . . playing the greater part of Bach's *Well-Tempered Clavier*, a feat which would be understood by the initiated. This young genius deserves some assistance so that he may travel," Neefe continued. "If he goes on as he has begun, he will certainly become a second Mozart."

Before long the youth became Neefe's assistant, playing the

harpsichord and leading the orchestra when his master was away. It was possibly Neefe who managed to have him sent on a visit to Vienna when he was seventeen. There Mozart heard him play the piano and may have given him a few lessons. "The world will hear more of him," Mozart is quoted as having said.

Back in Bonn after that, Beethoven's mother died. "She was so good to me," he wrote, "so worthy of love. The best friend I had." And his father was drinking so heavily that the archbishop-elector made Ludwig head of the family, though he was only seventeen, and paid him part of his father's salary so that he might support his younger brothers.

Beethoven now was depressed and gloomy, and life for him would have been miserable indeed had it not been for the friendship of the von Breuning family. He called them his "guardian angels" and spent much time at their house. There were a mother, three boys of about his own age, and a girl Eleonore whom he called "Lorchen." He gave her piano lessons, read romantic English poetry with her, and kept in touch with her all his life, even after she had married his friend, Franz Gerhard Wegeler.

Beethoven had also another friend in those years—Count Waldstein, a young nobleman who gave him that much-prized gift, a piano. The count came often to his house to hear him play.

When Beethoven was twenty he was playing with the archbishop-elector's court choir when Haydn visited Bonn, and the choir performed one of the old master's Masses. Haydn complimented the singers on the performance and invited them all to supper at his lodgings. Beethoven must have liked him, as everyone always did.

Haydn visited the city again a year later, and Beethoven, though he was usually shy, showed him a cantata he had written. This composition has since been lost, but it served its purpose, for Haydn praised it highly. He spoke to the archbishop about it, and the archbishop, impressed, made it possible for Beethoven to return to Vienna.

In Vienna he began to take lessons with Haydn. He paid him only a very small fee but often treated him to chocolate in the Viennese coffee shops, writing down these expenses in a little notebook. Master and pupil never got along very well in spite of the chocolate they consumed together. Haydn was grieving over Mozart's death, and compared his new pupil unfavorably with the genius whose music was the greatest he had ever heard. He liked neither Beethoven's manners nor his way of playing, and must have found him pompous, for he called him "The Great Mogul."

Beethoven, on the other hand, thought Haydn careless in correcting his written exercises. "He taught me nothing," he said, and secretly he employed another teacher, Johann Georg Albrechtsberger, who was a master of counterpoint. He also studied with Antonio Salieri, the Italian who had been Mozart's rival. These teachers found him self-willed and headstrong and said it was very difficult to teach him. He had to learn slowly by hard experience.

Nevertheless, though he was uncouth and rough in his manners, the Viennese discovered before long that he had a wonderful way with the piano, especially when he sat down to improvise. He was invited to play in many aristocratic houses, though he hated doing it and gave way to outbursts of temper when he thought the listening audience was inattentive.

One lady, Frau von Bernhard, wrote:

When he came to us he used to put his head through the door to make sure that no one he disliked was there. He was small, ungainly, with a pock-marked face (as a boy he was nicknamed "Spaniard" for his dark complexion). His hair was very dark and he spoke in dialect.

He was very proud. I have seen the mother of Princess Lichnowsky, countess then, go on her knees to beg him to play, but Beethoven would not. I still remember how Haydn and Salieri used to sit on the sofa, carefully dressed in the old style with hair bags [wigs], shoes,

and silk stockings, whilst Beethoven was accustomed to come carelessly dressed in the upper Rhineland style.

He was indeed a nonconformist; he would not dress like those
around him. Nor had he any wish to act like them. His aristocratic
friends wanted him to change his ways. They tried to teach him
how to behave in society and tutored and instructed him until he
could stand it no longer. After a while he went to the young Archduke Rudolph, who was his friend as well as his pupil, and said
he would not have them plague him. The archduke only laughed
and told his friends to let Beethoven go his own way.

Yet though he was scornful of the society of men, he was often
lonely as he moved from one uncomfortable lodging to another,
and often he fell in love. In 1801 it was Giulietta Guicciardi. "Now
I see things in a better light," Beethoven wrote Dr. Wegeler.
"This change has been brought about by the charm of a dear
girl; she loves me and I love her. These are the first happy moments I have had in two years." In 1802 he dedicated the "Moonlight Sonata" to Giulietta, but nevertheless she married someone
else.

It was the same with his other loves. One of them was the
Countess Therese von Brunswick, another Therese Malfatti. There
may have been others besides these. Three undated letters by
Beethoven have been preserved; they are known as his "Letters to
the Immortal Beloved." No one can decide to which of these
ladies they were addressed, or whether the beloved was some
other nameless person. Beethoven was continually wanting the
sympathy and companionship of a woman, but it was never completely his.

Troublesome etiquette, unsatisfactory lodgings, and unfortu-
nate love affairs were not the only things that bothered Beethoven
in those years. There were financial worries. He had some small
revenue from giving music lessons, and he published some music
and gave a few concerts in Prague and Berlin. Still he never had
quite enough to live on.

Nevertheless, with all his various difficulties, Beethoven never lost confidence in his own genius. "Courage!" he wrote in his notebook. "In spite of all my bodily weaknesses, my genius shall yet triumph. . . ."

The bodily weakness that was beginning to worry him most was his deafness. It came intermittently. Sometimes for quite long periods he could hear perfectly well, and then the deafness would come back again. He tried to keep his difficulty to himself at first; he would never speak of it to his friends.

At last, however, he did write of it to Dr. Wegeler:

I lead a miserable life indeed. For the last two years I have avoided all society, for I cannot talk with my fellow men. I am deaf. Had my profession been other, things might still be bearable; but as it is my situation is terrible. . . . At the theater . . . I cannot hear the high notes of the instruments or the voices if I am a little distance off. If anyone speaks quietly I only hear with difficulty. . . . On the other hand, I find it unbearable if anyone shouts at me.

He was filled with sadness at his own condition. He wrote the "*Sonata Pathétique*," and it is filled with sorrow. But at the same time there is tranquil tenderness in the slow movement and a tremendous rush of excitement in the finale.

In 1802 he was overwhelmed with depression and despair, for his deafness returned to him with renewed intensity. He had been in the habit of changing from one doctor to another, and now he sought an eminent new specialist, who advised him to leave Vienna for a time and take a vacation. He chose Heiligenstadt, a summer resort which lies in a quiet valley among wooded hills, for he loved the beauty of natural surroundings. "No one loves nature as much as I," he wrote.

But though nature comforted him in Heiligenstadt, he was often in deep despair. There he wrote a letter to his brothers, asking that it should not be opened until after his death. The letter has been called the "Heiligenstadt Testament." In it he laid bare the tragedy his deafness had brought upon him.

Men who think him malevolent, stubborn, and misanthropic do him wrong, he tells his brothers; from his childhood his heart has been disposed to a gentle feeling of good will. But he was compelled early to isolate himself from others because of his deafness:

> It was impossible for me to say to men, speak louder, shout, I am deaf. What a humiliation when one stood beside me and heard a flute in the distance, and I heard nothing, and again someone heard the shepherd singing and again I heard nothing. . . . I would have put an end to my life—only art it was that withheld me. It seemed impossible to leave the world until I had produced all that I felt called upon to produce.

Then he asked that his doctor attach a note to his will describing his malady, declared his brothers to be the "heirs to my small fortune (if so it can be called)," admonished them to "bear with and help each other," and bade them farewell.

The Heiligenstadt Testament was highly charged with emotion and filled with despair, yet that very year Beethoven resolved again to be happy, to throw trouble aside. He was beginning to realize his own power. Later he wrote, "Power constitutes the morality of men who distinguish themselves above the ordinary."

So, in those years when the disaster of his deafness was pressing on him, and he was worried and unhappy in love, somehow he managed to withdraw from all these things into his own world, to hold away his difficulties by strength of will. He worked very slowly and carefully, putting down all the musical ideas that came to him in a little sketchbook. Often inspiration came while he was walking in the country, and he would pause to take his sketchbook from his pocket. Then in the evening after he had reached home, he would develop three or four notes he had written into a melody, alter and change it, and put it away to be worked on again at a later time.

Working thus in his painstaking and deliberate way, he brought forth one magnificent composition after another: the Fourth and Fifth (*Emperor*) Piano Concertos, the Violin Concerto in D, ten sonatas for violin and piano, the best known of which is the "Kreutzer Sonata," and many piano sonatas, among them the "*Appassionata*," of which Bismarck once said, "If I heard that often I should always be valiant."

He was adept in all forms of instrumental music, but the one that interested him most perhaps was the symphony. This form had started long before Beethoven's time with the simple instrumental overture which the Italians played while the audience was settling down before the opera began. This overture developed into the instrumental sonata, and as the form evolved the number of instruments performing it gradually increased. Finally these instruments were replaced by a whole orchestra. Haydn had worked out symphonies of this kind, Mozart had written them, but in Beethoven's hands they attained gigantic stature; they addressed not a chosen audience but all humanity.

Beethoven's First Symphony followed the pattern laid down by Haydn in its simple exuberance, but as time passed and one symphony followed another, he lengthened the movements, changed the minuet into a scherzo, enriched the sonority of the orchestra and enlarged the coda until it became the dramatic résumé of a whole movement.

In 1802 Beethoven wrote a symphony of grand proportions, his third, and dedicated it to Napoleon Bonaparte, whom he regarded as a hero. But in 1804, when the symphony was finished, news came that Napoleon had announced himself Emperor. "I see he is just an ordinary man," Beethoven said, scorning Napoleon's ambition, and he tore out the dedication page and wrote simply, "To a hero," on the score. The symphony has been called the *Eroica* ever since.

More symphonies followed later. In the Fifth, Beethoven sweeps everything before him in a great onslaught of rhythm, basing the first movement on the opening motto of four notes which are taken up, echoed and re-echoed by the various instruments. "Fate knocks at the door," the instruments seem to be repeating.

In the Sixth Symphony he tried program music. The symphony describes a pastoral scene—a man walking in the country, the quiet murmur of the brook; a flute impersonates a nightingale, a clarinet a cuckoo, and there is the sound of a bagpipe, a vigorous wooden-shoed dance, and the patter of rain as the storm approaches. Even without the program, however, the composition is filled with musical enchantment.

It appears that Beethoven did not consider a "program" necessary, for in his next symphony, the Seventh, which he called the Grand Symphony in A, he returned to absolute music, and the listeners were thrilled by the beauty and glory of it, by the throbbing of the bass as fragments of melody were tossed from one instrument to another. The Seventh Symphony, although it is built on a grandiose pattern, is bright and filled with irresistible rhythmic life. It has been called the "Apotheosis of the Dance." "The Grand Symphony in A is one of my best," Beethoven himself said.

Music to Beethoven, after all, meant for the most part instrumental music. But people had been urging him for a long time to write an opera, and he finally agreed to try it. The opera was *Fidelio*. Its libretto was a rather poor one, but Beethoven took great pains with the music. He wrote four different overtures for it, and all of them were so beautiful that they are frequently played as concert pieces today. The third, known as "Leonore Number 3," is the best known and most exciting one. Donald Tovey, an English musicologist, says, "It is as dramatic as anything . . . put on the stage." And Karl Bekker, the German music critic, wrote, "Beethoven set out to write an opera, but ended with overtures." However that may be, some of the music of *Fidelio* is magnificent. Perhaps it achieves its greatest heights in a chorus of prisoners who are crying out for the light.

Napoleon had entered Vienna in November 1805, the very week that *Fidelio* was produced. Most of the Austrian nobility had fled the city, so the audience consisted for the most part of French soldiers. It was performed again in 1814 after the Austrians had come back. They greeted it enthusiastically.

Gradually, while Beethoven continued to produce his music, more people in Vienna noticed him. Most of the older generation were shocked at his emotional intensity, but the younger ones were stirred by his passionate compositions. Perhaps they felt guilty because Mozart had been so neglected. They did not want to let another musical genius slip through their fingers. In 1809 when the King of Westphalia offered Beethoven the post of chapel master at Cassel, and he had almost made up his mind to go, a group of his fellow citizens sent him a letter urging him to remain in Vienna. Three young noblemen, thereupon, offered him a yearly income which he accepted, and though death and bankruptcy interfered with their plan and only one of them, the Archduke Rudolph, continued it, Beethoven remained in Vienna. There his reputation grew steadily, and soon people were coupling his name with the names of Haydn and Mozart.

Yet despite his apparent success Beethoven was unhappy. After a long series of expensive lawsuits he had obtained custody of his nephew Karl, whose father had died, and he needed money to bring him up. The boy gave him little satisfaction, but Beethoven scrimped and saved and tried continually to get money for him. Added to this he had great difficulties with his servants and was continually scolding them and accusing them of petty thieveries.

He was now completely and permanently deaf. Those who came to see him wrote what they had to say in little conversation books, and he answered in writing. To one of his callers, Dr. Karl von Barsy, he wrote, "I am chained here by circumstances, but everything here is so sordid and shabby that things could not be worse."

Yet once again, as he had done before, he turned from the

shabby, sordid world into his own glorious world of music. Now he wrote the immortal Ninth Symphony and that great work, the Mass in D, which is called the *Missa Solemnis.*

All Beethoven's work came to him slowly and with effort, and the Ninth Symphony was composed only with the greatest difficulty though it was perhaps the most magnificent of his works. For a long time he had considered composing a symphony with a choral finale, but he had not been able to find a suitable theme. Finally one day he rushed into the room where his friend Schindler was sitting, his hands full of the papers on which he had been working. "I have it! I have it!" he cried. "Let it be Schiller's 'Ode to Joy'!"

And the great symphony with its ringing words, "All men in the world are brothers," was completed.

The Ninth Symphony and the Mass in D were performed in Vienna on May 7, 1824. A contemporary wrote:

No circumstance could have been more symbolic of the master's situation in life and in art than the occasion of the first performance and the tableau presented to the audience—Beethoven standing on the stage, his head sunk on his breast, beating time for the orchestra (which had been warned to disregard his motions); surrounded by silence; unware that the music had ceased, when he was turned about by one of the singers, Fraülein Unger, to perceive the multitude shouting and with many persons in tears.

The symphony had ended with the triumphant shout: "Hail the Joy from Heaven descending . . ." Beethoven had put his dream of the free and advancing brotherhood of mankind into his music.

Only a little time was left to him now, but he made the most of it, for he wrote his last sublime series of string quartets. And he was full of plans for the future. He left notes for a tenth symphony, and he wanted to write an overture on the name of Bach, and another for Goethe's *Faust.*

But these were never done, for he died on February 17, 1827. There was a violent storm at the time of his death. Snow fell and lightning ripped across the sky. It seemed a fitting accompaniment to his departure.

"Kings and princes can bestow titles and decorations," he had once said. "But they cannot make great men or minds able to rise above the base turmoil of the world." The boy so humbly born in the attic in Bonn had done this for himself, without the help of kings or princes. In spite of all his struggles with deafness, poverty, and loneliness, his voice still rings out in a mighty triumph. And who can sum up all that he has done for music?

For he raised instrumental music to new, unimagined heights. He combined the thematic development of Haydn's sonata pattern with the songfulness of Mozart and added an emotional sweep and grandeur that overwhelmed those who listened. Out of a small cluster of notes, like the four notes of the first movement in the Fifth Symphony, he knew how to raise a magnificent cathedral of sound. His piano sonatas command a new freedom and depth of expressiveness.

The precious element of humor that bubbled in Bach and sparkled in Mozart and Haydn has many faces in Beethoven. It ranges from witty laughter to brooding sarcasm, and finally to a play with thunderbolts in the "scherzo" of the Ninth Symphony.

His last quartets have a quality of mystery and remoteness that has baffled many listeners. These quartets have been compared to abstract painting and are among the most compelling music of all time. They are full of dramatic contrasts in mood, tempo, and texture. Their themes are often fragmented, prophetic with meaning.

And finally there is his great Ninth Symphony. It has often been performed at the United Nations and at other international gatherings and always it has appeared as a symbol of humanity's yearning for peace and international brotherhood.

CHAPTER FIFTEEN

Franz Schubert and His Songs

I N E U R O P E, with the coming of the nineteenth century, a new spirit was stirring. It moved in the shadow of the
German forests and marched with the armies of Napoleon. Now
poets, painters, and musicians shared new aspirations and new
dreams. Down with all barriers—social, moral, and political—

they said. Men must be free to create in whatever way they will.

The century before had been rationalistic—versed in logic, mathematical exactness, and scientific clearness—but now there was a reaction against these things. Long-pent-up emotions seemed to burst their barriers, and not precision, but whatever was beautiful and strange was sought after. Now men listened to the wind that stirred the branches of the trees, to the chattering of little brooks and the rush and whisper of the surf. They read old stories and half-forgotten legends and talked of Spain and the Orient. Kings and princes were no longer admired in this new age. Followers of the new ideas adored geniuses and heroes and considered Napoleon the greatest hero of them all. They talked of death and the ineffable peace that follows the struggle of life. Many young men committed suicide. "Him alone will I praise who living aspires to die by fire. . . ." the poet Goethe wrote. So poets, politicians, philosophers, painters, and musicians —all strained against the old fetters and joyfully claimed a new birth of freedom for individual men.

The musicians took up this movement later than the poets and the painters. Beethoven had started it—Beethoven, with his titanic struggling, his independence, and his great power. Now many musicians, inspired by the literature of the day, broke away from the classic forms. They impressed a new style on music—a style that is still felt.

One of the first of the romantics in music was Franz Schubert. But this statement must be qualified, for much of his music was composed on formal, classic lines. It would be better to say that Schubert's music was a kind of bridge that joined the old classical and the new romantic music.

Schubert has been described as a "short, stout man with round shoulders, thick blunt fingers, low forehead, projecting lips, stumpy nose, and short curly hair." His friends called him affectionately "Schwämmerl," or the "little mushroom."

He was born in 1797 in a suburb of Vienna where his father

was the village schoolmaster. His mother, like Haydn's and Beethoven's, had been a cook before her marriage.

Schubert's father saw to it that his son had a good musical education and, when he was old enough, sent him to the Viennese School for Imperial Choristers, which was called the Convict. The famous Antonio Salieri, who had been Beethoven's teacher, had founded it. At the Convict the boys laughed at Franz Schubert at first because of his homespun clothes, his bashful manners, and his spectacles, but soon they began to admire him, for he had a beautiful singing voice. He made warm friendships at the school that lasted all his life.

As a farewell present to the Convict when he left there Franz Schubert wrote his First Symphony in D Major, adding after the last major chord *"Finis et Fine."*

And when his voice broke (he had been singing in a church choir) he wrote into the alto part of his music book, "Franz Schubert crowed for the last time."

He tried teaching in his father's school for a time, but he did not stay there long. He wanted above everything else to write music, to set down on paper the melodies with which his head was filled.

He was very poor. Through most of his life he had literally no money at all. He hated to teach, and, though he published his songs, the music publishers paid him hardly anything. He gave only one public concert and that was not until nearly the end of his life, March 1828. The occasion was the anniversary of Beethoven's death, and the concert paid very well, but the money was soon spent on his friends, and Franz Schubert was poor as ever.

Unfortunately he had very little business sense. He enjoyed Vienna with his friends, and his friends wanted him there. In a rather haphazard way they paid for his food and lodging and bought his tobacco and beer. They did not consider this charity, for Schwämmerl repaid them with his comradeship.

Schubert composed almost continuously. He did not even take off his spectacles when he went to bed, for he was afraid he would mislay them, and he could not afford to spend time looking for them when he woke up.

In 1814 his friends urged him to write an opera. They pointed out that all successful composers wrote operas and that he might become rich. So Schubert wrote *Des Teufels Lustschloss,* but it was not a success. The libretto was poor. Like Beethoven, Schubert could write dramatic music but he lacked a sense of theater. That same year he wrote his Mass in F Major, three string quartets, the first movement of the Symphony in B Flat, and seventeen songs. Among those early songs were the lovely *"Gretchen am Spinnrade"* and *"Der Taucher."*

The next year he completed three more operas. (His friends must have been insistent.) But he also wrote, among other things, four sonatas, two symphonies, two masses, and a hundred and forty-six songs. Eight of these songs were dated October fifteenth and seven October nineteenth. It did not seem to matter that the music publishers gave him no encouragement. He went on writing music anyway.

It was in 1815 at a friend's house that he came across Goethe's poem, *"Der Erlkönig."* It tells the odd story of a father riding through a dark forest with a sick baby in his arms, and how the two were pursued by a demon spirit. Schubert was immediately fascinated by the strange, haunting poem. In a white heat he began putting notes down on paper. When he had finished combining the romantic words and the lovely melody with its weird, hectic accompaniment, he had written a "lied," or art song, filled with beauty. Words, melody, and accompaniment produced an effect that no one of them separately could attain. It was an original achievement, and many more lieder of this kind were to follow it.

After the *"Erlkönig"* Schubert turned to other music. In 1816 he wrote three ceremonial cantatas, two new symphonies, some church music, another opera, and over a hundred songs. Most of these latter were settings for poems by the German poets, Schiller and Goethe.

Gradually his fortunes improved. His friend, the famous baritone Heinrich Vogl, sang some of his songs in the salons in Vienna, and Joseph Gahy, who was an excellent pianist, began to play his sonatas before Viennese audiences, while a rich burgher organized musical parties for him which were called *"Schubertiaden."* For a time he had a post in the household of Prince Esterházy, but he was not happy in this work. Not long after that he went on a holiday to Upper Austria with his friend Vogl, and there he wrote the irresistible *Trout Quintet,* using one of his own lyrics, "The Trout," as a theme in one movement. His successes emboldened him, and he sent three of his songs to Goethe, but apparently Goethe never acknowledged them.

So he reached maturity, and still the music kept coming. He did not have to labor at his music as Beethoven had done. He had ideas by the hundred, and it was easy to give them form. The unfinished work, *Lazarus,* the setting for the Twenty-third Psalm, the Piano Fantasia in C on the theme of his song, "The Wanderer" —there seemed to be no end to his music. In 1821 the publishers agreed to take some of his works on commission, but they paid him very little.

He went to see Beethoven in 1822. The deaf musician pushed the conversation book toward him, but Schubert was so covered with confusion that he could think of nothing to put down, and went home in great embarrassment.

Schubert liked especially to write four-hand piano pieces, for he enjoyed the sociability of two people seated close together while they performed. This form did not appeal to the unsociable Beethoven at all, for he could never adjust himself to other people. An example of the form is the Grand Duo in C Major (op. 140), written in 1824. Schubert wrote his Mass in A Flat, and the exquisite *Unfinished Symphony* in 1822.

The *Unfinished Symphony* has been called the first romantic orchestral work. It has in it something of the severe classicism of Beethoven, but at the same time there is the glow of the romantic age. It was called "unfinished" because it has only two movements. It is a fragment whose perfection makes it complete in itself. The world did not hear it performed until 1865, however, for Schubert lent the manuscript to a friend, Joseph Hüttenbrenner, who put it in a drawer where it lay for forty-three years.

Song pervades all Schubert's music. This was true of his own piano playing. "Several people assured me that my fingers had transformed the keys into singing voices," he once wrote. "If this is true I am delighted since I cannot abide the damnable thumping."

So he succeeded in transforming the keys into singing voices in his *Impromptus* and his *Moments Musicaux*. These are intimate, spontaneous songs for the piano alone, the first of their kind which later Schumann, Brahms, and Chopin all cultivated with success. Technically they are not difficult to perform. The only long and difficult work of this kind is the *Wanderer Fantasie*, a composition that demands some brilliance on the part of the performer.

Schubert's piano sonatas, like his symphonies, are of a "heavenly length," and they demand a highly sensitive player who is capable of forgetting his audience.

There is a wistfulness in most of Schubert's music, a yearning for some happiness that never comes. But he was capable of a very different mood. The atmosphere of the post-Napoleonic times inspired him to write the quick-stepping, sparkling *Marches Militaires* (*Military Marches*).

Fine though all his music was, Schubert's songs were what he loved most. Whenever he read a poem it seemed to turn itself into a lied. It did not even necessarily have to be a good poem: it has been said that he "could set a handbill to music." However, most of his lieder were composed as settings for good poetry.

Sometimes he combined his songs into cycles, and these contain some of his finest music. In them he set poems on related ideas to music. Some of the cycles were built on long ballad-like stories, in which each song was a different scene in the plot. One cycle, called *Die Schöne Müllerin,* tells the story of the unhappy love of a young miller for a beautiful but fickle girl who rejects him for a handsome huntsman. The famous "Ave Maria" occurs in another group called *Songs from Sir Walter Scott.*

In 1826 Schubert wrote some songs using Shakespearean lyrics. "Hark! hark! the lark!" from *Cymbeline* is one of these. He had been on a walk in the country when he conceived it, and wrote it while he rested at a little inn. That same evening, after he reached home again, he wrote the lovely setting for "Who Is Sylvia?" from *The Two Gentlemen of Verona.*

Schubert was an innovator in the matter of piano accompaniments for his lieder. Up to his time the harpsichord and then the piano accompaniment had little importance in relation to the vocal line of a song. But Schubert gave the piano equal status with the voice. His accompaniments were no longer merely background for the singing, but rather equal partners which set the mood for the singer, and in a sense summed up the story of the song in the concluding epilogues.

As Schubert grew older his music became sadder. He was habitually hungry; a cup of coffee and a roll were often all he could afford to buy for his dinner. He became ill and dejected, and his mood was reflected in his songs. The cycle called *Die Winterreise* is filled with deep melancholy. It describes the winter journey of a broken-hearted man—the journey toward death. One of the most poignant songs in the cycle is "The Linden Tree"— the tree which the singer sees in all its beauty and knows he will not see again.

Schubert was correcting the proofs of *Die Winterreise* when he died in 1828. He had not completed his thirty-second year.

One of his friends said, "Schubert is dead, and with him has gone our happiest and loveliest possession."

With his death all Schubert's fresh, vivid, and spontaneous music seemed to disappear from the world. No one played his *Impromptus* and his *Moments Musicaux;* his songs were seldom sung.

His father and brothers kept his manuscripts carefully put away, for they were modest people and had no way of bringing them before the public, nor did they realize what musical genius the manuscripts contained. Then a young man named Robert Schumann came to Vienna from Leipzig and called on the Schuberts. Since his boyhood days Schumann had been an enthusiastic admirer of Franz Schubert's songs. Now he was making a pilgrimage to the place where the great song writer had lived. In the house of Schubert's brother, Ferdinand, on the first of January, 1829, Schumann found the pile of manuscripts which the family had treasured so carefully. Among those papers was Schubert's grandest symphony, the C Major. He took it back to Leipzig where it was performed in the great concert hall, the Gewandhaus, with Schumann's friend Felix Mendelssohn conducting.

CHAPTER SIXTEEN

The Versatile Robert Schumann

I N 1830, in Frankfurt, Germany, the famed violinist, Niccolo Paganini, was giving a concert. He was very thin—his arms and legs appeared to be mere bones, and his hands were long, with fingers that were like talons. When he played, he hunched over his violin like a giant bat, his long black hair streaming, his coat tails swaying and flapping, while he hypnotized his audience with feats of skill, and produced effects never heard before.

Robert Schumann, twenty years old, sat in the audience that day and listened and was enthralled. The son of a bookseller in a small Saxon town, he had been studying law at Leipzig and then at Heidelberg. But when he heard Paganini play he decided that the legal profession was not for him. He, too, would be a musician. He set his law books aside and began long hours of practicing on the piano. Before long he became impatient with the weakness of his third finger on the left hand so he made a device to strengthen it. And in doing this, he crippled the finger for the rest of his life.

He could not be a piano virtuoso with a crippled finger, but this fact would not prevent him from composing. He took lessons in composition with Friedrich Wieck in Leipzig, and Wieck said he had talent and encouraged him. He also took a course in theory with the conductor of the Leipzig orchestra, whose name was Heinrich Dorn. ("I shall never be able to amalgamate myself with Dorn. He wishes me to believe that music is fugue—heavens! how different men are!")

While he was studying with Friedrich Wieck, Schumann boarded at his teacher's house, and there he grew to know young pianist Clara Wieck. She was only thirteen when he first saw her, but he watched her grow, heard her perform in concerts, appreciated her talent and her spirit more and more. At last he asked her to marry him.

Clara's father objected to the marriage. True, Robert Schumann was a good young man and seemed to have musical talent, but Friedrich Wieck was stubborn and ambitious for his daughter. At last the young couple took their case to court (for that was permitted in those days), demanding to know why they should not wed. The court granted them permission, and they were formally engaged.

Schumann's letters to Clara Wieck at this time are filled with joy. "Since yesterday morning I have written twenty-seven pages of music," he wrote. "And I can tell you nothing more about it, except that I laughed and cried with delight." And a month later, "Here is a slight reward for your last two letters—my first published songs. While I was composing them I was quite lost in thoughts of you. If I were not engaged to such a girl, I could not write such music."

The year 1840 was what Robert Schumann himself called the "Song Year," for then he and Clara were finally married, and her father relented at last.

Up to the time of his marriage he had written much piano music: the *Carnaval, Kreisleriana, Symphonic Etudes, Fantasie in C*. These well-loved masterpieces are in the repertory of every pianist now. Perhaps his *Carnaval* is his most popular piano piece. It portrays a masked ball where various characters Schumann has imagined mingle with Pierrot, Columbine, and Harlequin while Paganini and Chopin follow them in the gay dance.

But now in 1840 Schumann turned more and more to songs. He wrote musical settings for the lyrics of the German poets, Johann Wolfgang Goethe, Friedrich Rückert, and Heinrich Heine, and also for the English poetry of Lord Byron, Robert Burns, and George Moore. He wrote about a hundred and fifty songs in the year of his marriage, a great outpouring of his happiness.

But if 1840 was his "Song Year," the year that followed led him to the orchestra, and 1841 has been called the "Symphony Year." That year he read a poem, a single line of which vibrated in his mind and would not leave him. The line was, "In the valley blooms the spring." In four days he sketched out a symphony on the coming of spring—his Symphony in B Flat.

When it was finished and about to be performed in Berlin he wrote in a characteristic letter to the conductor, Wilhelm Tauber:

Could you infuse into your orchestra a sort of longing for spring? The first entrance of the trumpets, this I should like to have sounded as if from above, like unto a call to awakening; and then I should like reading between the lines, in the rest of the introduction, how everything begins to grow green, how a butterfly takes wing, and in the allegro, how little by little all things come that in any way belong to spring. True, these are fantastic thoughts, which only came to me after the work was finished; only, I tell you this about the finale, that I thought of it as a good-by to spring.

So time passed. Clara continued to grow as a concert artist, achieving success throughout Europe. And gradually Schumann himself was granted recognition. He had been made "Doctor" by the University of Jena in 1840, and was given a professorship at the Conservatory in Leipzig in 1843. And all the time he was composing. There was chamber music now, a quintet for piano and strings in 1842, and in the next year *Paradise and the Peri*. He said this last was an oratorio "not for a prayer meeting, but for cheerful people."

Schumann's music, whether in the form of songs, symphonies, or chamber music, had the same fresh, exuberant quality. It seemed to be the very incarnation of the romantic spirit, for by some magic it could make tears rush to the eyes or stir the listener to outbursts of delight.

Most of the compositions he wrote were short, like quick, hot flames. He could not organize long, monumental works with the sustained intellectual power of a Bach, a Handel, or a Beethoven. Yet his symphonies were beautiful. And who could conceive more lovely melodies or grander fantasias for piano? Who could paint more exquisite little tone pictures?

He was deeply absorbed in his composition, and his lips were continually drawn together to whistle new melodies that came to his mind, but nevertheless he felt that his responsibility toward music did not end with his own composition. At that time, he observed, most people looked on music merely as a recreation, and enjoyed the thrill of idolizing some virtuoso. Only a little time had passed since Beethoven and Schubert had died, and already people were forgetting them, Schumann thought. And he wrote, "Let us not look on idly; let us lend our aid to progress; let us bring again the poetry of art among men."

And with this same end in view in 1834 he had started a critical review of music, *Die Neue Zeitschrift für Musik*. This review published the first serious musical criticism, and was bold and outspoken in its comments. "The critic who dares not attack what is bad, is but a half-hearted supporter of what is good," Schumann wrote. He had the greatest scorn for what he called the "honey daubers." The review often mentioned the "David Club," a fictitious club whose members had pledged themselves to fight like modern Davids against the giants of Philistinism (mediocre routine).

For about ten years, while he was busy composing, he wrote frequent reviews for *Die Neue Zeitschrift*. He liked to sign his articles with *noms de plume*. Those that were fierce and passionate he signed "Floristan," but the dreamy ones he signed "Eusebius," and the firm, masterful ones, "Raro."

The influence of his fresh approach in this music review was very great. It demolished what was merely ostentatious and fashionable, and lent a helping hand to the young musicians of the day whose work was genuine and sincere. Writing in *Die Neue Zeitschrift,* Schumann introduced Chopin to Germany. "Hats off, gentlemen, a genius," he said of him. He was among the first to acknowledge the talent of Felix Mendelssohn, of Hector Berlioz, and of Richard Wagner, and he took joy in the discovery of that gifted German, Johannes Brahms: "the young eagle," he called him. He was delighted, too, when he visited Schubert's family and brought to light Schubert compositions which had not been performed before.

Schumann's music criticism was fresh, sympathetic, and original. "No one has written so lovingly of lovely things," Ernest Newman, the English music critic, wrote. He continued to write musical reviews until 1845, and all the while he kept on with his composition.

He was composing music for Goethe's *Faust* when he was stricken with a severe nervous malady. But he recovered and went on with his work, and the scenes from *Faust* which he had completed were performed on the centenary of Goethe's birth, at Dresden, Leipzig, and Weimar.

He had been very sensitive and high strung always, but with Clara's help he had managed to lead a quiet, normal life even with six children. In 1850 he accepted the directorship at Düsseldorf, and he continued to compose and make concert tours. Now, however, his nervous symptoms increased. He imagined that he heard voices continually sounding in his ears. One night he suddenly left his bed saying that Schubert and Mendelssohn had sent him a theme which he must write down. He wrote five variations for that theme, and they were his last work. He threw himself into the Rhine not long after that, was rescued by some fishermen, and sent to a private asylum in Bonn, where he died two years later.

Sad though its ending was, Robert Schumann had a successful and happy life. He had created beauty, and he had generously helped other musicians to fulfill themselves. Clara Schumann, acknowledged as the leading woman pianist of her time, continued her concert tours. She put more and more of his music on her programs and was proud of the affection and warmth with which her audiences listened as she played.

CHAPTER SEVENTEEN

Felix Mendelssohn Discovers Bach

HANDSOME and young, with a dark-eyed, intelligent face and a slender, graceful figure, a Jew, beloved by his family and all who knew him, a happily married man who was proud of his beautiful children—this was Felix Mendelssohn. Robert Schumann was very fond of him and wrote of his music in glowing terms, and wherever he went men spoke of him happily and with affection. He died when he was only thirty-eight, but he lived long enough to make his contribution to the romantic music of his day.

Mendelssohn's father was a prosperous banker in the city of Berlin to which the family had moved from Hamburg where Felix was born. His mother wrote poetry, read Greek and Latin, and entertained noted artists, writers, and musicians.

The boy's parents were delighted when he appeared to show musical talent, and they obtained the best possible teachers for him. His sister Fanny was musically gifted, too, and the children studied together, working very hard, getting up at four o'clock in the morning to practice.

Was it really true that Felix was as gifted as his teachers said? the father wondered. In 1825 he took the boy to Paris to get the opinion of Luigi Cherubini, who was the head of the Paris Conservatory. Cherubini was a kind of musical czar then and his opinion was considered law. He was sure of young Felix's talent and urged him to come to Paris to study. But the father, proud of his son, brought him home again. He would find the best teachers in Germany for him.

Probably more important to Mendelssohn than any teaching, however, was an opera that he heard as a boy. This was *Der Freischütz* by Karl Maria von Weber. The opera was filled with realistic effects and was amazing because of the way in which its music brought to life the German forest with its countless dark trees, its clouds and winds, its mysterious shadows and bright sunlit glades. The music had a weird, fantastic atmosphere, and it evoked in the listener all sorts of romantic imaginings. It set young Mendelssohn dreaming, and his dreams were not of the German forest, but of fairyland. As he grew, his music, too, seemed to come from some other world.

In 1825 Mendelssohn's father bought a large estate in a suburb of Berlin. The beautiful old mansion had a music room and was surrounded by terraces and gardens. Here he built a *Gartenhaus* large enough to accommodate several hundred people. Friends drove from some distance to hear the musicales given there on Sunday afternoons. It was for one of these the following summer that Felix Mendelssohn, now seventeen, composed the ever-fresh, young music of the overture to Shakespeare's *A Midsummer Night's Dream*. The audience listened enthralled, for the music glowed with poetry.

"At the beginning, a few wind-blown notes sounded the 'Open Sesame' of a deep buried fairyland," one writer said of the overture to *A Midsummer Night's Dream*. "The realistic braying of Bottom on the bassoon added confusion to the proceedings, and Oberon's repeated song strewing blessings through the palace of Theseus . . . returned the overture to the brink of the spirit-infested wood. From there the same wind-blown notes heard at the beginning ushered back the world of reality, and the dream was over!"

Mendelssohn's overture to *A Midsummer Night's Dream* por-

trayed the elfin quality of Shakespeare's play. Written by a seven-teen-year-old it was a masterpiece in form and in scoring. Later the same fairy-like quality was found in Mendelssohn's bubbling scherzos. These had a fantastic play of delicate tones that seemed to float in the air like clouds, and all his music had a sweetness, delicacy, and a refinement of good taste. His beautiful Violin Concerto in E Minor was followed by more chamber music and by his symphonies, and they all bore his magic touch.

A brilliant pianist and one of the foremost conductors of his time, Mendelssohn was constantly on the road giving concerts. Fortunately he loved to travel. He often went on trips to Switzerland, France, Italy, and England, to Scotland and the

Hebrides, taking his paintbox with him, and coming home not only with the water colors he had made, but also with vivid memories he sought to put down in music. So he wrote the *Italian* and *Scotch* symphonies and the "Hebrides Overture" ("Fingal's Cave"), and in all these his music reflected the places he had seen. In "Fingal's Cave" his romantic imagination recalled the sound of the waves dashing against the rocks, the cries of the sea gulls, the odor of the salt air, and the melancholy of the northern coast. *Songs without Words* and *Calm Sea and Prosperous Voyage* also describe scenes of his travels. The *Reformation Symphony*, in which he used Lutheran chorales, is a tribute to Martin Luther.

Mendelssohn's grandfather, Moses Mendelssohn, had been forced to live in a Jewish ghetto and had suffered the sorrows which prejudice brought on him, but he had nevertheless succeeded in making a name for himself as a philosopher, a writer, and a respected member of his community. Mendelssohn was extremely proud of him, and, though he himself had been brought up as a Christian and had married the daughter of a Protestant clergyman, he never forgot he was a Jew. For this reason he wrote the oratorio *Elijah*, which proclaims the greatness of the Jewish people.

The city of Leipzig was the musical center of Germany at that time, and Mendelssohn went there in 1835 to become the conductor of the Gewandhaus orchestra. As an orchestra leader he was a great success. Up to his time most orchestra leaders had been seated at the piano or had played the first violin. Mendelssohn, however, stood up to lead. Slender, handsome, and energetic, he conducted the players whom he had disciplined to beautiful precision, and swayed with the music that he drew from them.

Two years after he went to Leipzig, he founded the Conservatory of Music there, and it quickly became one of the most distinguished music schools in all Europe.

But he did much more than create his fresh, finely chiseled

music, and more than direct his orchestra and organize his conservatory. He brought back to the people's notice the music of Johann Sebastian Bach, which had been neglected and forgotten.

As a boy of twelve Mendelssohn had first discovered the forgotten master. He came upon an autographed copy of the *St. Matthew Passion* in a dusty heap of old manuscripts that belonged to one of his teachers. He was so excited by it that he could not sleep. His mother had the music copied for him and gave it to him for a birthday present.

Later, when he entered Berlin University, he heard one of his friends say that Bach's music was like a mathematical exercise. The statement shocked him, and he set to work to correct his friend's opinion. He persuaded sixteen of his friends who had good voices to organize themselves into a choir, and they practiced singing Bach chorales every Saturday night. They did so well that after some hesitation Carl Zelter, the leader of the Berlin *Singakademie*, turned over his chorus of three or four hundred voices to them, and they began to rehearse Bach's *St. Matthew Passion*. The soloists for it were engaged from the opera.

The city seethed with gossip when the performance was announced, and the house was sold out well in advance. On March 11, 1829, the twenty-year-old conductor took up his baton, and the performance was a tremendous success.

Mendelssohn's sister, Fanny, reflected the general excitement when she wrote in a letter soon afterwards, "What used to be a dream has now come true: the *Passion* has been heard in public, and now belongs to the world!"

Thanks to the enthusiasm of the young Mendelssohn, Johann Sebastian Bach, who had been forgotten for a hundred years, took his place again as an inspiration and an example to later composers.

The critics say that Felix Mendelssohn is not among the greatest European musicians, that his music is sentimental. They wonder if his life was too happy to give his music depth. They say that he never achieved anything more beautiful than the overture to *A Midsummer Night's Dream,* which he wrote when he was seventeen.

Still, if he had never written any music at all, he would have served its cause with his conducting. And if he had never conducted an orchestra, there was still the fact that he rediscovered Johann Sebastian Bach. Perhaps that was his greatest achievement. What would the music of the nineteenth and twentieth centuries have been like without the influence of that organist and choirmaster of Leipzig?

CHAPTER EIGHTEEN

Johannes Brahms and the Shadow of Beethoven

"HOW CAN I write a symphony when I feel the shadow of the great Beethoven treading constantly behind me?" Johannes Brahms once said.

In the second half of the nineteenth century when Brahms lived and worked, the music of the Romantics was admired by everyone. But Johannes Brahms could not join in the universal fashion of the day, for he wanted to go back to the forms of the classic masters. He wanted absolute music that needed no story and no explanation, but only its perfect form. He was very modest in his approach, and would not even try to write a symphony until he was middle-aged. To try to imitate Beethoven seemed to him presumptuous.

Yet when he did finally produce his First Symphony the eminent conductor, Hans von Bülow, was so impressed that he called it "The Tenth," meaning that it was worthy to succeed Beethoven's Ninth. Since then Brahms' name has been linked with that of Bach and Beethoven: they have been called "the three great B's."

He was born in the disreputable district of the Hamburg waterfront. His father was a happy-go-lucky vagabond. His mother, a seamstress, crippled in one leg, was a spiritually strong and artistic woman. Perhaps Brahms learned from his father to love music, for at one time the elder Brahms was a double bass player in Hamburg's city orchestra, and he also played in a band with five other musicians on the Hamburg street corners.

Both parents came from the German province of Holstein, which is in the southern part of the Danish peninsula. The North Sea lies on one side of that peninsula and the Baltic Sea on the other. The grandeur of the North Sea and the brooding mists of the Baltic seem to sway and drift through much of Brahms' music.

As a child Brahms showed great skill at the piano. His father, wanting to exploit this ability, used to take him to the harbor taverns to entertain the customers. And one day an agent offered to take him to play in America.

Fortunately the child was rescued from these exploitations by a piano teacher, Otto Cossell, and a composer, Eduard Marxsen. Marxsen was an excellent teacher and an idealistic man, and as the boy grew he exercised a strong influence on him. By the time he was fifteen Brahms was giving piano recitals and playing with remarkable technical skill, though he was embarrassed if anyone praised his performance.

Once a man he did not know sat in the audience, and when

the performance was over came up to speak to him. It was the Hungarian violinist Eduard Reményi. Would the young Brahms act as his accompanist? he asked. He expected to go on a tour, playing gypsy music, traveling like a gypsy from one place to another.

The youth agreed to go, and soon he was playing accompaniments for the gay, wild gypsy songs while Reményi played the violin. These songs impressed themselves on Brahms so strongly that he never forgot them. Later he used them in the piano duets called *Hungarian Dances* and wove them into other chamber music works where they blended with his natural North German somberness.

Reményi's performances were, of course, not confined entirely to Hungarian music. Often he played the compositions of the classic composers. One day in Göttingen the "Kreutzer Sonata" of Beethoven was on his program. But when Brahms sat down at the piano he found that the instrument had been tuned a half step below the required pitch. An inexperienced accompanist would have been completely discomfited by the discovery, but Brahms knew the sonata so well that he could transpose it from A to B Flat without difficulty.

The concert went off smoothly, and the incident might have been forgotten, but it happened that the violinist Joseph Joachim was in the audience, and after the performance he talked with Reményi, who told him what had occurred. Joachim was impressed with the versatility of the young accompanist. Here was a pianist out of the ordinary, he thought. He wanted to see more of him.

So the friendship between Brahms and Joachim started, and Joachim was determined to help the youth in every way he could. He gave him a letter of introduction to Franz Liszt, and he introduced him also to Robert and Clara Schumann. Brahms played his youthful "Scherzo" for the Schumanns as well as his three sonatas. The third of these seemed to give promise of the future splendor of his music.

Before long the young Brahms was a frequent visitor at the Schumanns' house, and both Robert and Clara became very fond of him. Robert wrote glowing criticism of his music in *Die Neue Zeitschrift*. "Graces and Heroes have watched the cradle of this young genius. . . ," he wrote in his characteristically romantic style. Clara Schumann loved to play Brahms' music at her recitals. After Robert Schumann's death the young Brahms helped and comforted her. They were devoted friends for the rest of their lives.

When he was about thirty Brahms went to Vienna. The musical atmosphere there seemed so delightful to him that he stayed the rest of his life. Still, in Vienna he maintained his North German way of living—very systematic and modest, never quite trusting himself, though he has been called the greatest musical craftsman since Bach.

Though his tastes were simple, Brahms lived very comfortably in Vienna. He did not need a patron, for he was probably the first composer who earned enough by having his music published to be well off. His *Hungarian Dances,* which were originally a piano duet, were the basis of his financial success.

Like so many of the Viennese, he was fond of outdoor life and often walked in the country with his friends. He directed a singing society in Vienna, and liked to hold its meetings in the nearby country. He directed from the limb of a tree where he sat in order to raise himself above the chorus, for he was short—a plump little man with a long brown beard that fell down on his chest.

What kind of man was he, this North German musician who lived out his life so quietly in Vienna while his fame spread across Europe? He grew more and more solitary as time passed, uneasy in conventional society. On his sixtieth birthday he fled all the way to Italy for fear he might be expected to take part in some sort of celebration.

True, he had many devoted friends who were important and prominent men. Besides Joseph Joachim, the violinist, there were the Viennese surgeon Dr. Theodore Billroth, and Hans von Bülow, the conductor. Brahms quarreled with all these men and broke his friendly ties with them, and though he attempted to restore them again, he was lonely.

He disliked answering letters, and his mail generally went unanswered. Only when a letter contained a plea for help did he sit down and respond generously. Antonín Dvořák, the Czech composer, who at that time was unknown and poor, wrote him, and Brahms immediately used his influence to find him a publisher. This was characteristic of the kind of thing he did.

Brahms was extremely fond of children and enjoyed being called "Uncle Brahms" by them. He had a number of friendships with women who were singers, and these inspired him to create some glorious songs. (The famous "Lullaby" is dedicated to a woman of whom he had once been fond; it was intended to celebrate the birth of her second child.) He continued to be devoted to Clara Schumann all his life, but he never married.

Just as he avoided the bonds of matrimony, he avoided official positions. He was director of concerts and the choral society at the court of Lippe-Detmold only four years; and later, director of the Vienna Conservatory. He sought no other official post. He would have been pleased if his native city of Hamburg had offered him one; but it never did.

That was the man—and in contrast there is his music. There are the piano pieces, short poems of meditation and gentle humor; there are the two piano concertos, epic battles between piano and orchestra fought with passion and robust humor. There is, too, his difficult violin concerto of which someone has said that it was "written not *for* the violin but against it." And the monumental piano works called *Variations on a Theme by Handel,* and *Paganini Variations.* They bring this form to new imaginative splendor.

Besides all these there is the *German Requiem,* a composition for vocal soloists, chorus, and orchestra, on words which he himself selected from the Bible. He wrote it in his grief at his mother's death. It was first given in its entirety in 1868 when he was thirty-five years old.

More than ten years after the *German Requiem* had appeared, the University of Breslau offered Brahms an honorary degree. He was such a very modest man that everyone expected him to decline it, and there was general surprise when he accepted and said he would write music for the occasion. It took him a long time to decide what form this music should take. Finally he collected a number of convivial student songs and combined them into a sparkling overture. The "Academic Festival Overture" is still popular—more popular, perhaps, than when the composer first conducted it at Breslau on February 4, 1881.

His chamber music had a symphonic grandeur, but he was over forty when he started to write his first symphony. Then, three symphonies followed the first one, and each of them was different, yet they were all alike in their lyric beauty and emotional gravity. In the final movement of the last symphony he created a "Passacaglia" or form of variation on a few bass notes, which is the parting seal of a great master.

Each time he wrote a symphony he was not sure he had succeeded. He wrote a friend after he had finished the second one, "I don't know whether I have a pretty symphony. I must inquire of learned persons." Yet the music he spoke of so modestly was some of the greatest that has been written, and each symphony he produced surpassed the one that had gone before. Each brought something new into the realm of symphonic literature.

So at last Johannes Brahms, who had felt the shadow of the great Beethoven treading constantly behind him, had come the whole circle of music; he had written songs and chamber music, symphonies and choral music worthy to succeed the classic masters whom he admired.

He died at sixty-four of an ailment that was aggravated when he took cold standing in the rain at Clara Schumann's funeral.

CHAPTER NINETEEN

Chopin: Cannons Under the Roses

I N T H E nineteenth century, after Napoleon's defeat, men put off their wigs and satin knee breeches to wear the coats and trousers that were the symbols of democracy; they set aside also their harpsichords and claviers and began to play that new-fangled instrument, the pianoforte.

These instruments had first been made in Florence, the Italian

Bartolommeo Cristofori having produced the first practical one in 1709. They combined the strings which had come down through the long centuries from the Greek monochord, with a keyboard that developed from the old Roman water organ, and a sounding board like those of the ancient psalteries and dulcimers which were mentioned in the Bible.

After Cristofori's time such pianos were greatly improved with new placement of the strings and a larger sounding board to give more sonority and power. Now they could be played either soft or loud, as the name *piano-forte* implied. And they were capable of a great diversity of touch and shading; the notes could be held and mingled together, giving all sorts of remarkable effects.

By 1768 pianos had developed to such a degree that Bach's youngest son, Johann Christian Bach, gave a recital on one of them for fashionable Londoners—the first piano recital in history.

As the piano slowly became a popular instrument it supplanted lutes, viols, and harps in many middle-class homes. Then gradually the musicians took it up and found it useful in sketching out their compositions and in rehearsing singers and ensembles. Before long it became *"ein Mädchen für alles"*—a servant for all musical chores. The musicians of the romantic movement made the piano their favorite solo instrument, and of all these musicians Frédéric Chopin was the one most closely identified with it.

Chopin, it is said, was born to the sound of the violins that were playing at a country wedding near his parents' low-roomed house at Zelazowa Wola, a little Polish village not far from Warsaw. The year was 1810. His father was a tutor in the family of Count Skarbek and had been born in Nancy, France. His mother before her marriage had been a lady-in-waiting to the countess. They were intelligent, affectionate, not rich, not poor, and they all spoke French, followed French manners and customs, and read French books, as did all educated families in Poland then. Poland had had a tragic history; it had been split and divided among Prussia, Russia, and Austria, but France had been steadily sympathetic to it. Most of the Polish people, therefore, felt an affection for France.

The Chopin family loved music. The father liked to play the flute, the mother to sing, and one of Frédéric's sisters learned with some pride to play the piano. Everyone expected little Frédéric to be musical, too. They were distressed when he responded to music with floods of tears. Then they discovered that he wept not because he disliked music but because he loved it so, and they hastened to find a teacher for him.

Chopin's first teacher was a solid Czech music master, Adalbert Zywny, who trained the boy with Bach's *Well-Tempered Clavier* and taught him so much that he was ready to give a recital for the friends of the Count and Countess Skarbek when he was only eight.

"What did they like best?" his mother asked the little boy when he returned home after the concert. She was sure that he had played all his pieces well. "My collar, mamma, my collar," the young virtuoso answered, proud of that collar, which was made of lace. But the members of the nobility who had heard him play assured her that the fragile little pianist had a magic touch, and his mother was proud when he was invited to play before the Czar.

After that, his father, perhaps because he was himself a teacher, saw to it that Frédéric was well educated. At fourteen he was sent to the Warsaw Lyceum, and he was also taught musical composition by Joseph Elsner, the foremost composition teacher in Warsaw. Elsner sensed that the boy was gifted with a unique and rare style. He recorded: "Lessons in musical composition: Chopin, Frédéric, third year student—amazing capabilities, musical genius."

The slight, blond-haired boy was full of fun and mischief in those years. He was a great mimic, and delighted his friends with impersonations of the Austrian emperor, of an Eastern Jew, of a sentimental Englishman. Most of all he liked to imitate a piano player, throwing his hands into the air in a way that he called "catching pigeons."

With all his gaiety he had his serious moments. He was passionately stirred by the idea of freedom, and he loved to read. The rich store of Polish poetry appealed to him most, especially the epic poems of the poet Adam Mickiewicz. That poet's "Lithuanian Poems" were later to become the source of inspiration for his four great ballades.

But the young Chopin was attracted, too, by the Polish folk songs and dances. These were distinctly heard in the rondos that were his first compositions. He loved to write stately music for the polonaise, which was a characteristically Polish dance. Many eighteenth-century composers had written polonaises before now, but he gave them their character of patriotic exuberance.

Chopin first left Poland when he was sixteen. He wanted adventure, and cosmopolitan cities held a fascination for him. At first he took some short trips with his mother and sister, and then, when he was seventeen, a friend of the family invited him to pay a visit to Berlin.

He heard much music on that visit to Berlin, listened to many operas, and wrote home to his parents that Handel's *Ode for St. Cecilia's Day* "most nearly approaches my ideal of sublime music." In Berlin he saw Felix Mendelssohn, but was too shy to speak to him, and, like every other artist of his time, he was entranced by Paganini's playing.

So the fledgling learned to fly. And the old nest in Poland was too small to hold him. His father managed to get together some money to send him to Vienna. And there he found a publisher for his variations for piano and orchestra on a theme from Mozart's *Don Giovanni*.

In his portfolio he also had his two concertos for piano and orchestra. Although the orchestra part of these is considered inferior, the piano part has great beauty, and the concertos are still performed by many famous artists. Perhaps he realized the shortcomings of his orchestral composing; after this he devoted himself to piano composition almost exclusively.

He had not been long in Vienna when he was persuaded to give a concert. He said that he undertook with some hesitation to play "in a city which can boast of having heard a Haydn, a Mozart, and a Beethoven." But he was needlessly nervous; the concert was a success. People stood up on their seats to applaud.

About a week after that he gave another concert and this time Count Lichnowski, Beethoven's friend, lent him his own piano to play upon. Chopin's playing was brilliant though not very robust. The critics were friendly, but some of them thought his tone "too small."

So he returned home a second time, stopping at Teplitz, where he met a "courtful of princes," and at Dresden where he stood in line two and a half hours to get tickets to Goethe's *Faust*.

Now he was more restless than before. He wanted to travel. But he was afraid to go—"afraid," he said, "of dying in a strange land, in a strange bed, among strangers."

He went to Vienna again. But when he got there he heard that the revolutionary attempt of the Polish people to shake off their foreign yoke had failed. Should he go back and join in the fighting? His father urged him not to, and he decided to stay on in Vienna. He was very unhappy there, for the Poles were unpopular in Austria. His sensitive nature could not tolerate the slights and small insults he encountered continually; he decided that he would leave Austria and go to France.

So he set off again, stopping at Stuttgart on his way. There he heard that Warsaw had been captured by the Russians, and he was overwhelmed with grief. He found consolation in writing his "Revolutionary Etude."

Perhaps he would go to London now, he thought. But he would stop in Paris on the way. He stopped in Paris—and stayed there the rest of his life.

In Paris the slender, blond youth was lonely and lost at first.

But a concert was soon arranged for him in Ignaz Pleyel's room at 9, rue Cadet, and though none but a few Polish emigrés came to hear, the critic François Fétis praised his playing in the *Revue Musicale*, announcing that his style was perfect and that he showed great originality. Fétis' praise and his own charm quickly won the Parisians to him, and he became a great society favorite. "I move among the best people, I sit with ambassadors, princes, ministers; and I have not even a notion how it all came about. I didn't even try for it."

The well-bred youth with his charming presence had no need to try. He was soon invited everywhere, and fashionable pupils flocked to him. "I have five lessons to give today; do you think that I am making a fortune? Carriages and white gloves cost more, and without them one would not be in good taste."

He was a severe teacher who demanded a great deal of his pupils. He insisted on a thorough musical foundation, a daily study of Bach, and rhythmic accuracy. And though he made them work hard his pupils were greatly attached to him. "He is turning the heads of all the women," one gentleman said. "The men are jealous of him. He is the rage."

So Chopin worked at his composition and his teaching, and he loved Paris. He lived there like a man of fashion, keeping a carriage and a manservant, and wearing suits, hats, and gloves which he bought at the most exclusive shops. He surrounded himself with beautiful things: in his apartment were rich carpets, fine furniture, and a profusion of flowers.

One day Franz Liszt, the great piano virtuoso, came to visit him, wearing his green gloves and his Hungarian pelisse, and with his medals dangling on his breast. After he had taken off his cloak and run his fingers through his long golden hair, Liszt sat down at the piano and began to play one of Chopin's études while the composer listened. And while he listened Chopin wrote a letter to a friend in Poland: "I write to you without knowing what my pen is scribbling, because at this moment Liszt is playing my études and transporting me out of my respectable thought. I should like to steal from him the way to play my own études."

Liszt, however, was only one of Chopin's many friends, for all the great Parisian world of art and literature visited Chopin in his beautiful apartment. There were women as well as men, and he was often in love. He would have liked to marry, but some disaster always befell his love affairs.

That was how he lived in Paris. And all the time he was composing. He wrote twenty *valses* in varying moods, some of them gay and carefree, some languorous and sad. He wrote fifty-six mazurkas filled with Slavic feeling. In these mazurkas he introduced his most exotic harmonies, his most original melodic intervals and melodies reminiscent of Polish folk songs. He wrote a great many polonaises—difficult pieces of music that are amazingly exciting. He wrote nocturnes, serenades, preludes, and études. But beautiful though these works are, his immortality rests also on his greater works, on his ballades, his fantasies, his sonatas and scherzos.

Chopin was no weakling in either his music or his character. Schumann said there were "cannons under the roses" when he played. And James Huneker, the American music critic, wrote, "Chopin was weak in physique, but he had the soul of a lion."

Chopin's ballades and fantasies are like great epics filled with dramatic suspense. They start with a simple narrative and gradually conjure up a tremendous storm of passion, beautifully controlled and molded, and filled with grandeur.

He rarely played in public. "I am not fitted to give concerts," he said. But in a small room, slight and poetic-looking as he sat before the keyboard with a few friends around him, he could produce exquisite music.

"There is nothing to compare with the enjoyment he affords us when he improvises on the piano," Heinrich Heine the poet wrote. "He is then neither a Frenchman, nor a German; he reveals a higher origin; he comes from the land of Mozart, Raphael, and

Goethe; his true land is the land of poetry." And another listener said, at one of his performances, "Everyone went away full of sweet joy and profound meditation."

In 1835 Chopin fell in love with Maria Wodzinska and was engaged to be married to her. But the engagement was broken, probably because of Chopin's delicate health. He was overcome with grief, and, at the insistence of his friends, decided to take a trip to London. There he gave a recital at James Broadwood's under an assumed name, but everyone who listened knew who he was. Nothing could disguise his unique style, and no one else could play like Chopin. Mendelssohn, who heard him, reported: "One day he played magnificently at Broadwood's, then fled. It appears that he is very ill."

It was true. Weakness, ennui, and despair were building up in him, and Mendelssohn's observation was well founded. He was indeed very ill. The first signs of tuberculosis were beginning to appear.

Just at this point he met George Sand. Her real name was Amandine Aurore Lucie Dupin, a woman whom many men admired and the author of a great many romantic novels. Chopin did not like her at all at first. She wore a suit of overalls, like those of a modern working man, and she smoked cigars. She sat up all night writing, and everyone in Paris seemed to be gossiping about her.

But she was kind to Chopin with a sort of maternal kindness, and gradually his friendship for her deepened. Now as he wrote mazurkas, polonaises, and nocturnes happiness came back to him again.

In 1838 he went with her to Majorca, an island off the Spanish coast, and wrote his friend Julian Fontana:

I am in Palma among palms, cedars, cacti, pomegranates, etc., everything the Jardin des Plantes has in its greenhouses. A sky like turquoise, a sea like lapis lazuli, mountains like emeralds, air like heaven. Sun all day, and hot. Everybody in summer clothes. At night for hours, guitars and singing. Huge balconies with grapevines overhead. Everything faces toward Africa as the town does. In short a glorious life!—I am close to what is beautiful. I am better.

But they had difficulty in finding lodgings in Palma, and after some search found a place in an old monastery called Valdemosa. Chopin wrote Fontana again describing it:

Built between the rocks and the sea, it's an enormous Carthusian monastery where you may picture me with no white gloves and with my hair uncurled, as pale as always, in a cell with doors larger than Parisian gates. The cell is the shape of a tall coffin, the enormous vaulting is covered with dust, the window tiny; outside the window there are orange trees, palms, and cypresses, opposite the window my bed on thongs under a Moorish filigree rosette. Near the bed is a square, rickety writing desk that I can scarcely use; on it (this is a great luxury) a candle in a leaden candlestick. Bach, my scrawls, old papers (not mine), silence—you could yell—still silence. In short I write you from a strange place. . . .

The winter in that strange place was damp, and Chopin became depressed. One day when George Sand had gone shopping in Palma in the rain he thought she would never come back. "I knew you were dead," he told her when she finally appeared. That day he had written the "Raindrop Prelude."

Gradually Valdemosa became a nightmare to them both. The peasants distrusted and avoided them, they were cold and uncomfortable, and they missed their friends. They decided finally to leave. But when they got as far as the coast Chopin had a hemorrhage and was deathly ill. The captain of a French sloop-of-war, *Le Méléagre,* took pity on them and brought them to Marseilles. The Spanish visit had been like a bad dream.

Chopin improved a little in the south of France. He wrote the Sonata in B Flat Minor that contains the famous "Funeral March." This is followed by the spectral "Presto Finale," which has been called "the wind moaning over wintry graves."

After a time he was well enough to go back to Paris, where

he played before King Louis-Philippe. But though he continued to compose, writing some of his greatest masterpieces—the F Sharp Minor Polonaise, a second and third ballade, and the third scherzo—his health was failing fast. Now he spent the summers at George Sand's estate, *Nohant,* and the winters in Paris. In 1848 he managed another trip to England, where he played in a private musicale before Queen Victoria.

But he was too weak and ill to go on teaching. "I think my cough is strangling me," he said. He quarreled with George Sand, who might have been a comfort to him. And now he began to think more and more of Mozart. He entrusted his favorite pupil, Auguste Franchomme, to the Princess Czartoryska, saying, "You two will play Mozart together, in memory, and I will hear you."

He died in the early morning of October 17, 1849. He had asked that Mozart's Requiem be played at his funeral as it had been played at Haydn's and at Beethoven's.

That, in bare outline, was the brief career of Frédéric Chopin, whose playing is a legend, and whose compositions are a goal and inspiration to all who study the piano.

CHAPTER TWENTY

Berlioz Paints Pictures in Music

G R E A T changes in instrumental music had been under way in the Romantic Age. The old symphonies which Haydn and Beethoven had perfected were going out of fashion. Music with a "program" was sought after now. Composers delighted in giving a description or an explanation for their music. They wanted music to be a vehicle for their emotions. They wanted it written with a descriptive title and sometimes a quotation from a poem. They no longer liked "opus" numbers.

Beethoven himself had once written this kind of music. His Sixth Symphony was called the *Pastoral,* and it describes a country scene. But, though he wrote program music in the Sixth Symphony, he did not depart from the classic symphonic form, for the form was important to him. The "program" was of secondary importance.

It was just the reverse with the romantic composers. Program and emotion mattered much more to them than did any requirements of musical form.

Emotions by their very nature are short-lived. In music it is hard to sustain emotions very long, and when you have once described a scene or a state of mind, it is done and needs no repeating. So composers now often wrote short compositions—songs, rondos, or overtures.

Beautiful though these short pieces were, however, they did not give scope enough for a full orchestra. Must the composers of orchestral scores continue to write in the old classic manner?

they wondered. Must they abandon "programs" and cease trying to express what they saw and felt? The genius of Beethoven had succeeded in doing both, but he had done it only once, and had gone back to the classic manner in his later symphonies. And, after all, not everyone had the genius of Beethoven.

Though none had that genius, still there were composers who succeeded in writing not classic but romantic orchestral music after their own fashion. The first of these, the man who conceived a new kind of orchestral music and a new kind of orchestra, was that strange, unhappy man, Hector Berlioz.

Berlioz had a hard struggle to become a composer at all. He was born in La Côte St. André in France, and his father wanted him to be a doctor. He did, in fact, go to Paris as a medical student. There his first session in the dissecting room was too much for him.

"The sight of that human charnel house . . . so filled me with horror that I leaped out of the nearest window and ran breathless all the way home, as if pursued by Death and all her train."

So he quarreled with his father and wrote him truculently, "I am voluntarily driven toward a magnificent career (no other epithet can be applied to the career of an artist), and I am not in the least heading for perdition. For I believe I shall succeed."

He did not play any instrument well enough to earn his living by teaching, but he could sing and read music at sight, so it was not hard for him to get a part in the chorus of the Théâtre de Nouveautés. The rehearsals at the theater were appalling to him. "It will make me into an idiot and give me cholera morbus," he said. Still he needed the money.

Meantime he was continuing his music studies. His teacher was the elderly Jean François Lesueur, the most celebrated teacher-composer in France at that time. Lesueur was very kind to him and for a time took him to live with his family. Under Lesueur's influence he composed a Mass, and although he had to borrow money to pay for its performance, it was finally produced at the

Church of St. Roch on July 10, 1825. The *Messe Solennelle* was Berlioz's first finished work.

The young composer was dizzy with excitement when the Mass was sung. He had not seen his teacher, M. Lesueur, in the church and rushed to his house afterward to ask why he had not come to hear it. Lesueur had been there after all, it turned out; he had listened standing behind a pillar.

"By heaven," the old man said. "You shan't be a doctor or an apothecary or anything but a great musician!"

Because of the success of his Mass, Berlioz was accepted at the Paris Conservatory. He had been refused there before, for Cherubini, who was its head, was a classicist, and he could not overlook Berlioz's lack of formal training.

The new student hated the drudgery and exercises at the Conservatory. If he could only win the Prix de Rome, he thought, he could escape them. This prize had been instituted by Louis XIV to permit artists and architects to study in Italy, but by Napoleon's order in 1803 it had been offered to musicians also. It provided for three years' study abroad, two of which were to be spent in Italy. The contestant must submit a cantata to the jury and must be dressed in formal attire to be interviewed by them.

Berlioz tried for the Prix de Rome three times in succession, and three times failed to receive it. Then in 1830 he made his fourth effort, and he succeeded. For the competition he wrote the cantata, *La Mort de Sardanapale,* and the judges liked it.

After he had succeeded in getting the Prix de Rome, he found that he did not like Italy. So he went back to Paris, and there he fell in love with Henrietta Smithson, an Irish actress who was playing Shakespeare. He arranged a festival of his own music in order to impress her.

One of the compositions he played at this festival was his autobiographical *Symphonie Fantastique.* The *Symphonie Fantastique* is composed of five dramatic movements and describes the romantic experience of a young musician in love. The lover has taken opium, and under its influence has dreamed. First then, there are the agonies and passions of his unrequited love and the consolations that religion brings; then his meeting with his beloved at a ball in the midst of a brilliant festival; then the shepherds playing their pipes in a pastoral setting. Now with the sound of the wind in the trees, the beloved appears, and his heart misses a beat, forebodings come—will she be unfaithful to him? In the fourth movement he dreams that he has killed her, and is marching to the scaffold. Finally she has joined the witches in their weird orgies. There are groans and bursts of laughter and funeral bells as she takes part in the witches' dance. A parody of the *"Dies Irae,"* that medieval liturgical chant for Requiem Masses, is interwoven into the dance.

Berlioz, himself a good music critic, said that his symphony was "now gloomy and wild, now brilliant and grand," and perhaps that is as good an estimate as anyone has given.

The *Symphonie Fantastique* was successful in its object for soon afterwards he married Henrietta Smithson, and they had a son. But Berlioz found it hard to support a family. He became art critic for the *Journal des Débats,* but he said writing critical articles was like having a cannonball chained to his leg.

So he went on with his composing. Now he wrote the symphony *Harold in Italy.* Inspired by Lord Byron's *Childe Harold,* it describes Berlioz's reminiscences of his own stay in Italy. Berlioz labeled the first movement "Harold in the Mountains, Scenes of Melancholy, Happiness and Joy," and went on to a movement in which is heard the "March of the Pilgrims, Singing their Evening Hymns." The final scene he describes as an "Orgy of Brigands."

All this time he was deeply in debt, but relief came when the Minister of Affairs commissioned him to write a Requiem to commemorate the victims of a bomb which in 1835 had been thrown by an Italian anarchist. The minister offered him 4000 francs. Berlioz hesitated. He needed the money, he wanted to write the

Requiem, but not unless he could do it in his own way. He wanted to write what he would call the *Grande Messe des Morts.* He wanted five hundred performers for it.

The minister compromised at last! he would have four hundred and fifty performers. So Berlioz set to work, and the musical ideas came to him so fast that he had to invent a kind of shorthand to put them down. The Requiem that he wrote demanded eighty sopranos, eighty altos, sixty tenors, seventy basses, many trumpets, horns, drums, gongs, and cymbals, as well as scores of strings and woodwinds.

With the Requiem, seventeen years after he had received his Prix de Rome, Berlioz experienced his first real success. Schumann wrote, "The 'Offertory' surpasses all!" And his friend Heinrich Heine, listening, said that Berlioz was "like an antediluvian bird, or a lark the size of an eagle."

Meantime his fame in France was growing. The small officials who were running the French government after Napoleon's downfall wanted to impress the people with grand displays, so they commissioned Berlioz to write the *Symphonie Funèbre et Triomphale.* It was intended to accompany the burial of the patriots who had fallen during the July Revolution at Constantine in Algeria, and it would be the largest composition ever written for a military band.

There were more than two hundred in the band, among them a group of Bavarian cornetists who had come to Paris to give a concert. They marched through the streets playing, Berlioz in the lead wearing the uniform of a national guardsman. But it was almost impossible for the musicians to keep together in this way, and the crowd that lined the sidewalks was so noisy that the music was almost drowned out. Finally they reached the Place de la Bastille and here, when they were ready to start the symphony, sixty thousand National Guardsmen tramped across the square beating their own drums. This went on for two hours, and of the symphony Berlioz said later, "not a note survived."

But the music of the *Symphonie Funèbre et Triomphale* was not really lost. Berlioz altered and revised it a little and announced that it would be played again at a hall on the rue de Vivienne, where a huge crowd filled every seat. Some years later Richard Wagner said that he had heard this performance as a young man, and that he remembered how Berlioz stood "at the head of his troops leading his orchestra like a Napoleon."

There are many more things that might be said of Hector Berlioz—Henrietta Smithson died, and he married Mlle. Marie Recio. (When she too died, her mother kept house for him. She could not speak a word of French, nor he a word of Spanish, but they got on well together.) He traveled, and the writer Honoré de Balzac persuaded him to go to Russia—"You will make much money there. I will lend you my fur coat."

He wrote his memoirs, *Evenings with the Orchestra*, and biographies of Paganini and of Beethoven, as well as the splendid *Treatise on Musical Instruments*, which musicians still study today.

He wrote *L'Enfance du Christ*, a delicate oratorio with a small orchestra which describes Mary and Joseph knocking vainly at the doors as they seek lodging. "It seems to me to contain a feeling of infinite, of divine love," Berlioz said.

And finally he wrote an opera on the fall of Troy, *Les Troyens*, and brought together all that he had learned of music through his long and turbulent life. But this was not performed successfully till over twenty years after his death. Then it was described as "gigantic" and "convincing."

All these things might be written of the romantic Hector Berlioz but more important than any of them was the fact that in writing his romantic music he became truly the master and founder of the modern orchestra. He loved to experiment with new instruments like the saxophone. (This instrument had been invented by Adolphe Sax in 1840 and had been first used in an orchestra by the French composer Jean George Kastner four years later.) He loved, too, to discover new possibilities of technique and color.

Sometimes he put bags over the horns or sponges at the ends of drumsticks. He hung up the cymbals and had them struck with sticks rather than clapping them together, and he tried new combinations of instruments, such as a trombone playing a duet with a piccolo.

Besides all this he managed to make the players "play better than they knew how," so that they revealed new splendors, shimmering colors, volcanic outbursts. No one had made an orchestra play like this before.

The violent music of Hector Berlioz's orchestra made its vivid impression on everyone who heard it play. Some were startled and outraged, but some were vividly impressed. Franz Liszt the Hungarian pianist and composer listened to the *Symphonie Fantastique* and was overcome by it. He would make program music like the music of Hector Berlioz, he decided. He would employ the piano so brilliantly that it would sound like an orchestra.

CHAPTER TWENTY-ONE

The Brilliance of Franz Liszt

O N T H E night of October 22, 1811, it is said that the people of the little town of Raiding in Hungary looked up and saw a comet hanging in the sky. That night a boy was born to Adam Liszt and his wife, and many of the village people said the comet was a portent: the boy would be brilliant as the star had been. For a time their prophecy came true; for several years he did shine like a comet in the social and musical life of the continent. He was to be an outstanding piano virtuoso, a teacher among whose pupils were counted the most eminent musicians of his time, a stimulator of new musical ideas, and a generous man. He was moreover to be a hard worker; his musical compositions were to number between thirteen and fourteen hundred. Many of these seem tawdry and outdated now and most of them are not performed at all today. Yet for all this it must be said that Franz Liszt was an original thinker and had an enormous influence on the composers of his time.

The little Hungarian town where Liszt was born was surrounded by wooded hills and there were gypsy encampments on its outskirts. Wild gypsy dancing and plaintive singing were fuel that fired the emotions of the growing boy, and the pageantry of the village church kindled them again. These things must have been quite as important to him as the reading and writing the village priest taught him.

He was passionately fond of music and heard a good deal of it at home, for his grandfather had been in the employ of Prince Esterházy and so had known Joseph Haydn. His father also was a steward on the Esterházy estate, a frustrated musician who longed for musical companionship in the little town of Raiding and played the clavier by the hour. Franz Liszt was still a very little child when his father taught him to play.

In time he grew from a child into a slender boy—tall for his age, blue-eyed, fair-haired, and handsome. He threw himself into his music with a passion; those who listened to his playing were filled with the sense of his promise.

One day his father took him to Ödenburg, the nearest large town, and there the boy performed at a little concert. A group of Hungarian nobles heard him there and agreed to pay for his musical studies for six years. That made it possible for his father to take him to Vienna, where he studied under Carl Czerny and Antonio Salieri, who in his earlier days had taught Beethoven and Schubert.

Finally he was ready to make his debut at a concert in Vienna, and it was a thrilling success. In 1823 he went to Paris, and there he set his audiences into an uproar. He hoped to study at the Paris Conservatory, but met with difficulty. The director of the conservatory, Luigi Cherubini, who ruled all Paris like a musical dictator, was himself Italian born, but now he insisted that Franz Liszt might not be admitted to the conservatory because he was not French.

There was therefore nothing that the boy could do but study with private teachers, and this he did with great energy and industry. When he was sixteen his father died, and his mother came to Paris to share his modest rooms with him. He supported her by giving music lessons and occasional concerts.

All this time he was practicing hard—probably few pianists have ever practiced as hard as he did! One day he had heard Paganini play the violin and just as Robert Schumann had been carried away by the great violinist, so now Franz Liszt saw new horizons when he heard Paganini play. He decided forthwith that just as Paganini was the greatest of all violin performers, so he, Franz Liszt, would be the greatest of all pianists. Having set himself this goal he lost no time in setting out to reach it.

Soon he was ready to start on concert tours, and even when he was traveling he took a little silent clavier with him in the stage coach so that no time might be lost from his practicing. Everywhere he went he was admired. Back in Paris people called him the "Ninth Wonder of the World," and women, particularly the ladies of the nobility, adored him. They gave him lavish presents and pelted him with flowers when he performed. In 1833 the Countess Marie d'Agoult fell in love with him, and it was now that he began to compose. He was traveling with her when he wrote the first volume of his descriptive pieces for the piano, *Années de Pèlerinage.*

Franz Liszt and the Countess d'Agoult lived quietly in Switzerland for four or five years and had three children. One of them was a daughter named Cosima, who grew up to marry the conductor Hans von Bülow and who was later the wife of Richard Wagner.

In time Liszt and the countess drifted apart. He continued with his concert tours and performed in Germany, Russia, Sweden, and Spain. Everywhere he went, admiring audiences looked up at him on the concert platform, and kings and princes showered him with jeweled orders. Soon he had more money than he needed, but he was generous in helping needy musicians and in aiding deserving causes. In Vienna he gave a series of six piano recitals —the first such series that had ever been given. The proceeds he announced were to be given to completing the Beethoven memorial at Bonn. Through his generosity this was finally unveiled in 1845 at a music festival which he and the German composer Louis Spohr conducted.

There were three thousand people in the concert hall for the first of these Vienna recitals, and among them was a group of Hungarian noblemen who were enchanted with his playing. They invited him to Budapest, and there he appeared in a thousand-franc Magyar costume bought for the occasion, and was presented with a jeweled sword.

For the most part Liszt played his own compositions in his concerts and often these were transcriptions he had made of other men's music. They might be military marches, or Schubert lieder, or even Beethoven symphonies. Often he ended his performances with what he called his *Grand Galop Chromatique,* a collection of difficult scales and exercises played in what has been called "an athletic bout of piano pounding."

For Liszt believed a piano performer ought to stir up and excite his audience. He dressed in the most romantic style, often wearing a long green cape. And he had the piano turned sideways to the audience so that his handsome profile could be seen to good advantage. Before his time performers had always sat with their backs to their audiences or faced them across the piano. One listener remembers how he strode to the platform, pulled off the doeskin gloves from his well-shaped white hands, and threw them carelessly to the floor before he sat down to play. Another describes how he "constantly tossed back his long hair."

Yet despite his exhibitionism Liszt was a very influential musician, one of the most influential in the nineteenth century. He enlarged and magnified the possibilities of piano technique, and produced a brilliance and sonority that had not been heard before. Under his hands the piano suggested a whole orchestra with harp, bells, trumpets, and kettledrums. This was a completely new way of playing the piano, and the influence of Liszt has extended down to the most modern composers.

So he played in city after city: in Berlin and Copenhagen, in Lisbon, London, and Madrid, in Moscow, St. Petersburg, and Warsaw. Then in 1847 he made his last concert tour, and after that he never took any money for his performances. He had decided to give up his concert playing, to settle down to composing and conducting. He went to Weimar where the Grand Duke Friedrich had invited him to be director of the court orchestra.

In Weimar he chose for the programs at the duke's court not only a wide range of the classics but also the music of his contemporaries. He gave enthusiastic performances of Schumann's symphony, not caring that Robert and Clara Schumann did not like his musical style. He also directed the court orchestra in Berlioz's *Symphonie Fantastique* and his *Harold in Italy*, both of which had impressed him so greatly.

Perhaps his most adventurous undertaking was the production of Richard Wagner's new opera *Tannhäuser*, a bold thing to do because Richard Wagner was a revolutionist and a political outcast at the time.

Besides his conducting in Weimar, Liszt found time for teaching pianists and for writing music criticism. He wanted to explain to the public, not only the musical work of his more advanced contemporaries, but his own compositions as well.

His own compositions must have taken a great deal of his time, for he was a prolific composer. He was a great apostle of program music and was first to use it in orchestral compositions which he called "tone poems." "*Tasso*," "*Prometheus*," "*Mazeppa*" and "*Les Preludes*" are among his best-known tone poems. Each consists of one long movement divided into sections. Liszt was inspired by Berlioz and his orchestration in composing these. In them he employed a recurrent phrase in what is called "cyclic form." This phrase wove through all the sections giving the composition a stunning effect of unity. Berlioz had used a similar device, calling it an *idée fixe*, and Wagner developed it further in the leitmotivs of his operas.

Liszt did not confine himself to tone poems in his longer works, for he wrote two symphonies, the *Dante* and the *Faust*. Although these are long and rhetorical, they are interesting for they contain an innovation which seems prophetic. The *Faust Symphony* opens with great harmonic boldness, for the first theme encompasses all twelve chromatic tones as if pointing toward the atonal system of the twentieth century. In the realm of harmony Liszt was far ahead of his time, and his new uses of chromatic harmonies were original and trail blazing.

Of all his many compositions, however, the piano pieces which he called *Hungarian Rhapsodies* are those for which Liszt is best known today. They are based on the gypsy melodies which he heard as a boy. But even more important than these are his poetical piano pieces, *Années de Pèlerinage* (Years of Wandering) and his Sonata in B Minor which he called "Sonata After Reading Dante."

For thirteen years Franz Liszt lived and worked at Weimar, and then he grew restless. In 1861 he went to Rome where his life took another new direction. He had always been of a religious and mystical turn of mind, and now on April 25, 1865, he entered the Third Order of St. Francis of Assisi. He wore a monk's garb and was called the "Abbé Liszt." His duties were those of door-keeper, reader, exorcist, and acolyte. But these duties did not interfere with his music, nor with an occasional game of whist.

He lived at first in the Vatican and later at the Villa d'Este at Tivoli. But during the last fifteen years of his life he divided his time among Italy, Budapest, where he taught in the Hungarian Conservatory of Music, and Weimar, where the grand duke was still his friend.

At Weimar in a little gardener's house which the grand duke put at his disposal, he surrounded himself with a crowd of adoring pupils, welcoming those who had talent and those who had none, often giving financial help to those who were needy.

Most of his compositions in those last years were for the piano, but his style changed as he grew older. One writer notes that the glittering arpeggios of his earlier works were no longer heard, the music was more simple and austere, and there were instances where the tonality seemed blurred.

One of these later compositions is called "The Angelus" and is said to have been inspired by far-off Roman church bells. Another, called *"Les Jeux d'Eaux à la Villa d'Este,"* suggests the play of waters in a famous fountain which the sculptor Giovanni Bernini designed for the gardens of the Villa d'Este at Tivoli near Rome. Another describes St. Francis of Paula walking across the waves, and another St. Francis of Assisi preaching to the birds.

In these years he also composed the Catholic oratorios, *St. Elizabeth* and *Christus*. And he turned from these to write the *Coronation Mass*, which was sung when Franz Joseph II was crowned King of Hungary.

He never finished his last oratorio—that on St. Stanislaus of Poland. At seventy-four his eyesight was failing; perhaps he was too tired to finish it. But he was still eager to hear great music, music that was new and startling for his day. He wanted to hear a performance of *Tristan und Isolde* at the Festival Theater in

Bayreuth. His widowed daughter, Cosima, was in Bayreuth, Richard Wagner having died in 1883.

He went to Bayreuth in July, 1886, and that was where he died. He was stricken during the performance of *Tristan* and carried to Cosima's house. It was to be written of him later, "The man was greater than his music." The light of the comet that had shone at his birth went out, and he was a legend—one of the finest pianists of all time, and a generous benefactor to a host of unrecognized composers.

CHAPTER TWENTY-TWO

The Triumph of Richard Wagner

BEETHOVEN started it—this breaking away from the old classic forms that Haydn and Mozart had followed, this giving way to tempestuous passion, this trying new ways to express strong personal emotions. Schubert, Schumann, Mendelssohn, and Chopin—each one had followed Beethoven in his own way, but it was Richard Wagner who was more romantic and more revolutionary than any of them. In the nineteenth century his operas set the whole world marveling.

Of course there had been many operas before Wagner's time, and he knew them well. There had been Monteverdi's and Gluck's operas, and Mozart's *Don Giovanni*. Karl Maria von Weber had produced *Der Freischütz*, with its romantic setting in the German forest, and Giacomo Meyerbeer, another German, had composed "grand opera" that was filled with glitter and staged with elaborate scenery. But Richard Wagner was to produce operas different from any of these.

He was to build his operas around German legends and people them with heroes of Teutonic mythology. He would tell the story of the Holy Grail, that shining mysterious cup from which Christ drank at the Last Supper. And he would tell, too, of dragons and of the treasure of gold that was hidden in the Rhine. From his boyhood days Wagner had considered himself a poet; for him these were the materials of poetry.

Music and poetry belonged together, Wagner thought. Painting and the dance ought to be bound up with them. He would combine all the arts and use them to express the great emotions with which he was overflowing. He would direct everything himself. He would write the poetry, direct the dance, paint the scenery, and choose the colors for the costumes—rich colors with plenty of shining armor. Above all, he would compose and direct the music.

Wagner dreamed of flowing music. He dreamed of taking the listener from one part of his performance to another as smoothly as a stream flows past its shore, of making the current of that stream grow imperceptibly stronger until the listener was lost in the overwhelming sea of emotion. His plans and ideas came to him gradually. One thought piled up on another until he had created the peerless structure of his "music dramas." He called what he had composed "the music of the future."

Though he was able to create such extraordinary music, he was not a very prepossessing man. He was aggressive, rather pompous, disagreeable to his friends, and, in the first part of his life, continually in debt, so that he had always to be running away from his creditors. For all that, however, he had two qualities that carried him through: indomitable confidence in his own ability and unfailing industry. These two, added to that intangible quality called genius, brought him success. His was some of the most moving and most original music of the nineteenth century.

He was born in Leipzig, May 22, 1813. His father, a police clerk, died when Richard Wagner was still quite small, and his mother took in boarders to support her family. One of these boarders was Ludwig Geyer, an actor, and from him the boy learned to love the theater.

The family moved to Dresden after Ludwig Geyer had married Richard's mother. Perhaps through Geyer's influence Richard's two older sisters became singers in the Dresden theater. In Dresden young Richard Wagner began to write plays. His first product was a tragedy called *Leubald und Adelaide*. All the characters in it were killed in the fourth act, so he had to bring them back as ghosts in the fifth act in order to finish the play.

All this time in Dresden he heard a good deal of music. He said music gave him a "mysterious joy" and that he felt "ghostly tremors" when violins were tuning. Then one day he went to hear Beethoven's *Fidelio*. The young soprano, Wilhelmine Schrö-der-Devrient, sang in the opera, and Wagner wrote, "From that moment, my life acquired its true significance." He, too, would write operas.

He borrowed some books and taught himself composition. He never learned to play the piano very well, but he thought that did not matter. By the time he was twenty-one he had embarked on his career. That year he produced *Das Liebesverbot*, his second attempt at opera. It was a failure and the company went bankrupt.

In 1836 he married a young actress named Minna Planer. She was in a stock company so he traveled with her from place to place, taking their huge dog "Robber" with them. In the following year he became chapel master of the German Theater in Riga. Then he wrote *Rienzi* in a grand, bombastic style. He and his wife left there in 1839.

On a slow, stormy journey across the English Channel with Minna Planer and Robber, he talked to some sailors who told him the legend of a spectral ship commanded by a Dutch sea captain who had sworn to round Cape Horn if it took him all eternity.

The romantic story appealed to Wagner and he wrote *Der fliegende Holländer* (*The Flying Dutchman*), and submitted it to the conductor of the Paris Opéra. It was promptly rejected. The conductor took the story and asked another man to write music for it, though parts of *Der fliegende Holländer* contain some of the most lovely melodies of all Wagner's music.

Rienzi was produced at Dresden very successfully, and Wagner was appointed chapel master there. He continued to compose.

Now he tried *Tannhäuser,* about a thirteenth-century minnesinger and how his love was divided between a chaste maiden, Elisabeth, and the goddess Venus. The opera was produced in Dresden and also later in Paris, but in Paris an antagonistic group called the Jockey Club made such a disturbance with booings and catcalls that it had to be shut down.

Still, in spite of failures, Wagner kept on working. Next he wrote *Lohengrin,* the romantic legend of a knight of the Holy Grail who is sent to rescue Elsa of Brabant, falsely accused of murdering her brother. *Lohengrin* was later well received, but Wagner could not stay to enjoy his victory, for he had been involved in the Revolution of 1848. He had written inflammatory articles in the press and supposedly had taken part in the street fighting in Dresden. A warrant had been issued for his arrest. He would have been imprisoned, but with his wife's help he managed to escape. Franz Liszt sheltered him in his house in Weimar and gave him money to go on to Switzerland.

Wagner spent twelve years in exile and in these years he laid plans for the operas which were to crown his career. Now he wrote *Tristan und Isolde* on the old Celtic legend about the ill-starred love of Isolde, wife of the Irish King Mark, and the handsome young courtier, Tristan. Now also he began to consider *Parsifal,* another legend which was based on the legends of the Holy Grail. And he made plans for the related cycle of operas called *Der Ring des Nibelungen.* These were really four operas to be played on four successive nights: *Das Rheingold, Die Walküre, Siegfried,* and *Gotterdämmerung.* Based on Teutonic mythology, all four were to tell the tale of a golden ring which was seized by the gods and taken to Valhalla, and which the warrior Siegfried succeeded in bringing back to earth, where it finally disappeared into the waters of the Rhine.

Not only did Wagner plan these operas during his exile, but he produced many famous books, including *Art and Revolution, The Art Work of the Future,* and *Opera and Drama.*

So the years of exile in Zurich and in London and Paris passed with amazing industry, and at last Wagner was granted permission to go back to Germany.

Things did not go well in Germany. He was a man of extravagant tastes, and before long he had mounted up a pile of debts. He went to Russia for a time, then he returned to Germany and again he was beset by creditors. There was talk of sending him to a debtors' prison. In Vienna *Tristan und Isolde*, after over fifty rehearsals, was abandoned as "unperformable."

Wagner was thoroughly disgusted. No one appreciated his music, he thought. His operas appeared to be getting nowhere, and the critics were all hostile to him. Yet he knew his music was great, and he proclaimed the fact loudly. He was right, of course.

Just at this point an extraordinary thing came to pass. He was sitting one day in a friend's house in Stuttgart, hoping that he might escape from his creditors, when there was a knock at the door.

He must have thought it was another bill, another creditor. He must have trembled as he opened the door, for he was a very high strung man. There, on the threshold, he saw a handsomely dressed individual who bowed and presented a card which bore the name "Herr Pfistermeister." This person did not arrest him as Wagner had expected. Instead, he presented him with the signet ring and portrait of King Ludwig II of Bavaria and a letter which bore the monarch's crest. Herr Pfistermeister was the king's representative. The nineteen-year-old king had heard Wagner's music and been overcome by it. He wanted Wagner to come to Munich to live there as an honored guest.

"So great was my joy that it crushed me," Wagner wrote later. The king agreed to pay all his most pressing debts, to give him an annual pension of 1200 gulden, and to provide him with a comfortable house in the suburbs of Munich.

But before long the king's jealous courtiers began to object to this arrangement. They spread damaging rumors about Wagner. Articles against him began to appear in the newspapers; there was a threat of an uprising against the king. Ludwig was not one to stand against this storm. He wrote Wagner ordering him to leave Bavaria. "Believe me, I had to do it," he wrote afterward. "Never doubt the loyalty of your best friend."

Wagner went to Switzerland. There he was joined by Hans von Bülow and his wife Cosima, the daughter of Franz Liszt. Later, after the death of Wagner's first wife, Cosima was divorced from Hans von Bülow, and she married Wagner. They were extremely happy, for Cosima admired him deeply and was ambitious to help his career. She called him "The Master."

The Wagners lived at a country estate called *Triebschen* on the shore of Lake Lucerne. There Wagner completed *Die Meistersinger*, an opera based on the old story of Hans Sachs, the poet-shoemaker of Nuremberg, and the singing contest of the musicians' guild. It is bright and gay, filled with life and joy, and very different from Wagner's other works.

Before very long the four operas of *The Ring*, on which he had worked so long, were finished. Some time before, King Ludwig had promised to build an opera house suitable for them, but now he had abandoned the plan, and Wagner wondered where he could find a building grand enough for such gigantic productions.

It was Cosima who came to the rescue. The operas must certainly have a building especially suited to them, she said. And it ought not to be in any city, but in some little place amid beautiful surroundings, where people were free and unhurried. They settled at last on a spot about a mile above the town of Bayreuth in the foothills of the Bavarian Alps.

Wagner Societies were founded in many widely scattered places —in St. Petersburg and Cairo, in London and New York. By 1872 they had collected enough money to lay the cornerstone of the new structure. They chose a special performance of Beethoven's Ninth Symphony to celebrate the occasion.

Four years later the Bayreuth Festspielhaus was finished. A distinguished audience gathered from miles around to hear the first performance of *The Ring*. Not quite enough money had been raised, but King Ludwig had advanced the necessary sum for the completion of the opera house. And a comfortable house, called *Wahnfried*, was built for Richard and Cosima Wagner. It was surrounded by a nicely landscaped garden.

The Bayreuth Festspielhaus was beautiful and impressive. In it the orchestra was concealed from the audience, and when the stage was lighted the house itself was plunged in darkness, and the hushed people watched and listened with awed attention.

Here in 1882 the second festival was held, and Wagner's opera *Parsifal* was performed. The performance lasted five and a half hours. Wagner wanted Bayreuth to be the only place in which this opera was to be performed, and for about thirty years his wish was observed. But afterward performances of *Parsifal* were held annually in other music centers—London, Paris, Vienna, and New York. It was generally produced during the Easter season.

Now Cosima and Wagner both were working very hard, she helping with the Wagner Societies, he producing and rehearsing the operas. He was explicit and exacting in directing every rehearsal. He selected the singers and instrumentalists himself, and directed every detail of scenery and costume. All this time ideas for new operas kept coming to him, and he employed his secretaries to carry on exhaustive research. Tired at last, he consented to go with Cosima for a short rest in Italy before starting a new piece of work. There he died in an old palazzo on the Grand Canal in Venice. It was February 13, 1883. Cosima brought his body back to *Wahnfried* to be buried in the garden.

After Wagner's death more and more people took the journey

to Bayreuth, and in many musical centers they crowded the houses where *Tristan, Tannhäuser, Die Meistersinger,* and his other operas were performed. So in the end the composer who had been ignored and neglected triumphed. His operas, which had once been called "unperformable," were now heard almost with reverence, and people began to recognize their power and to appreciate their newness.

What were the things that Wagner introduced into his music that impressed his audiences so strongly? First of all, he used a very large opera orchestra—three times as big as the orchestra Beethoven used for *Fidelio.* And he used this orchestra not merely as an accompaniment, but to hold his music dramas together and to explain the action on the stage, in somewhat the same way the Greek chorus had defined and explained the action on the ancient stage at Athens.

The music itself was new and different, too. It was woven out of short, combustible, melodic phrases, each one suggesting either a character, an incident, an idea, a mood, or an object. A musical phrase might suggest a bird, for example, or a dragon, or some piece of stage property—a sword, a ring, or a hammer. These leitmotivs combine into a broad, solemn, magical stream. At times the stream flows along, shimmering in luscious combinations; at other times it roars like a mighty waterfall.

The new use of the orchestra and the leitmotivs was not the only innovation that Wagner made, however. There was also the new effect of continuity which he achieved in his music. It may be explained in this way: just as in a prose sentence there are different parts separated by commas and semicolons, even so in music there is a kind of punctuation, though there are no punctuation marks. Instead, there is a progression of two or three chords played according to a certain pattern. These are called cadences. They create a moment of rest or relaxation. Wagner blocked this moment of rest and so produced the effect of continuity. He made the phrases overlap so that the last note of one phrase became the first note of the next. No one had done this so extensively before Wagner's time.

There were changes not only in the music of Wagner's orchestras, but in the singing as well. The characters in his operas did not sing in the Mozartean melodious sense. Rather, he wrote "song speech" for them. This reflected the intonation of German speech and was very strong and expressive.

Beyond all these musical innovations, Wagner made another which was perhaps more far-reaching than any of them. Most music since 1600 had been written in a definite key, or series of notes forming a given major or minor scale. It started in this key and returned to it, leaving the listener, as one writer said, with a sense of coming home. This "key feeling" is tonality. In *Tristan,* Wagner used chromatic tones which were foreign to the given scale, and he used them so extensively that the key centers became fleeting and blurred, and the music took on a sense of vagueness. By blurring tonality, Wagner pointed the way to the modern "atonality."

All these adventurous changes brought to Wagner's audiences a sense of his great power. But this alone was not responsible for the impression his operas made. There were the tremendous depth and variety of the characters in them. Hans Sachs, the poet-shoemaker in *Die Meistersinger,* combines wisdom with noble resignation; King Mark, in *Tristan,* though he is deceived by his wife and her lover, is generous and gentle. Even the despicable, dishonest Beckmesser in *Die Meistersinger* is portrayed with impersonal aloofness and dignity. (Beckmesser was suggested to Wagner by Eduard Hanslick, a Viennese critic who had dealt with his music harshly.) Not only the human characters but the Teutonic gods are ably dealt with. Like real human beings, they are afflicted with human frailties.

All these things taken together, and the elaborateness of the settings, and richness of the costumes, gave to the Wagnerian operas a uniqueness and grandeur that no one had seen before. People watched and listened, and marveled at their extraordinary power and beauty. Poets, artists, politicians, and common folk— all came under Wagner's sway, until all Europe and America were filled with "Wagnerites" and every serious composer of the nineteenth century was influenced by him in one way or another. Some composers imitated his style. Others reacted violently against it. But none could avoid thinking about the powerful changes Wagner's music had created.

CHAPTER TWENTY-THREE

Maestro Verdi: The Peasant of Le Roncole

"THE PEASANT of Le Roncole," Giuseppe Verdi liked to call himself, but the Italian people called him their "grand old man." They crowded the theaters to hear his operas, and stood shouting and waving when the curtain fell on his productions. To them his spirit reflected the very spirit of Italy.

Italians have always loved music; in Italy opera is a national institution. Opera is as natural and abundant with Italians as is bullfighting in Spain, highland dancing in Scotland, or baseball in the United States. Peasants, craftsmen, small tradesmen, their wives and their children—all love to sing and to listen. And in the nineteenth century there was much new Italian music for them to hear. The roads leading into Milan, Rome, or Venice were crowded on every holiday with people eager to hear an opera.

Gioacchino Rossini was one of their favorite composers. He was a great master of *opera buffa* and had written no fewer than thirty-two operas and two oratorios before he was thirty years old. They were enough to delight the Italians, and it did not matter if he lived out the rest of his life without composing anything else. The music he had written before he was thirty overflowed with a joyous wealth of melody and rhythmic charm, and it bubbled with wit and originality. His *Barber of Seville* was the one among his operas that they loved best of all, and the rest of Europe agreed with them.

But Rossini's were not the only operas in which they rejoiced, for there were also Vincenzo Bellini's *Norma* and Gaetano Donizetti's *Lucia di Lammermoor*. A bottle of wine, some bread and cheese, a few grapes or figs, and the Italians needed no other sustenance save this glorious music.

They listened with joy to every performance, but for Giuseppe Verdi's music their feeling reached a higher pitch. He was the master of their music, the voice of their feeling for Italy. They loved him and he loved them.

At Le Roncole near Parma in Italy Verdi's parents kept a little inn that was combined with a small village shop. In the autumn of 1813 Giuseppe Verdi was born there only five months after the date of Richard Wagner's birth.

He was a very quiet boy, seldom stirred by anything. Only when the hand-organ man passed through the village he showed great excitement, so that he could not be kept indoors but ran to follow after him.

He was still quite young when he went to work for Antonio Barezzi, a merchant in the town of Busseto, three miles from Le Roncole. His master was a thorough musician, and Giuseppe learned a great deal from him.

Impressed by the boy's musical talent, Barezzi arranged to have him study with Ferdinando Provesi, the chapel master of the cathedral in Busseto, who was also the conductor of the town orchestra.

Giuseppe learned quickly. Before long he had written some marching songs for the orchestra, and Provesi said he showed promise. Encouraged by both the marching songs and the teacher's praise, the generous Barezzi decided that the boy must be given more opportunity. He provided money so that Giuseppe could study in Milan.

But Giuseppe met with disappointment in Milan, for the conservatory there would not admit him. Still he stayed in the city anyway, studying with Vincenzo Lavigna until at Provesi's death he went back to take his place as leader of the town orchestra at Busseto. The post of organist in the cathedral there was also vacant, so the boy filled that as well.

All this time Barezzi, the merchant who had been so good to him, continued to befriend him, and when Verdi was about twenty he married Barezzi's daughter.

Now he was filled with ambition; the village orchestra, the cathedral organ, were not enough for him. He must write an opera. So he wrote *Oberto,* and it was produced in 1839 at La Scala, the opera house in Milan. Verdi and his wife went to Milan to hear it and were jubilant, for both audience and critics liked it. The producer ordered three more operas from the promising young man.

Filled with enthusiasm, Verdi started on his second opera. But now his two beautiful young sons died and then his wife, and the blow was more than Verdi could bear. He finished the second opera, but it was a complete failure. He would never write another opera, he decided. There was no more music left in him.

But Bartolemeo Merelli, impressario at La Scala, was Verdi's friend, and patiently he sought to encourage him. One day he brought him a libretto to read, the libretto of a proposed opera, *Nabuchodonosor*. As Verdi read it, musical phrases and melodies came to his mind. He started to work on *Nabucco*.

Nabucco is based on a Biblical text. It tells the story of an uprising of the Jewish people against the wicked Babylonian king, Nebuchadnezzar. The Italians who heard Verdi's opera seized upon it eagerly, for they, too, were trying at that very time to get their freedom, to break loose from the ruling hand of Austria and to unite into a strong nation. At the first performance of *Nabucco* its militant tunes aroused their patriotic fervor. Verdi became famous overnight. The Italians were frantic in their enthusiasm.

Now they asserted proudly that their own Giuseppe Verdi was in the front rank of European composers, and his operas followed each other in quick succession. *I Lombardi* in 1843 was followed by *Ernani* in 1844. In 1847 there was *Macbeth* and in 1849 *Luisa Miller*.

The excitement of revolution was in the air then. The Italians, led in turn by the mystical Giuseppe Mazzini, the red-shirted Giuseppe Garibaldi and the statesman-like Camillo Cavour, were struggling for freedom from Austria and for the unification of Italy under King Victor Emmanuel. The people sang and whistled Verdi's melodies up and down the peninsula.

As the political struggle intensified Verdi's name was heard everywhere. "Viva Verdi!" was written on the walls of houses from north to south. The Italians made an acrostic of the first letters of his name and daubed it on the fences:

VITTORIO

EMMANUELE

RÈ

D'

ITALIA

It was the unifying symbol of the new nation.

Before long the government censors began to consider Verdi dangerous. He produced *Rigoletto,* based on a story by Victor Hugo, in 1851, *Il Trovatore* in 1853, and *La Traviata* also in 1853.

The night *Il Trovatore* was first produced in Rome (January 19, 1853) the Tiber had overflowed its banks, and the audience waded in ankle-deep water to reach the theater. Lines of people stood at the doors from nine o'clock in the morning until evening when the curtain rose. Some listeners thought they had found hidden meanings in *Il Trovatore* and began to question Verdi's loyalty to the Austrian government. The censors watched him eagerly after that.

Finally in 1859 when Verdi applied for a license to produce *Un Ballo in Maschera* (The Masked Ball) the government refused permission to perform it until he had changed the locale of the opera and altered the names of all the characters. The King of Sweden, for example, became "Governor of Boston." But though the libretto was changed, the music was stirring as ever.

All Verdi's operas up to this time were violent melodramas with fast action and quick pulsations, and they were now so popular that Verdi prospered. He had always considered himself a peasant, so now he bought a farm near his native village of Le Roncole. It was called *Sant' Agata.* There he rode out every day to inspect his fields and vineyards and took great pride in breeding a fine strain of horses. It looked as if the musician in him had been altogether submerged by the peasant.

But he was not destined to stay long in the quiet of the Italian countryside. In 1871 the Suez Canal was to be completed, and Ismail Pasha, the rich khedive of Egypt, planned a musical celebration for the opening. What could be more natural than that he should invite Giuseppe Verdi to compose an opera? Verdi refused at first, for he was busy with the affairs of his farm. But he was persuaded at last.

No amount of money was spared in the production of *Aida*, for Ismail Pasha was extraordinarily rich. An eminent Egyptologist, Mariette Bey, was employed to make sketches for scenery and costumes. He was responsible for the realistic Nile scene, for the mammoth Egyptian temple from which the voice of the priestess issued, for the specially made and authentic Egyptian trumpets that sounded in the famous march. But though Mariette Bey had credit for scenery and costumes and Antonio Ghislanzoni for the libretto, the music of *Aida* was Verdi's—the richness of his treatment of the orchestra, the wealth of melody, the massive ensemble.

When *Aida* opened in Cairo, Verdi himself was afraid to cross the Mediterranean to hear it. He heard it later when it was produced in Italy, and he heard the enthusiasm of the audience and read the praises of the critics. *Aida* was indeed one of the most successful and popular operas ever written.

After the distraction and excitement of *Aida*, Verdi returned to the quiet fields and vineyards of *Sant' Agata*, and wrote no music for about three years. Then the Italian novelist and poet, Alessandro Manzoni, died, and Verdi broke his silence by composing a Requiem for him. The Requiem was not like any sacred music that had been written before. It was dramatic and theatrical, and the critics assailed it, saying that it broke all the rules of sacred style. But Verdi cared little for their opinion, for he had written the Requiem as he wanted it to be. He must have been pleased when the German composer, Johannes Brahms, praised it.

He was seventy-three years old before he wrote another opera. That year *Otello* was produced in Rome, and both musically and dramatically it was a great advance over anything he had done before. There are still arias in *Otello*—for instance, the famous "Willow Song" of Desdemona and Iago's "Credo"—but the music of the orchestra flows into an almost symphonic continuity. Some people said Verdi had been influenced by Wagner in this music, but he denied it.

Great though *Otello* was, it was not the final crown of Verdi's career. In his eightieth year he wrote *Falstaff*, an opera-comedy which sparkles with youthfulness and fanciful humor, and recalls Mozart in his gayest mood. *Falstaff* resembles an opera by Mozart, for it attains a perfect combination of drama and music, yet it is not like Mozart, for it is essentially Italian in the power of its vocal melody.

Perhaps a little of the credit for the success of Verdi's last two operas should be given to Arrigo Boito, himself a writer and composer and author of a fine opera, *Mephistofele*. He adapted the texts of the Shakespearean dramas for the Verdi operas.

Falstaff was a happy climax to Verdi's life. He lived on at *Sant' Agata*, gave a large amount of money to a hospital that was doing research in malaria, founded "A House of Repose for Musicians" in Milan which he said was his "finest opera," and wrote a little religious music—an Ave Maria, a Stabat Mater, a Te Deum, and a hymn to the Virgin on the words of Dante's *Paradiso*.

He died January 27, 1901, having lived a full life and given Italy not only his music, but also his pride in her destiny.

Other operas were, of course, to follow Verdi's. His country, having found joy in operas, could not stop producing them. Now Pietro Mascagni, a baker's son, wrote *Cavalleria Rusticana*, a spine-tingling drama filled with entrancing melody; and Ruggiero Leoncavallo produced the short, shock-filled *I Pagliacci*. Together these two operas form the high point of the *"verismo"* school of Italian composition. *Verismo* means realism, and "veris·tic" operas were as filled with melodrama as any murder mystery play or horror film.

Of all the later Italian composers Giacomo Puccini was most talented. In 1893 his opera *Manon Lescaut,* with its lush, romantic melody and sweetness, displayed calculated harmonic and dramatic effects. Three years later *La Bohème* appeared. Lovely and sentimental, it soon became one of the world's most popular operas. And following that, Puccini produced *Tosca,* his third great success. In it he experimented with the whole-tone scale and made some bold harmonic innovations. It is another veristic thriller.

And now Puccini wrote *Madama Butterfly,* the story of an American naval officer who married a Japanese girl and left her; and *The Girl of the Golden West,* in which he collaborated with David Belasco and which was produced at the Metropolitan Opera in New York with Arturo Toscanini conducting. *Turandot,* with its modern overtones and its Chinese atmosphere, was another great success.

All these operas were highly dramatic in their treatment, exotic and romantic in their effect, and all were based on good librettos. Puccini's music heightened the dramatic characterizations of his heroes and heroines and made them unforgettable. Soon he became a popular idol; his operas rivaled Verdi's in their popularity.

In that Italy where audiences once had marveled at the grandeur of Monteverdi's operas and taken Verdi to their hearts, opera still is a living force. Announcements of new productions are continually posted on the billboards outside the opera houses, new music thrills the listening audiences. For Italy still loves its opera as it has since Monteverdi's time.

PETER ILICH TCHAIKOVSKY

CHAPTER TWENTY-FOUR

Romantic Music Reaches Its Zenith

R OMANTIC music reached its zenith in the late nineteenth century. Tone poems, gigantic symphonies, operas—
all were vividly colored and filled with personal emotion; many
of them were autobiographical. Almost all the composers of that
time were followers of Liszt and Wagner, and there were many
gifted ones among them. Three composers towered above the

others, however. There was the sensitive Russian Peter Ilich Tchaikovsky; the Austrian organist Anton Bruckner, with his profound yet childlike religiousness; and Bruckner's pupil Gustav Mahler, a Bohemian Jew who grew out of a childhood of desperate poverty to include a conception of cosmic grandeur in his symphonies.

There were of course many others, but these three will serve to show the passion and the color of romantic music at its peak.

Tchaikovsky was extremely gifted. His life, like his music, was full of ups and downs, of failures and successes. Enthusiastically he abandoned his study of law for the piano. One of his teachers was the great pianist Anton Rubinstein. The young musician was so fluent and able that when Rubinstein gave him a theme and asked him to write variations on it, he sat up all night and in the morning had written two hundred variations! Rubinstein was ecstatic in his praise, but later Tchaikovsky wrote: "I took him an overture, *The Storm,* guilty of all kinds of whims of form and orchestration. He was hurt and said it was not for the development of imbeciles that he took the trouble to teach composition. . . ."

Tchaikovsky married, was incompatible with his wife, and parted from her. But he found fulfillment in writing letters to Madame Nadejda von Meck, the widow of a wealthy railroad man. She sent him generous financial help, but they agreed never to see each other, for he did not wish to be disturbed in his work. Still, he was devoted to her and dedicated to her some of his finest compositions. Toward the end of his life she stopped sending him money and he resented it greatly, though by then he no longer needed it.

The same unstable pattern repeated itself where Tchaikovsky's music was concerned. First he was carried away by the beauty of what he had composed. He wrote Madame von Meck, "It would be vain to try to put into words that immeasurable sense of bliss which comes over me directly a new idea awakens in me and begins to assume a definite form. I forget everything and behave like a madman. Everything within me starts pulsing and quivering. . . ." But then he was filled with remorse because he thought what he had done was not good enough. He destroyed dozens of his own musical scores.

The music which this unhappy man created was gorgeously colored, sometimes delicate and fairy-like, sometimes almost hysterical in its tragic passion. *The Nutcracker Suite* is one of his most popular and typical compositions. The ballet for which it was written is based on a story by E.T.A. Hoffmann called *The Nutcracker and the Mouse King*. The ballet music starts with a march of assembling wedding guests. The "March of the Sugar Plum Fairy" follows, and someone has said that this "seems to drop note by note like the tinkle of dew drops falling from a rose leaf." There are dances ending with a Flower Waltz in which "poppies and marguerites sway gracefully to several charming melodies, after an elaborate cadenza from the harp."

"The Snow Maiden," which is also very popular, was written as incidental music for a play based on a fairy tale. And perhaps best known of all is *Swan Lake,* which contains some of the most graceful, lovely ballet music anyone has ever written.

Not all Tchaikovsky's music was graceful and fairy-like, however. He wrote powerful "absolute" music, pouring his passionate feeling into the great Piano Concerto in B Flat Minor, the first great Russian piano concerto.

And he also wrote many brilliant compositions for orchestra: the sparkling Violin Concerto in D, the *Rococo Variations for Cello and Orchestra,* several striking shorter pieces including "Romeo and Juliet," and "Mozartiana," which is a delightful work patterned after the music of Mozart, his favorite composer.

Stirring and beautiful though all this music was, it was to his symphonies that he gave himself most fully. The Sixth Symphony was the climax of his creative life. He had a good deal of difficulty in finding a name for it. He thought of calling it the "Program

Symphony," and when this did not suit him he tried the "Tragic Symphony." At last the words *Symphonie Pathétique* occurred to him, and this was the title he put down before he sent it to the publisher. The name was suitable, for in this music he had expressed all the pathos and tragedy of life as he saw it.

In spite of his gift for melody, Tchaikovsky was less successful when it came to vocal music. Most of his operas are failures, although *Eugen Onegin* is still performed in Russia, and is occasionally included in the repertoires of European and American opera companies.

Nine days before his death (he died of cholera on October 28, 1893) he heard his *Symphonie Pathétique* and left the concert hall saying he had a feeling of "complete content." His last composition was "the best, the most open-hearted" of all his works, he said. Many critics have thought his work lacked perfect form, for the transition sections are often weak and labored. Tchaikovsky agreed with the critics. Nevertheless, he will be remembered and enjoyed, for he had extraordinary gifts both as a melodist and orchestrator.

Peter Ilich Tchaikovsky had made his own life miserable, lonely, and unhappy. In one of his best known songs whose music is written on Goethe's poem, *"Nur wer die Sehnsucht kennt,"* he sang of his haunting sorrow and declared with poignant melody that all happiness has been taken from him. But Anton Bruckner, the Austrian organist, found no room for self-pity in the work he was doing. A familiar figure on Vienna's Ringstrasse, he walked in baggy clothes, his strong head with its Roman nose set on broad peasant shoulders. The elite of Vienna cared little for him, and indeed he was not at home in their society. He liked coarse peasant food and Pilsener beer, and was never without his snuffbox.

Bruckner had been born at Ansfelden, a little town in Upper Austria near the Bohemian border. Son of a poor schoolmaster, he had been a chorister at St. Florian's Monastery in Linz. St. Florian's had the finest organ in all the Austrian monasteries, and under it Anton Bruckner lies buried.

He was deeply religious, a devoted Catholic, and he was no doubt proud when he was chosen to be organist at Linz. From there he went on to be organist at the *Hofkapelle* in Vienna and professor at the Vienna Conservatory. He was a magnificent organist and improviser, a master of counterpoint, and a great composer.

At first Bruckner's compositions were classical in form though romantic in feeling. He disliked innovations in music and looked askance at Richard Wagner's "Music of the Future." But later Wagner became his idol and his inspiration, and he tried to use Wagnerian methods in symphonic form. His Seventh Symphony in its slow movement is an elegy on the death of Wagner.

Altogether Bruckner wrote several Masses, a Te Deum for Chorus and Orchestra, a string quartet, and nine symphonies. He created chorale-like song themes for his symphonies and from these he built great symphonic structures, magnificently orchestrated. They were so large and long that conductors objected to performing them at first, but gradually Bruckner's compositions gained recognition, so that he became known as one of the greatest church and symphonic composers since Beethoven, Brahms, and Schubert.

Bruckner's music is indebted to Beethoven in formal design (the Beethoven Ninth Symphony seems to have been a particular influence) and to Wagner in instrumentation. His love of massive blocklike expanses of sound reflects his knowledge of the organ, where keyboards and stops are frequently contrasted and combined.

All Bruckner's music reveals his profound yet childlike religiousness—one piece is dedicated simply to "My dear God"—and his music reflects also his love for his native landscape.

Anton Bruckner was a teacher as well as a composer, a very

great teacher of counterpoint. One of his pupils, who was also his ardent admirer, was the German song writer Hugo Wolf, the foremost composer of lieder since Schubert and perhaps the finest song writer of all time. Not only was he intensely absorbed in the text of his songs but through marvelously subtle melody, shading of the words, and the accompanying piano part, he brought every detail of the poems' meanings to the surface.

Gustav Mahler was the third great romantic composer of his period, and he was a pupil of Anton Bruckner. His music swayed between joy and despair, for it mirrored the times in which it was written, the years before the First World War.

Like so many other musicians Gustav Mahler had a miserable childhood. He was born in the little town of Kalischt in Bohemia of an extremely poor family, so poor in fact that they had no windowpanes in their house. His grandmother was a street peddler, his father a coachman, until later when he ran a distillery. All this might as well be forgotten and dismissed as unimportant, save that it gives contrast to the glamour of Gustav Mahler's career.

The little boy is said to have played folk songs and marches on an accordion when he was four. When he was about seven he found an old piano in an attic and taught himself to play it. Later he managed to get to Vienna where he won a scholarship at the conservatory, and that was the beginning of his success. It was there that Anton Bruckner was one of his teachers.

Mahler was in his early twenties when he became a conductor. Hans von Bülow recognized his talents and made him his assistant. After von Bülow's death in Cairo, Mahler took over the conducting of the Hamburg Opera with great success. He was invited to conduct in Prague, Budapest, Hamburg, and London. After that he came back to be director of the Vienna Opera, a task at which he worked with great zeal and energy. As director he exacted so much from his singers that they called him "tyrant," but, nevertheless, the Vienna Opera had never been so fine.

In 1908 Mahler was offered the directorship of the Metropolitan Opera in New York which he accepted, and in 1909 he was elected conductor of the New York Philharmonic Orchestra. He quarreled with the orchestra's directors in the 1910–11 season, for he was a nervous, high-strung man, and he returned to Vienna. He died at the age of fifty; it was said that his death was caused partly by overwork.

It is hard to understand how any one man could possibly have left behind him as much music as did Gustav Mahler. He composed only in the short intervals between concert tours and during brief vacations, and he called himself a "summer composer." Yet the amount of his output was enormous.

He wrote many songs which he combined into song cycles on romantic subjects. He composed also nine great symphonies and part of a tenth. Materials from the song cycles were incorporated into these symphonies. Themes from *Lieder eines fahrenden Gesellen* (*Songs of a Wayfarer*) appeared in the First Symphony; songs from *Des Knaben Wunderhorn* (*The Boy's Magic Horn*) were used in the Second, Third, and Fourth. All the symphonies were outwardly patterned on the classic tradition but their content was arch-romantic. They were outpourings of his cosmic yearnings and in them at times his deep despair dissolved into triumphant ecstasy.

Mahler's symphonies were laid out on a gigantic scale. The number of performers in his orchestra was double the number that had been used heretofore. His Eighth Symphony required a thousand performers. It was called the *Symphony of a Thousand*.

Not only did Mahler make the orchestra bigger than it had been before, but he made the symphonies longer, introducing additional chorale movements into them. Aaron Copland, the American composer, writing of Mahler's symphonies, says that there were new contrapuntal textures in them and new orchestral colors "without which the modern symphony would be inconceivable."

Mahler's greatest work was his symphonic song cycle *Das Lied von der Erde (The Song of the Earth)*. He composed it after his doctor had told him that he was fatally ill with a heart ailment. "I see everything in a new light," he wrote then. "I thirst for life more than ever before and find the habit of existence more sweet than it ever was." His music combines resignation with a heightened sense of the joy of life.

Das Lied von der Erde describes the awakening of earth to spring. It is typical of his work, for it depends on a poetic narrative for its background—this time an ancient Chinese poem. But though in this as in his other music Mahler was an advocate of program music, still he objected violently to having these programs printed for his hearers to read while they listened. "Down with all program books," he was wont to say. He thought the audience ought to be free to listen to his music without trying to read at the same time.

Peter Ilich Tchaikovsky, Anton Bruckner, Hugo Wolf, and Gustav Mahler—theirs was great music at the end of the nineteenth century. But theirs were not the only romantic voices that sounded then. In France Georges Bizet was charming his audiences with the immortal opera *Carmen,* and Belgian-born César Franck was writing romantic symphonies and chamber music with a strong religious feeling, while his pupil Vincent d'Indy was making a secure place for himself.

Camille Saint-Saëns was also composing then. An influential administrator, Saint-Saëns is remembered today for his eerie *Danse Macabre* and the charming *Carnival of the Animals,* as well as for his piano concertos.

The greatest of this French group was Gabriel Fauré, who through his lovely *chansons* carried on the song tradition in France, much as Hugo Wolf had done in Germany. His songs have a soft-hued glow with their graceful melodies and flowing modal accompaniment. Equally great are his Requiem and his chamber music.

With the work of all these distinguished men the vivid romance of an age came to its colorful close. Richard Strauss was to open the way for a new style of music. In his work startled listeners heard harbingers of the music of the twentieth century.

CHAPTER TWENTY-FIVE

Richard Strauss and the Afterglow

BORN in Munich, son of Franz Strauss, an eminent horn player, Richard Strauss showed great promise as a child. He was something of a pianist at four, a composer at six, and studying music under the Munich *Hofkapellmeister* at ten. Soon his songs were heard on the concert stage and his Quartet in A (op. 2) and his Symphony in D Minor were being performed.

Hans von Bülow heard him conduct his "Serenade for Wind Instruments" and, quick to recognize new talent, invited him to be his assistant. In 1885 Richard Strauss succeeded von Bülow as conductor of the Meiningen Orchestra. After that, Strauss had many important posts: he was *Hofkapellmeister* at Weimar, and in Berlin; he conducted at Covent Garden in London; he traveled in Italy and married an eminent singer, Pauline de Ahna. A tall man, with kindly blue eyes and an informal manner, before the end of the nineteenth century he had become the most eminent composer in all Europe. Yet for all this he remained intensely human, loving his glass of beer and an occasional game of cards called "Skat."

Like Bruckner, Strauss did not start as a romantic composer; in fact, he disliked Wagner's music at first. When he was still quite young he went to hear the opera *Siegfried* and he wrote a friend about this music, "It would have killed a cat and the horror of musical dissonance would melt rocks into omelettes."

However, this judgment of Wagner's music changed. Only about a year later his friend Alexander Ritter, the violinist, persuaded him to listen to more of Wagner's music. After he had heard *Tristan* he was completely converted.

Now his own music became romantic in its feeling. He started to write tone poems patterned on the symphonic poems of Liszt, and he experimented with the cadences of Wagner's musical speech. Soon he had given up Brahmsian classicism altogether, and his music was wonderful in its use of discordant new sounds. It dazzled and scandalized the musical world with its brilliance and noise.

Richard Strauss wrote nine tone poems altogether; the first of them, which he called "*Aus Italien*," appeared in 1886. The subjects of his later tone poems were varied and dramatic. "Macbeth" was one of them, and after it came one of his best, "Don Juan." This he called an "opera without words," and a recent writer describes it as "a continually unfolding music drama."

"*Tod und Verklärung*" followed. It describes the thoughts of a dying man. The romantic music was strongly influenced by Liszt, and the composer's friend Alexander Ritter wrote the poem after the music had been composed.

Six years after "*Tod und Verklärung*," the public was astonished with "*Till Eulenspiegel's Lustige Streiche*." This is an exceedingly clever though complicated score. Strauss's orchestra was growing ever larger now, and the music seemed to overflow with youthful creative power.

Till Eulenspiegel was a semi-mythical character who lived about 1350. In the fifteenth century a book was published about him. The word *Eulenspiegel* means the owl's looking glass, for in this book he held up a mirror before human owls, making fun of their follies and pretensions.

Gradually he took his place in German legend as the imp of fantasy and the perverse, a wandering fellow who lived by his wits. He turns up in one place after another. Now he is a butcher, now a baker, now a wheelwright, and then a joiner, or a monk. Everywhere he rejoices in plaguing honest people, in robbing the rich and helping the poor. The music starts with a Mozart-like theme, then a few sharp chords and Till is off on his deviltry. The orchestra echoes laughter and pathos, and the whole is so skillfully composed that as the American critic Olin Downes has said, "not a note could be added or taken from it without destroying its beautiful proportions."

Strauss was bitterly reviled for *"Till Eulenspiegel,"* but this did not matter to him. In 1897 he produced another tone poem, "Don Quixote," and in it he reached one of the high points of his music. Here in his fresh interpretation of Cervantes' great novel is the attack on the windmill, the sound of bleating sheep, the singing of passing pilgrims, and the deeply touching scene of Don Quixote's death. The tone poem is written in rondo form, for it is a series of incidents with a return to the main theme after each episode. There is an exquisite appreciation of the essential conflict between the real and the ideal which is the essence of Cervantes' book.

And now, his ambitious imagination soaring, Strauss wrote a tone poem intended to describe the whole development of the human race from the primitives to superman. *"Also Sprach Zarathustra"* was inspired by the book of the same title by Friedrich Nietzsche.

"Ein Heldenleben" is autobiographical. The hero in it is Richard Strauss himself as he is attacked by critics. In this music he answers them, is attacked again and again, is defeated and triumphant.

Such were some of the exciting and varied subjects which Richard Strauss chose for his tone poems. But this was not the only kind of music that he wrote. He composed a great many songs, and though some of these were merely pretentious and bombastic, some like his *"Ständchen"* and *"Morgen"* are exquisite and may be placed beside the greatest of the German lieder.

Besides all this Strauss wrote operas, and three of them are outstanding. First there was *Salome,* based on the play by Oscar Wilde. It made a sensational success with the fashionables of

Dresden, and scandalized audiences both in Europe and America. Besides giving Richard Strauss his greatest international fame, it made him a great deal of money. With some of this he built a house in the Bavarian Alps.

Another opera, *Elektra,* was a tremendously loud, discordant work. Critics of the time called its creator a madman, but *Elektra* is now considered one of the finest tragic operas since Wagner's. Critics speak of it today as a work of genius, streaming with musical beauty.

Finally, in 1911, Richard Strauss produced *Der Rosenkavalier,* and this was another surprise. "This time I shall write a Mozart opera," he said. The "Mozart opera" is a farce satire laid in the Vienna of the mid-eighteenth century. It is gay and melodious with depths of tenderness and romance and at the same time it is risqué, witty, and urbane. It was soon popular everywhere, and particularly in the United States. It is said that at the end of the Second World War when American occupation forces were about to take over his house in the Bavarian Alps, Richard Strauss stopped them at the front door saying, "I am the composer of *Der Rosenkavalier.*"

After *Der Rosenkavalier* Richard Strauss, now rich and famous, continued to compose, but nothing could rival the success of his earlier work. The music with which he had dazzled and scandalized the world had brought the romantic movement to a close. Perhaps, as some critics now say, the brilliant sun of romanticism had already set and his music was merely the brilliant afterglow.

CHAPTER TWENTY-SIX

Patriots' Music

THE NINETEENTH century in Europe was a time of intense national feeling. A man owed his allegiance to the nation into which he had been born, it was said. The people whose language he spoke, whose traditions he inherited—these were the people he loved. The nation whose hills and rivers, fields and forests were familiar to him—this was the nation he must preserve and cherish, and this was the country he must fight for if necessary, serving not the king but his own people. He must treasure his own nation's ways, its legends and customs, its songs and dances. He must take part in its parades, and honor its flag, and celebrate its national heroes. A new kind of music was needed to proclaim these new beliefs.

In one country after another the flames of this national feeling flared up. In Denmark, Niels Gade, son of a musical instrument maker and friend of Schumann and Mendelssohn, wrote eight symphonies whose inspiration sprang from his love of his native country. Not far away, in Norway, that land of fjords and short, lovely summers, of lark songs and sturdy folk, Edvard Grieg composed music inspired by native legends. His incidental music for Ibsen's *Peer Gynt,* his piano concerto, and lyric piano pieces all have the ease and simplicity of Norwegian peasant songs. Some of his works are gay and lighthearted, others brood with melancholy.

Jean Sibelius, the great Finnish symphonist, lived on into the twentieth century, but his name should be added to the list of nationalist composers. His tone poem, *"Finlandia,"* and his Second Symphony, with its exultant climaxes, are the very essence of his country's spirit.

Of course there were many others; it would be impossible to name them all. The Czechs, for example, were proud of Bedřich Smetana and said his music was the true expression of their feeling.

Smetana was the friend of Liszt, and had come to public attention during the Revolution of 1848. Then the men of the National Guard had fought on the barricades in the streets of Prague, and Smetana, stirred with revolutionary spirit, had written rousing songs for them. After that his fame was assured. His opera, *The Bartered Bride*, was very popular, and another opera, *Libuša*, was played on all national festival occasions, as it is still.

But his cycle of symphonic poems, called *My Country*, contains some of Smetana's finest work. The part called the *"Moldau,"* which describes the river as it rushes along through fields and past little towns, is the best known section of this work. Alfred Einstein in his book *The Music of the Romantic Age* said of Smetana's *My Country:* "Never has a country, its character, its nature, its heroic or awe-inspiring historical memories, received purer glorification than in this cycle. . . . Smetana has thus become the rhapsodist of his people."

Smetana's young compatriot, Antonín Dvořák, the son of a butcher in a little Czech town, composed a sheaf of chamber music and opera. But no one paid any attention to him until he wrote a patriotic hymn. This was called "The Heirs of the White Mountain," and the Czechs hailed it joyfully. After that they welcomed his symphonies and his operas and his beautiful cello concerto. They were proud when he was invited to New York in 1892 to be head of the National Conservatory of Music, and proud, too, when he composed the symphony *From the New*

World, in which he employed melodies and rhythms characteristic of American Negro and American Indian folk music. But most of all they were proud because they identified him with their own country.

In England the evidence of national pride came later than in the other countries. This may have been because the impact of Handel's music was so great that no English composer felt he could equal it. After Purcell's time there had been no English composer of international fame until toward the end of the nineteenth century, when Edward Elgar appeared. After that, at the turn of the century, there was a glorious blooming of musical creativity in England.

It was headed by Ralph Vaughan Williams, who has been rightly called the father of modern English music. Born in Gloucestershire in 1872, Vaughan Williams studied with Max Bruch in Berlin and Maurice Ravel in Paris. He did not really begin to find himself as a composer, however, until he returned to his native England and combed the seashore, valleys, and villages for ancient folk songs. Soon he had become active in the National Folk Song Society, and spent a good part of his life in annotating, transcribing, arranging, and lecturing about the ballads, chanteys, morris dances, and love songs of the British Isles. He had many of these songs published and used some of them in his own works, where they took on a very personal quality, reflecting the rugged, individualistic stature of the composer himself. He wrote a great many outstanding choral works, stage works, chamber pieces, and songs, but he is best remembered for his gigantic symphonies and particularly the *London Symphony.* In this he has reproduced the sounds and atmosphere of London in a memorable way.

While it was Vaughan Williams who re-educated the English to the great Tudor and folk music of their past, there are other English composers who have made significant contributions to the present. Vaughan Williams' friend Gustav Holst is best known for his imaginative orchestral work, *The Planets.* Sir William Walton has written many colorful orchestral scores including two symphonies, several concertos, and the striking choral work, *Belshazzar's Feast*.

Another of England's composers must be mentioned here, a mystic dreamer whose music, filled with wonderful melody, was perhaps too refined to command a wide audience. This was Frederick Delius, who was born in England though of German parentage. The quality of his music is reflected in the two beautiful compositions for a small orchestra, *On Hearing the First Cuckoo in Spring*, and *Summer Night on the River*. Two large choral works are *Songs of Farewell* and *A Mass of Life*. *Appalachia*, a large composition for orchestra and soloists, is perhaps, his best-known work. He wrote it after a short stay in Florida, where he tried unsuccessfully to grow oranges.

Of all the English composers living in the second half of the twentieth century, Benjamin Britten is most gifted. He has added a great deal to the oratorio and opera literature of our time. His best known works include the operas *Peter Grimes, The Turn of the Screw*, and *A Midsummer Night's Dream*, the choral work called *A Ceremony of Carols*, and the song cycles for tenor voice and piano on poems by John Donne and Michelangelo.

Certainly with the work of all these men, English music has come into new flowering. Other new and talented composers will doubtless add to the legacy of modern English music which Vaughan Williams began.

CHAPTER TWENTY-SEVEN

Glinka, Moussorgsky, and the People of Russia

T HE MUSIC of the Russian people was sad, wild, colorful. It had come down from both Slavs and Tartars.

Western Europe knew very little about the native Russian
music until the middle of the nineteenth century. People who
traveled to Russia heard the ancient Byzantine chants which the
priests of the Greek Orthodox Church had sung since the tenth
century, and they knew that the czars employed Italian composers, singers, and ballet dancers, and later French and German
musicians. But the West knew nothing of the music of the Russian
peasants. That was the music the Russian Michael Glinka heard.

When he heard the peasant music, Michael Glinka realized that
the songs and dances the Russian people knew had a vitality that
was not to be found either in the liturgical music of the Greek
Church or in the imported music of the czar's court. Here were
melodies and rhythms that belonged especially to the Russian
people. He did not realize how much they meant to him until
he went abroad. Once, on a visit to Italy, he wrote, "Homesick-
ness for my native land led me to think of writing Russian music."

After some study abroad, Glinka wrote an opera, A Life for
the Czar. It tells the story of how Ivan Sussanin sacrificed himself
to save his sovereign: how when the monarch was attacked by a
group of marauding Poles, Ivan led them into an impenetrable
forest, and died there, but the Czar escaped.

The opera was performed December 9, 1836. It used native folk
songs, some in 5/4 and 7/4 time, that had not been heard in
art music before. It was a great success.

After that many Russian students and scholars began to discuss their country's music. What they heard at the court and at the theaters was foreign, they said. They wanted to do away with the showy splendors of the stage and ballet, with the opera singers who cared more for displaying their own talents than for the music they produced.

A group of young friends, later called "The Five," took these ideas very seriously. They met every Saturday night at the house of the pianist, Mili Balakirev. Besides the host there were César Cui, an engineer; Alexander Borodin, who wrote symphonies; Nicholas Rimsky-Korsakov, a naval officer who had been in the Far East and who brought oriental sumptuousness to the music he composed; and Modeste Moussorgsky, a dashing, hard-living army man who resigned his commission for the musical life.

Every Saturday night "The Five," whom someone has called "a mighty handful," speculated, arranged, discussed, and planned new music. Sometimes they read the works of the writer Nikolai Gogol or of the poet Aleksandr Pushkin, sometimes they played Beethoven quartets or four-handed Schubert sonatas on the piano.

Each member of "The Five" was important in his own way, but it was Moussorgsky who was to have the greatest influence on music. He was born in the Russian village of Karevo, and his parents were well-to-do, although his grandmother had been a serf. He earned a meager living as an ill-paid clerk while he devoted himself to his music with a pure passion. At first he was intimate with the other members of "The Five," but gradually his friendship with them petered out, and he worked alone.

He had been inadequately trained in composition, which left him with little ability in orchestration. Yet this lack of training proved a blessing in other ways, for he escaped the influence of Western music. His aim was to bring the music of the Russian people into his own compositions.

"It is the people I want to depict," he wrote. "Sleeping or waking, eating and drinking, I have them constantly in my mind's

eye. Again and again they rise before me in all their reality . . .
with no tinsel." He thought of the music of the people, not as
something picturesque, but as the true expression of their life.
He did not want to uplift the people or purify their music, he
wanted to transcribe it faithfully, and this he did. The flavor of
his compositions is enhanced by its stark simplicity. He often
used the ancient modes of the Greek Orthodox Church and sometimes the whole-tone scale, and his use of modal harmony was
original and advanced for his time.

No human being was too humble to interest Moussorgsky, no
scene too crude. He observed healthy people in high spirits, and
people who were ignorant, miserable, and sad. In his music were
the drunken coachman, the homeless tramp, the miserable serf—
these were important to him.

There was great variety in Moussorgsky's music, as one might
expect. He started an opera called *The Marriage,* on a poem
by Gogol, and in its music he tried to imitate the inflections of
the speaking voice. Liszt admired most of all his *Nursery Songs,*
a collection of miniature dramas seen through a child's eyes. His
Songs and Dances of Death are masterpieces still awaiting full
public homage.

But perhaps Moussorgsky's greatest achievement was the opera
Boris Godunov, which was first performed in 1874. *Boris Godunov*
had been simmering in Moussorgsky's mind for a long time before
he wrote it. When at last it was finished after a number of difficulties with the Russian government (the addition of a love scene
which Moussorgsky did not want, and the deletion of several
scenes which he did want), the audience saw a drama of brooding splendor and heard a new style of singing, half recitation, half
chant, that sprang from the Russian speech.

The opera is based on Pushkin's drama. It tells the story of
Boris Godunov, Czar of Russia in the sixteenth century, and of
how he was suspected of having murdered the brother of Ivan
the Terrible in order to gain the throne. A monk named Gregory

headed an uprising against him which was wildly acclaimed by the people. In the excitement the half-insane Boris died.

The dramatic scenes of this opera gave Moussorgsky great opportunities. He portrayed a crowd crying to the czar for bread; a drunken friar telling a wild story of an ancient battle between Russians and Tartars; a coronation scene with clanging bell harmonies. Moussorgsky loved the sound of bells.

"What kind of music is this?" the critics asked. They did not like it. But younger Russians crowded the house when the opera was performed, and the students were fired by it.

Perhaps the political implications of the opera were not lost on the students. Evidently they were not lost on the Russian government either, for before long an order came that *Boris Godunov* must be shut down.

Moussorgsky began another opera after that—*Khovanstchina*—and started several more that he did not finish. He also wrote a piano suite to commemorate the work of his friend, a Russian painter, Victor Hartman. It was called *Pictures at an Exhibition*. The suite describes Hartman's paintings in short piano studies which seem to be filled with the talk of the Russian people, their roughness and their sweetness, their tragedy, and their humor. With its inventive contrasts, it is a highly original work.

So Moussorgsky worked on until 1881, when he died. And after that he was almost forgotten for about thirty years.

But thanks to Rimsky-Korsakov's orchestration and his interest in promoting Moussorgsky's great opera *Boris Godunov*, and thanks to Maurice Ravel's orchestration of *Pictures at an Exhibition*, Moussorgsky's work came to be regarded as some of the world's most original music. His songs and choral works, as well as his operas, reflect the life, speech, and feelings of the Russian people. His music is national music, but it is more than this, for it transcends boundaries. As time passes it continues to have meaning to an international audience.

WOODWINDS. LEFT TO RIGHT: DOLCIAN, OBOE, BASSOON, OBOE DE CACCIA, BASSET HORN

CHAPTER TWENTY-EIGHT

In the Century of Airplanes

"THE CENTURY of airplanes deserves its own music. As there are no precedents I must create anew."
It was the Frenchman Claude Debussy who said these words.

223

A poor and very modest man, he had won the Prix de Rome in his youth, and, after three years in Italy, had come back to Paris to live. There he supported himself in a rather meager way by giving piano lessons and playing accompaniments for singers. In his spare time he often went to the house of the poet Stefan Mallarmé, and there he talked with poets, painters, and musicians, the avant-garde of Paris.

There was a new art movement in Paris then. In poetry it was called Symbolism. The Symbolists held that it was not necessary to describe an act or an object but merely suggest it in words. If the words were rightly chosen they would convey to the listener the effect that the poet desired.

The painters in this movement were called Impressionists. They held reproduction of objects in scorn; it was the *impression* they made on the viewer that was important to them. They thought drawing not as significant as reproducing color by breaking light into tiny fragments.

Stirred by the work of the Symbolists in suggesting whole moods with a few words and of the painters who abandoned themselves to the joy of pure color, Debussy resolved to work with fragments of pure sound.

And just as the painters had broken down the light into the hundreds of colored fragments which they combined and recombined into new harmonies, so Debussy strayed away from the conventional scales to which music had been confined since the days of Bach and explored the ancient Gregorian modes and the pentatonic scale.

In 1880 Debussy heard an Indonesian orchestra at the Paris Exhibition. It was then that he became fascinated with the whole-tone scale: the succession of C, D, E, F♯, G♯, A♯, and C. Now he began to build his harmonies out of this material. He built chords on seconds, fourths, sevenths, and ninths, and used them in a "chord stream." By using the damper pedal of the piano, he found he could create blurred, vague effects in which one chord drifted into another like so many clouds moving across the sky.

It was not only in his harmonies that Debussy found he could create a new kind of music. Melody for him was as exotic as harmony. Fragmented bits of tunes, motives, arabesques—all were ethereal, elusive, yet ultimately refreshing.

His orchestration suited this new kind of music. Muted horns and trumpets, flutes in low register, English horn and oboe solos, harps, many types of percussion instruments, and divided muted strings—all these were characteristic of the style which Debussy created for the new age.

It was on the evening of December 22, 1894, that the Parisian audience first became aware of this new kind of music. They had assembled that night to hear *Prélude à L'Après-Midi d'un Faune (The Afternoon of a Faun)*, which Debussy had described as a "musical eclogue based on a poem by Stefan Mallarmé." An eclogue is a pastoral piece. The composer's description of his music left the audience wholly unprepared for what they heard. It left them puzzled but enchanted, for it was not like any music they had ever heard before.

The *Prélude à L'Après-Midi d'un Faune* has no program; it tells no story, describes no scene. Instead it weaves a kind of spell around its listeners, stirring in them the mood of a summer afternoon and a faun asleep and dreaming. The clear notes of the flutes, the light strumming of the harps, the sound of strings and horns, all suggest warm sun and light breezes.

So new and so different from any music that had been created before was the *Prélude à L'Après-Midi d'un Faune* that it startled many listeners, but many hailed it with delight. Soon Debussy's enthusiastic friends wanted him to produce something larger, more impressive. But he would not be hurried; it was eight years before *Pelléas et Mélisande* was written on a symbolist text by the Belgian writer Maurice Maeterlinck. This is a great impressionist opera; words and music are matched in it to produce a dreamlike story veiled in allusions.

Debussy's outstanding orchestral compositions are the Spanish inspired *Iberia, Nocturnes,* and *La Mer,* which has been called the finest piece of music ever written about the changing sea.

In the realm of piano music Debussy was also a master. There was a new and sonorous beauty in his Preludes and a new pianistic subtlety in his Etudes. He wrote a cycle of delightful miniatures called *The Children's Corner* for his little daughter, the first of which, "Golliwog's Cakewalk," is filled with the rhythms of the American minstrel show.

Maurice Ravel contributed also to the new music of the new age. He was a friend and colleague of Debussy, though he was younger by about thirteen years. He loved the modal harmonies and exotic rhythms that Debussy used but he was influenced, too, by the eighteenth-century harpsichordists Jean Rameau and François Couperin. Like Debussy, he was much stimulated by Spanish dances and folk songs. All his work is polished, witty, and crystal clear; and yet gentle sadness pervades it. Like Debussy he sometimes creates in his music the illusion of guitars and castanets.

Ravel was born in the Basque country, which is in the southwest corner of France in the shadow of the Pyrenees. His father, a mining engineer, encouraged his interest in music, so when the family moved to Paris Maurice entered the conservatory. But his music was too unconventional for the pedantic authorities there; he never succeeded in winning the Prix de Rome though he tried four times.

Even if the authorities at the Paris Conservatory gave him no encouragement he was nevertheless rewarded by the enthusiasm of the poets and artists who recognized his genius. The group called the *Apaches,* whose heroes in painting were Paul Cézanne and Vincent Van Gogh, and in literature the poets Mallarmé and Verlaine, made Maurice Ravel their musical standard bearer.

In 1914 Ravel volunteered for service in the French Air Force but he was rejected and made to drive a military transport truck instead. At the front he saw many of his best friends killed, and returned after the war to write a collection of piano pieces called *Le Tombeau de Couperin*. These are six graceful French dances each dedicated to the memory of a friend who had been killed in battle.

Now one composition followed another. He drew much inspiration from literary sources and the sunlight of Southern France shone through his music. Sometimes he wrote compositions with the clean cut shapes of classical music as in *"Menuet Antique"* and *Pavan for a Dead Infanta*. But again he wrote impressionistic piano works such as *"Jeux d'Eau,"* *Miroirs*, and *Gaspard de la Nuit*. In *"La Valse"* he used Viennese dance rhythms, but there were jazz elements in the masterful Concerto in D for the Left Hand. This concerto was written for Ravel's friend Paul Wittgenstein, an officer who had lost his right hand in battle. Wittgenstein, a distinguished pianist, gave its first performance in Vienna in 1932 with Ravel conducting. Later in *Rapsodie Espagnole* Ravel brought melodic and rhythmic material from the Basque country where he was born.

In his orchestral work even the simplest motives were made to sound exciting. *Bolero* is perhaps his greatest orchestral *tour de force*. In it he repeats a theme again and again, each time with increasing intensity as it moves from instrument to instrument through the orchestra.

Like Debussy, Ravel wrote many unforgettable songs; the *Chansons Madécasses* (Songs of Madagascar) are most brilliant.

Recognition came to Ravel at last, and he found favor with the critics and with the public. He was invited to come to the United States in 1928 and liked it here except for the food. He said he was "dying of hunger" in America.

He stopped composing altogether during the Great Depression of the early 1930s, and severe illness prevented him from continuing his work. He died in Paris in 1937 after an unsuccessful brain operation. But he had taken music a step further away from the old pattern set by Wagner in the nineteenth century and along the road on which Debussy had embarked.

Eric Satie and those who followed him were to push music further still along that way. They wanted simple, unaffected music and hated the exaggerated emotions, the length, bombast, and self-pity of the late romantics.

Satie, an iconoclast, a friend of Jean Cocteau the playwright and Pablo Picasso the artist, lived in a poor suburb of Paris where he wrote the *Mass for the Poor*. With keen wit and deft satire he gave his music such whimsical titles as "Three Pieces in the Form of a Pear" and "Dried Embryos." Sometimes he left off bar lines and key signatures, and whatever he wrote was in a satiric vein.

Satie produced comparatively little, but his influence was great. Ravel gave him credit for artistic guidance, and a group of young composers called the "Six" took his principles to heart in their creative work. To Debussy, Satie, and the "Six" must go the credit for completing the liberation of French music from Teutonic romanticism. The "Six" wrote about Parisian street scenes and the night life of Paris, using much jazz idiom in a lighthearted, graceful, and witty, yet dry, music.

Henry Collet, the foremost French music critic of the time, had first called them the "Six." One of them is Darius Milhaud, the most prolific of the group. He was the friend of Paul Claudel who was both poet and French Ambassador to Brazil. At one time Milhaud went with Claudel to Brazil and there he wrote some charming piano pieces called *Sandades do Brazil*. Claudel also provided the poetry for his opera-oratorio *Christophe Colombe,* his greatest work so far.

Milhaud's first visit to the United States inspired a ballet called *Création de Monde*. In this jazz passages, with "blues" played by the saxophones, are combined with parts filled with French grace and polish.

Milhaud has composed over six hundred works altogether. His music has a very wide range, from heavy and complicated to light-hearted witty humor. And besides all this he has had great influence as a teacher, both in Europe and in America.

A very different member of the "Six" was Arthur Honneger, who was of Swiss parentage though he was born in France. An athlete, Honneger was fascinated by sports, and also by machinery. In 1924 he produced the well-known "Pacific No. 231," which was inspired by the sound of a locomotive. He also wrote the oratorio *King David*, a strong, clean cut work on a Biblical text. His music is harsh, angular, and expressive, yet there is also a conservatism in it.

"My great marvel is Johann Sebastian Bach," Honneger once said. Somehow he managed to fuse elements of Bach's counterpoint with a warmth of contemporary dissonance and rhythm. He liked the form of the symphony and his greatest symphony, the Fifth, was commissioned by the Koussevitsky Music Foundation to be performed at the music festival at Tanglewood, Massachusetts, in 1951.

Other members of the "Six" besides Milhaud and Honneger were Louis Durey, Georges Auric, Germaine Taillefere, and finally Francis Poulenc.

Poulenc, who died in 1963, was exquisitely French, a wonderful melodist whose glittering piano pieces are parlor music in a sophisticated modern vein. He wrote a tragic opera, *Les Dialogues des Carmelites*, about the martyrdom of some Carmelite nuns during the French Revolution. And he wrote another and subtle little musical drama called *La Voix Humaine* (*The Human Voice*) on a text by Jean Cocteau in which a woman talking on the telephone bids farewell to her sweetheart before his marriage to another woman. Her lamentation lasts for forty-five minutes—the whole duration of the opera.

Debussy, Ravel, Satie, and the "Six"—in all these composers the French artistic tradition was deeply ingrained. There was a tradition of clarity of utterance, economy of means, elegance. Yet they succeeded in finding a new kind of musical expression for the age in which they found themselves. Meantime, in the years between the two World Wars, the revolutionary movement in music reached a peak. Two giants were creating a musical upheaval whose repercussions still go on. They were Igor Stravinsky and Arnold Schoenberg.

CHAPTER TWENTY-NINE

Stravinsky Startles His Audience

WHILE Claude Debussy and Maurice Ravel were producing their new music in France and Satie and the "Six"
were striving to get away from the conventions of the Romantic
Age, a new voice began to be heard in Paris. This was the voice
of a Russian, Igor Stravinsky, who began his career by writing
ballet music for the Russian producer Sergei Diaghilev. Diaghilev
had great ambitions for his ballet. He wanted to combine the

very finest in poetry, art, and music with the dancing of his beautifully trained performers. He had already engaged the promising
artist Pablo Picasso to paint scenery, and in 1909 he brought
Igor Stravinsky from Russia to compose his music.

In Russia Stravinsky had been a brilliant young student of the
Russian composer, Rimsky-Korsakov. But in Paris he was just one
more struggling young composer. With the production of his first
ballet, *The Firebird* in 1910, however, he suddenly became the
talk of Paris. *The Firebird* made a great sensation. It had some
of the qualities of his teacher's music—exotic melodies and warm,
colorful orchestration.

Delighted at the success of *The Firebird,* Diaghilev encouraged
Stravinsky to write music for another ballet. This was *Petrouchka,*
the ballet that tells the story of a puppet at a Russian village fair.
Here are the noise and excitement of peasant folk on holiday,
and the dancing puppet dominates the other sounds with the
rhythms of his mechanical movements.

There were no vague mists of impressionism in Stravinsky's
music as there had been in Debussy's. His rhythms were vital.
The orchestral colors of *Petrouchka* were raw, and the stream-
lined texture was filled with unexpected sounds which the Parisians found harsh and dissonant; if people had been startled by
Debussy, they were dismayed by Stravinsky. But with *Petrouchka*
his work was only beginning.

Now Stravinsky went back to Russia, and there in March 1913
he finished the ballet called *Le Sacre du Printemps* (*The Rite of
Spring*). It tells of the loveliest girl in a Russian village and how
she was chosen to invoke the spirit of spring and fertility, by
dancing and dancing until she fell down dead.

The music has the harsh, vibrating power of primitive music,
yet it is extremely complex. In a way it is like an international
convention in which people of all languages are talking at once.
A variety of meters, rhythms, textures, and instrumental timbres

all sounded together at once. They produce an earth-shaking world of new sound.

The Russian dancer Vaslav Nijinsky directed the choreography of this ballet, and he kept trying unsuccessfully to make Stravinsky alter his music to suit the dance steps. This caused a good deal of delay, but finally *Le Sacre du Printemps* was produced at the Théâtre des Champs-Elysées in Paris, on May 29, 1913.

The premiere caused a riot. Although there was order and logic behind every note of the score, many in the audience felt that the music was chaotic. Hissing and booing and derisive laughter greeted it. Jean Cocteau in Paris wrote, "Standing up in her loge, her tiara awry, the old Comtesse de Pourtalès flourished her fan and shouted, scarlet in the face, 'It's the first time in sixty years that anyone has dared to make a fool of me.'"

Unnerved, Stravinsky drove around Paris in a taxicab all night after the performance, and he never returned to the style he had used in *Le Sacre du Printemps*. He probably did not realize at the time that this masterpiece of sophisticated primitivism would go down in history as the most famous work of the early twentieth century. Yet for Stravinsky it was not the end of his stylistic road. Like a scientist he has continued to explore every important musical device of the twentieth century.

By the time Stravinsky's admirers had finally absorbed *Le Sacre du Printemps,* its composer had already turned in a new direction. In the war years and the early twenties he produced *L'Histoire du Soldat* for a very small orchestra (violin, double-bass, clarinet, bassoon, cornet, trombone, and percussion) and the brilliant *Les Noces* (*The Wedding*) for chorus, four pianos, and percussion. In both these compositions as well as in *Ebony Concerto* and *Ragtime* there are elements of jazz.

But he was again not content to be chained to one style. He had already explored the neo-romantic in *The Firebird*, the complex primitive in *Le Sacre du Printemps,* and jazz in works like

Histoire du Soldat. Now he turned his sights to the past, to classicism. The opera-oratorio *Oedipus Rex* which he wrote in 1926–27 is one of the landmarks of the twentieth century. It is based on a translation in Latin of Jean Cocteau's adaptation of Sophocles, and its stark, ice-cold polyphony builds up to the strong inevitable dramatic climax. The structure is so clear and convincing that it could almost be built out of marble.

The other masterpiece of this time is the *Symphony of Psalms,* which he produced in 1930. This, too, is classical, yet it has a subtle warmth in the choral passages and an over-all feeling of religious devotion.

Now other works followed in the classical vein: Symphony in C (1940), *Appolon Musagetes,* The Symphony in Three Movements (1945), and *The Rake's Progress* which was produced in Venice in 1951 and had been suggested by some engravings of the English artist Hogarth.

These works are impressive, and a host of younger men began to imitate Stravinsky's neo-classical style. They too tried spare writing, off-beat accents, and angular melodic lines. But meantime the master turned once again in a new direction. This time he began to combine the complex polyphony of the late Middle Ages and early Renaissance, with the twelve-tone method which Arnold Schoenberg had recently developed. These two seemingly divergent ideas Stravinsky somehow fused into a whole, and the works of his latest period are in this style. They are the *Canticum Sacrum* written "in honor of St. Mark," the *Threni* on texts of the Lamentations of Jeremiah, and the ballet *Agon.*

Perhaps in a few years Stravinsky will have abandoned this style, too, yet it is sure that in whatever way he works, the characteristics of Stravinsky's style will remain.

CHAPTER THIRTY

Schoenberg and the Twelve-Tone System

STRAVINSKY has influenced three generations of composers, yet in his last period he himself was influenced by Arnold Schoenberg, whom some have called the greatest musical genius of the twentieth century. Schoenberg's twelve-tone system was eventually to disturb the very foundations of the Western tonal system.

The idea of tonality which Schoenberg sought to do away with had been accepted since the days of the Greeks. Since their time it had been assumed that seven of the twelve tones belonged to a given key and the other five lay outside it. All tones in this key, moreover, gravitated toward a central or "home" tone. This relationship was called "tonality." To abandon it was both strange and revolutionary.

The accepted tonality was not abandoned all at once; revolutions seldom come suddenly. In the nineteenth century in Wagner's music the idea of a key center had lost more and more of its meaning. Debussy had created harmonies not intended to take the listener from one key center to another, but to create a mood. Richard Strauss in *"Ein Heldenleben"* had written some difficult passages in which the tonal centers were hard if not impossible to find, but Schoenberg now brought this trend to its logical conclusion.

Schoenberg claimed freedom to use any combination of sounds whatever. He abandoned the old practice of resolving his phrases to "consonant" or "nice sounding" chords. He made no distinction between consonance and dissonance.

By abandoning the old rules of tonality Schoenberg achieved immense harmonic enrichment. Instead of the few dozen chords that could be worked out in the old classical harmony, Schoenberg's system offered more than two thousand new chords. Some of these, to be sure, were very unpleasant to the unaccustomed ear. But Schoenberg was sure that when people became accustomed to these harsh sounds, they would like them.

He was a native Viennese, so it was natural that his music had its roots in the Viennese musical tradition. He was influenced by both Mahler and Wolf and above all by Wagner. His first well-known composition, *Die Verklärte Nacht,* shows a clear relationship to Wagner's *Tristan.*

After that he began to create his own individual style—*Gurre-Lieder* is a work of gigantic size and difficulty. It was composed from 1899–1901 but was not performed until 1913. In it he used wide leaps in the melodic lines and extreme ranges. Meantime he was composing other music.

As might be expected, Schoenberg's new music took the public by surprise. The first performance of his Quartet in F Sharp Minor was given in Vienna in 1908. It was not a twelve-tone work, but pointed in this direction, and the audience made such a demonstration against it that his friend, the composer Gustav Mahler, stepped up to the platform and begged them to allow it to be finished. The critics rejected it with one voice, although now the work is regarded as an outstanding achievement.

Now Schoenberg began to realize that with constant dissonance, blurred tonalities, extreme ranges, and wide leaps, he had brought his music to the verge of chaos. He knew that he had destroyed, and felt he must create something new to replace what he had destroyed.

In his book *Manual of Harmony* he explains the twelve-tone system. He worked it out slowly with painstaking experiment. The system has sometimes been called "atonal" but Schoenberg himself did not like this term: he preferred to call it dodecaphonic or twelve-tone music.

Schoenberg's twelve-tone system is called serial music, because it is based on a series of notes which become the nucleus of the whole composition. The series which is sometimes called the "Basic Set" is composed of the twelve chromatic tones within an octave arranged in a special order. These tone rows may be used as melodies or in combination to form chords, but no given tone may be repeated until the entire row of eleven more notes has been sounded. They may, however, be sounded backwards or in any prescribed order.

Besides the maze of strident chords in Schoenberg's composition there are wide skips in melodic contours that jar the ear accustomed to the steplike rise and fall of conventional melody.

The result of all this is a kaleidoscope of warm, romantic, dissonant sound. The music is in direct contrast to the impressionism of Debussy and his followers. The impressionists sought to depict impressions of the outside world—the sea, the mountains, and so on—but Schoenberg and the expressionists directed attention to their inner feelings. Their music was self-centered like that of the romanticists, but it was fiercer and more violent. This intensity necessitates short, concentrated works, for violence spends itself and cannot last long.

In 1912 Schoenberg wrote a well-known cycle of twenty-one songs for contralto called *Pierrot Lunaire* in this style. It uses *"sprech stimme,"* or speaking voice, in which the voice does not sing but chants in a singing fashion in rhythm to the music, with a weird and witchlike effect. And he wrote Variations for Orchestra and the Violin Concerto in this same style.

With the advent of Hitler to Germany, Schoenberg, like so many other noted artists and musicians, was forced to flee from Germany, and he took refuge in the United States. Here he lived in California and continued to compose. He taught a great many promising composers there and exerted a strong influence over them.

As he grew older his music became somewhat orthodox again, and he wrote a number of works in "the olden style" which combined twelve-tone elements with classical tonality. In this way he wrote Piano Concerto and "Ode to Napoleon." Probably his greatest work is the opera *Moses and Aaron,* which is based on the Old Testament. It was left incomplete, for Schoenberg died in 1951, but its music has tremendous power, color, and dramatic effect.

Schoenberg's music has had an enormous influence on all modern composers. One of his followers was Alban Berg, who does not use the twelve-tone rows strictly and whose music is therefore easier to listen to than his master's. His greatest works are his operas *Wozzeck* and *Lulu,* in both of which Berg linked the new twelve-tone method with forms of the past.

Anton von Webern was another great disciple of Schoenberg. Although his musical output was small, he has had a tremendous influence on the musical world, particularly in the last fifteen years. Whereas Berg's music had been warm and emotional, Webern's was cool and intellectual, as finely cut as a diamond. He was a miniaturist; whole sonatas and symphonies took only a few minutes under Webern's pen. He wrote a symphony which took eight minutes to perform, a concerto and a string quartet each of which took nine minutes. Each note in his work was important, for it symbolized whole phrases of music, and each note spoke as an expression for an idea.

Webern followed the twelve-tone system more strictly than did Schoenberg himself. His music is full of complex canons, invertible counterpoint, yet it is not difficult. Perhaps this is because its texture is so transparent. It is full of "space" and rests. Often only one instrument plays at a time while the others rest.

Webern has been called a pointillist in music. He used the "dot" technique which the French painter Seurat had first used in painting. The tiny dots which Seurat placed on his canvas gave a beautiful effect of light, and the tiny sparks of sound which Webern assembled gave a new kind of beauty to the music which he wrote.

So Schoenberg and his followers changed Western music, and it was never to be the same again. Though he encountered resistance that bordered on downright hostility and revulsion, the touch of his genius may be traced in the work of almost every modern composer.

CHAPTER THIRTY-ONE

Béla Bartók and His Recording Machine

E A R L Y in the twentieth century the young Hungarian Béla
Bartók tramped from village to village in the Carpathian
Mountains of southeastern Hungary. His friend Zoltan Kodály
was with him; he also was to become an eminent composer. The
pair carried a recording machine, and here and there they stopped
for a few days in some tiny village, to watch the village people
dance and to make recordings of their strong, vital songs. Bartók
wrote later that these years were the happiest of his life.

Hungarian folk music was a discovery and a source of joy to
the young Bartók. The Hungarian government had recently proclaimed gypsy music the national music of Hungary. But Bartók
maintained that gypsy music had been commercialized and cheap-
ened for use in the cafés. The real Hungarian folk music was
centuries old, far more beautiful, more vibrant and imaginative
than gypsy music.

Soon Bartók was publishing articles on the ancient folk music
he had discovered. Official authorities were furious at his statements, and angry when he pointed out similarities between the folk
music of Hungary and that of Rumania. Bartók was then a piano
teacher at the Royal Hungarian Musical Academy in Budapest,
and the officials did everything they could to ruin his career. As a
result the young musician could afford to publish only about two
thousand of the songs he had collected. There were many more.

Nevertheless Bartók kept on collecting his tunes. He crossed

over from Hungary to Rumania and began to collect folk music
from the Arab countries of the Near East and North Africa. He
made no attempt to prettify the tunes as musicians of the Romantic Age had altered and embellished the folk songs they knew.
Bartók kept the folk songs genuine, honest, crude, and beautiful.
When he composed he used the primitive, pure music in his own
work.

Early in his career Bartók had been influenced by Debussy
and under this influence had written suites for orchestra. But soon
he broke away from Debussy toward music of a more purely Hungarian nature. He absorbed the folk-tune rhythms and the folk
melodies with exotic scales which were related to Gregorian modes
and to the scales of the Near East. In the inspired collection of
piano teaching pieces *Mikrokosmos* he imitated the drone of a
Balkan bagpipe as well as the stomping of boots in a Hungarian
dance.

Now he wrote other piano music: the percussive *Allegro bar-
baro* and the Sonata for Two Pianos and Percussion. His six lovely
string quartets many musicians today consider among his greatest
works; they are a logical extension of the last Beethoven string
quartets.

His large-scale works began with the one-act, spine-chilling
opera, *Duke Bluebeard's Castle,* based on the old fairy tale, and
then a pantomime, *The Marvelous Mandarin.*

Bartók's writing for voices, though it was effective, never reached
the level of genius of his writing for instruments. His orchestral
works are brilliant; they teem with originality and life. Concerto
for Orchestra, with its colorful orchestration, the beautiful violin
and viola concertos, the three piano concertos, and the electric
Music for Strings, Percussion and Celesta—all these are masterpieces.

In some of his music Bartók manages to give a vivid reproduction of the sounds of the outdoors: the insects chirp, bees buzz, and
birds sing and chatter. The chirping and croaking cacophony of

insects and animals are heard both in the rhythm and in the relation of the sounds to each other.

Those happy days when Bartók was collecting folk music and composing were all too short. He was out of sympathy with the Hungarian dictator Nicholas Horthy and the regime of the Nazis, so he was eventually forced to flee from Hungary. In 1940, during World War II, with the help of his English publishers he managed to escape and came to the United States. His genius was not generally recognized here; his works were seldom performed, and he was greatly discouraged. He died of leukemia in a New York hospital in 1945.

It is ironic that a few weeks after his death forty-eight major performances of his works took place throughout the country, and today his music is hailed for its fire, its rhythmic drive, bold harmony, and exotic melody. Today he is considered one of the really great musical geniuses of the twentieth century.

CHAPTER THIRTY-TWO

Other New Voices in Europe

B É L A Bartók was a towering figure, but he was not the only
great composer in twentieth-century Europe. Many men in
many widespread places took the heritage of music which the
centuries had given them and each in his way made new music.

Leoš Janáček, the Czech, was one of the great twentieth century composers. A teacher, he traveled widely during his vacations collecting folk songs as Béla Bartók had done. But Janáček
collected not only the songs the people sang, but the inflections
of their speaking voices. He heard and put down the singsong
of simple, unsophisticated country folk, and carefully indicated
the rise and fall of their voices when they were surprised, or
pleased, or angry. He noted the voice of a woman as she called
her children home across the fields, and the tones of one old lady
telling a story to another. These for Janáček were the material
of music. The melodic fragments which he collected in this way
were highly charged with emotion; he combined them into a
musical mosaic that was irresistibly direct in its impact.

The truth and realism of Janáček's operas is reminiscent of
Moussorgsky. *Její Pastorkyna* (*Her Foster-Daughter*), or *Jenufa*,
the German title, is his most successful one. But he wrote choral
compositions. Perhaps the best known of these is his *Glagolitic
Mass* based on an ancient Slavonic text. It is strikingly original;
some critics think it the best of all modern sacred works.

But Eastern Europe has, of course, no monopoly on modern

music. New music is being heard now in many parts of Europe. The orange groves, the Moorish walls, and gypsy dances of southern Spain were all inspiration to Manuel de Falla, one of the greatest of all the Spanish composers. Falla fell under the spell of impressionism at first, for he lived for several years in Paris. Despite this fact his music is exquisitely Spanish and the Spaniards were enormously proud of him. Franco, the Spanish dictator, showered him with honors. Falla was not impressed with all this adulation. When the Spanish Revolution broke out he left Spain, and died eventually in Argentina.

Falla's first success was the opera *La Vida Breve* (*The Short Life*), first performed in 1915, and *El Sombrero de Tres Picos* (*The Three-Cornered Hat*). The revival of harpsichord playing in the twentieth century inspired him to write the exquisitely stylized Concerto for Harpsichord.

As Janáček had found his inspiration in the speaking voices of his own Czech people and Falla had been inspired by the traditions of Spain, so Ernest Bloch, although he was born in Geneva, Switzerland, was deeply nourished on the spiritual heritage of the Jewish people, and he wrote music which reflects the rich, elaborate ritual songs of the synagogue. His is impassioned rhapsodical music with bold harmonies and rugged rhythms. His Jewish cycle includes *Schelomo,* which is a rhapsody for cello and orchestra, and also the *Israel Symphony* and *Trois Poèmes Juifs.*

Not all the twentieth-century composers were nationalists, of course. Olivier Messiaen, a French mystic, is influenced by the Far East and uses Hindu and Balinese motivs in his original and intricate compositions. A devoted Catholic, his compositions are primarily organ works, and even his orchestral works seem to have an organ-like quality. Many of them are unusual because they employ birdlike melodies, for Messiaen has made a careful study of bird song.

Perhaps the most striking quality of modern European music

is the great variety of styles its composers have chosen. Their music is, of course, as different as are the men themselves. After the First World War there were some who found new creative strength in the impersonal objective music of the eighteenth century. Some even went back to the age of Monteverdi or to the work of the Flemish masters of the fifteenth and sixteenth centuries. They garlanded their compositions with elaborate counterpoint though their music was filled with strident, dissonant boldness. Bach became the supreme idol of these moderns. Their compositions bore all the discipline and restraint of the old master as they produced dance suites, fugues, passacaglias, and variations—forms which the romanticists had long thought outworn. Stravinsky had been one of the first of these so-called "neo-classicists" and he had great influence in swaying other composers to this point of view.

Perhaps the composer who cares most for the old, classic forms is the German Paul Hindemith. A prolific composer, he also writes extensively on theory and on music. Before Hitler's advent he carried out a great many musical projects both in the German public schools and in the labor unions. Hindemith is a great believer in what was called *Gebrauchsmusik*—that is, "music for everyday use" to be played or sung by amateurs. He has written many works of this kind for both children and adults. He said, "People who make music together cannot be enemies, at least not while the music lasts."

Unfortunately, however, Hitler did not like Hindemith's music. The Nazis proclaimed him "spiritually non-Aryan" and said he was a "cultural Bolshevik." So he came to America at the beginning of the Second World War and taught for a time at Yale University. Later he taught at the Berkshire Music Center at Tanglewood, Massachusetts. He lives in Zurich, Switzerland, now, but sometimes comes back to the United States to visit and to conduct.

Hindemith has resisted Schoenberg's twelve-tone system. With tremendous creative energy, he has inherited the German counterpoint, ponderous yet flowing. His music has the moral sturdiness of the early Protestant reformation and melody that grows out of old German songs and Protestant chorales. Yet it was Hindemith who was one of the first to employ jazz elements in his work. Many sonatas and chamber works for all combinations of instruments have come from Hindemith's pen but one of his most beautiful works is the setting for *a cappella* choir of *Six Chansons* by Rainer Maria Rilke. They are warm and sensitive: little gems of choral sound.

Perhaps his greatest music is the score of his opera, *Mathis der Mahler* (*Matthias the Painter*). This music he later made into a symphony. The hero of the opera is Matthias Grünewald, a late fifteenth-century painter. Hindemith took three orchestral movements from this work and named each one after a panel of Matthias' mystical altar painting at Colmar.

Hindemith's serious, deep philosophical course has been matched by a great outpouring of music of another kind in Russia. Many distinguished composers have been working under the Soviet government in Russia and adding their contribution to the grand sum total of twentieth-century European music. Among them was Serge Prokofiev, who graduated from the St. Petersburg Conservatory in 1914, and after that began producing a large number of compositions. His first compositions were an opera, *Love for Three Oranges*, two piano concertos, the *Scythian Suite* and the *Classical Symphony*, several sonatas, some piano pieces including "Sarcasms," and some songs, including "The Ugly Duckling." His work was filled with propelling motor rhythms, bold bittersweet dissonances, and passages of grotesque satire that he called "jests," "laughter," and "mockery."

The *Scythian Suite*, which was originally a ballet, was his first mature orchestral work. Its theme, based on Russian mythology, was suggested to him by his friend Diaghilev. The critics and the public were indignant when they heard it. They disliked its "harsh noises."

Prokofiev, however, did not listen to their complaints. He wrote his *Classical Symphony,* and although this was ostensibly in the style of Haydn and Mozart it abounds in twentieth-century surprises. There is much charm in its abrupt illogical changes of key and texture, which would not have occurred to a composer of the classical period. It is a masterpiece.

While the young composer was growing to maturity, the Russian armies were mobilized to fight the First World War, and in 1917 revolution was added to war. When the Czar and his family were killed, those of the nobility who could not escape were massacred, and unrest and uncertainty were everywhere as the people struggled with the task of bringing the war to a successful end and setting up a new government. Order had to be restored across the vast sweep of the Russian lands; cities leveled by bombs had to be rebuilt, fields planted, industries begun. And all these things had to be done by the working people who had no experience to help them in what they had to do.

The new Soviet government realized it must somehow unify the various peoples who were spread out across the great stretches of Russia. They must encourage the citizens to work, and give them courage to face self-denial and hardships. For this reason the Union of Soviet Composers was organized. Its members pledged themselves to support the socialist program with their art, to bind together the widely scattered and disparate people with music of which they could all be proud.

Prokofiev did not join this movement at first. He crossed Siberia and took a ship across the Pacific to America. He made several appearances as a pianist in New York and in 1921 went to Chicago, where his opera *Love for Three Oranges* was well received.

That year he went on to Paris, where his friend Diaghilev produced his ballet *Chout* (*The Clown*). After that he wrote another ballet, *Le Pas d'Acier* (*The Steel Leap*), a stirring musical account of the growth of industry under the Soviets.

The producer and conductor Serge Koussevitsky was in Paris at that time, and he helped Prokofiev by giving performances of his work. In 1930 Koussevitsky commissioned him to write a work to be performed in Boston for the fiftieth anniversary of the Boston Symphony Orchestra. This was the Concert Music for Strings and Brass (op. 50), which contrasts strings and brass in a striking way.

Prokofiev returned to Russia in 1934, and two years later he wrote his *Russian Overture,* based entirely on Russian themes. The next year he asserted his faith in Soviet ideas with a cantata written for the celebration of the twentieth anniversary of the Russian Revolution. The text was chosen from speeches by Karl Marx, Lenin, and Stalin.

So Prokofiev reached the zenith of his career and now he wrote music of almost every kind—music for films, ballets, cantatas. One of his operas bore the title *I Am the Son of Working People* but he later changed it to the name of its hero, *Simeon Kotko, a Soldier of the Red Army.*

Perhaps the best known of all Prokofiev's work both in Russia and in the West is *Peter and the Wolf.* Prokofiev himself called it *An Orchestral Fairy Tale for Children;* audiences of all ages enjoy it.

Prokofiev wrote the text of his "orchestral fairy tale" himself and interwove it skillfully with the music. "Early one morning Peter opened the gate," it begins, "and went out into a big green meadow." Then the story tells how Peter encountered various characters, and each is represented by a corresponding instrument in the orchestra: the bird by a flute, the duck by an oboe, the cat by a clarinet in the low register, the grandfather by a bassoon, the wolf by three horns, and Peter himself by a string quartet. The gunshots of the hunters are sounded by kettledrums. The story tells how the wolf threatened all the animals and how

Peter finally succeeded in catching him. Then there is a triumphal procession of all the animals as Peter takes the wolf to the zoo. Peter's grandfather and the cat bring up the rear.

Besides this engaging fairy tale, Prokofiev wrote two violin concertos, the third piano concerto, the *Lieutenant Kiji Suite,* the cantata *Alexander Nevsky,* the nine dynamic piano sonatas, and the giant-sized Fifth Symphony which many people consider his greatest work.

Dmitri Shostakovich, another brilliant Soviet composer, was only eleven years old at the time of the Russian Revolution. He was nineteen when his First Symphony was performed in Leningrad, but this composition is still one of his finest. Very dramatic in its feeling, it has been compared to the work of Beethoven, whom the Russians greatly admire.

The Second Symphony of Shostakovich has the subtitle "Dedication to October," and was performed on the tenth anniversary of the Revolution. It is composed with complicated counterpoint and uses polyrhythm. A factory whistle sounds in it, symbol of Russia's rising industry. His Third Symphony has a choral ending patterned on Beethoven's Ninth and the Seventh Symphony glorifies the siege and victorious defense of Leningrad in the Second World War.

But Shostakovich does not confine himself to symphonic music. He has written an amusing opera on the theme of one of Gogol's stories called *The Nose.* In it a nose leaves the face of a man seated in a barber's chair and begins to lead the life of a government official under the czar. The singer who takes the part of the nose is directed in the score to press his fingers against his nostrils to produce a nasal effect.

And there are ballets, too. One of these, *The Age of Gold,* was produced in Leningrad in 1930 and is intended to depict the degeneracy of a capitalistic city. And another, *The Limpid Stream,* pictures life on a collective farm.

Not all Shostakovich's work has been well received by the Soviet government. An opera called *Lady Macbeth of the District of Mzensk* shows sympathy for the heroine, and the government condemned it, saying that it "tickled the perverted tastes of the bourgeois audience by its jittery, noisy, and neurotic music." It had been well received in New York and Cleveland.

So in twentieth-century Europe, new voices have been heard. They are rich, vibrant, different from any that have been heard before. For the new composers have taken all the heritage of the past and added to this their own individual genius.

And meantime across the ocean in the Americas another music has been growing.

CHAPTER THIRTY-THREE

And in America

1. *The Overture*

"WE REFRESHED ourselves, after tears, with singing Psalms," wrote Edward Winslow describing how the Pilgrims spent the night at Leiden before they set sail for the New World. "We refreshed ourselves with singing of Psalms, making joyful melody in our hearts as well as with the voice, there being many of the congregation very expert in music; and indeed it was the sweetest melody that ever mine ears heard."

So the newcomers to America prepared for their adventurous journey with singing, and they continued to sing after they reached the new shores. The psalms the Mayflower passengers sang were those they had known in England; they brought with them a copy of the *Ainsworth Psalter*, and this contained thirty-nine tunes, but the people generally sang the psalms from memory.

The New Englanders printed a psalm book of their own in 1640. This was the *Bay Psalm Book,* the second book to be printed in the colonies. The first was an almanac. The *Bay Psalm Book* had no musical notation, but the congregations hardly needed notes. They knew the tunes well. One of them was the familiar "Old Hundred" which is still sung in our churches today.

Psalm singing in New England was not a dreary business. The settlers apparently believed in worshiping God "with singing mirth." Most of the clergy did not object to their fitting any tunes they pleased to the psalms, and some of these were dance tunes and sailors' hornpipes. The Reverend John Cotton and some of the other clergy railed against such liveliness, however. They spoke of some of the psalm tunes as "Geneva jigs."

Almost from the beginning the singing of psalms went hand in hand with the singing of ballads. "Vayne and trifling ballads" one stern Puritan minister called them. A young Harvard student copied out a number of these in his "commonplace book." Among them were "The Lovesick Maid, or Cordelia's Lamentation for the Absence of Her Gerhard," "The Last Lamentation of the Languishing Squire, or Love Overcomes All Things," and "The Two Faithful Lovers." The Reverend Thomas Symmes called such ballads as these idle, foolish, and pernicious, and said they were "trash"—but still they were extremely popular.

By the beginning of the eighteenth century, when the first rigors of settlement were over, interest in music had increased steadily. Now a good many gentlemen were importing delicate and costly instruments from England. An advertisement in the Boston *News Letter* read, "Flageolets, Flutes, Hautboys, Bass viols, Violins, bows, strings, reeds for hautboys, books of instruction for all these instruments, books of Ruled Paper, to be sold at the dancing school of Mr. Eustone in Sudbury Street near the Orange Tree, Boston."

Gradually music went filtering through the American colonies. Some Germans who were followers of Jan Hus and who called themselves "Moravian Brothers" went to Bethlehem, Pennsylvania, and brought with them copies of Haydn's quartets and symphonies. Soon they were performing *The Creation* and *The Seasons,* and neighboring people came from miles around to hear them.

Pennsylvania boasted the first church organ in America. It was made in Holstein, Germany, and the young minister of the Gloria Dei (Swedish) Church, which stood on the banks of the Wissahickon, in asking his friends for contributions for it, wrote, "The Indians would come running from far and near to hear such unknown melody." Members of the congregation were said to have accompanied the organ when it came "with music on the viol, hautboy, trumpets, and kettledrums." That was about 1700.

In 1713 an organ was sent from London for the Episcopal Church in Boston. It is said that no one unpacked it for seven months after it came, however, for many members of the congregation thought it wrong to have organ music at a religious service.

As time passed, Charleston, South Carolina, led the other cities in music. The first opera in America was given there in 1735; it was *Flora, or Hob in the Well.* Apparently, its composer has been forgotten.

The first musical society in America, the St. Cecilia Society, was founded in Charleston also. Josiah Quincy, who went to a concert of that society, wrote that "one Abercrombie, a Frenchman just arrived, played the violin, and a solo incomparably better than any one I ever heard. He cannot speak a word of English, and had a salary of five hundred guineas a year from the St. Cecilia Society. There were more than two hundred and fifty ladies present, and it was called no great number. In loftiness of headdress these ladies stoop to the daughters of the North —in richness of dress, surpass them."

Meantime, a few men were dreaming that their new country might some day become a leader in the world of music, a rank she was finally to attain in the twentieth century.

The charming Francis Hopkinson was one of these. A young

Philadelphia lawyer, he was one of the signers of the Declaration of Independence and active in the debates of the Constitutional Convention. He was also later a judge of the Admiralty Court of Pennsylvania.

Hopkinson found time for music also. He often substituted for the regular organist at Christ Church in Philadelphia, and tried his hand at composing. One of his compositions was *The Temple of Minerva*. He said that this was an "oratorical entertainment"; some people maintain that it was the first American opera. However that is, it was performed in 1781 "by a company of ladies and gentlemen in the hotel of the Minister of France in the presence of his Excellency General Washington and his lady."

The Temple of Minerva was strongly political in feeling; it had an overture, arias, ensembles, and choruses—all of which praised the idea of an American alliance with France. Its music has been lost, but the words are safely guarded now in the Library of Congress in Washington.

Francis Hopkinson's enthusiasm pointed out to the American people of his time that music might be a powerful force in the new nation, but his compositions when they are played today seem rather thin and conventional. Perhaps music is a mistress that demands the full strength of her followers, and Hopkinson had many different interests.

Benjamin Franklin, while not a true musician or composer himself, had an acute judgment and a discerning taste in musical matters. He played the guitar and harp, both of which were fashionable instruments in his time, and he liked very much to sing, enjoying Scottish songs particularly. It was his contention that folk songs should be sung simply and not embellished with elaborate accompaniments—a very modern point of view.

It was Franklin who was first to print and publish music in America, and it was he whose ingenuity created that extraordinary new instrument the "Glassychord" or "Glass Armonica."

Musical glasses whose tone depended on the amount of water

each held had been brought to Dublin in 1743 by one Richard Pockrich, and Gluck had played on them three years later in London. But the ingenious Benjamin Franklin had improved them and made them into a real musical instrument.

Franklin's invention was a series of thirty-five glass bowls, graduated in size and fitting inside one another. A horizontal rod passed through all the bowls to hold them in place, and this rod could be made to rotate by foot like a spinning wheel making the edges of the bowls pass through a trough of water. The sounds were produced by holding the finger tips against the moistened revolving edges of the bowls.

Franklin's new instrument impressed the Europeans very much. A German almanac for 1782 notes, "Of all musical inventions the one of Mr. Franklin of Philadelphia has created perhaps the greatest excitement." Gluck, Mozart, and Beethoven all composed special pieces of music for it. Many of the ladies who tried to play this instrument, however, said it affected their nervous systems, and there were rumors that some had even become insane. Was this perhaps why Franklin's instrument gradually fell into disuse?

Thomas Jefferson was perhaps the most passionate music lover among the early American leaders. He imported the printed music of a great many compositions from France and rose at five in the morning to practice it. He liked minuets especially. One of his slaves said he could hardly remember his master without a fiddle in his hand. Sometimes he played the chamber music of Haydn and Mozart with his friends at Monticello. Patrick Henry was one of those who liked to play the violin with him.

Sometimes Jefferson took part in a string quartet that gave little recitals at William and Mary College at Williamsburg, Virginia. He designed a special square music stand for use on these occasions which may still be seen at Monticello, Jefferson's house.

In 1776, when the Revolution was at its height, Jefferson dreamed of forming a little private orchestra at Monticello like

the one Prince Esterházy had at Eisenstadt. He had no great
wealth like that of the Austrian prince, but in his eagerness he
tried to make plans for a "domestic band of musicians." He wrote,
"I have thought that a passion for music might be reconciled with
that economy which we are obliged to observe." Then he went
on to explain how he thought a private orchestra could be arranged.

I retain among my domestic servants a gardener, a weaver, a cabinet-
maker, and a stonecutter to which I would add a *vigneron* [vine-
grower]. In a country [like Italy] where music is cultivated and prac-
tised by every class of man, I suppose there might be found persons
of those trades who could perform on the French horn, clarinet, or
hautboy, and bassoon, so that one might have a band of two French
horns, two clarinets, two hautboys, and a bassoon, without enlarging
their domestic expenses. A certainty of employment for half a dozen
years, and at the end of that time to find them, if they choose, a con-
veyance to their own country, might induce them to come here on
reasonable wages. . . .

It is a pity that Jefferson's dream of a private orchestra did not
come to pass.

Thomas Jefferson was the master of many slaves at Monticello,
though he maintained that he could not justify slavery and
worked out a scheme for having the slaves gradually freed in
Virginia. The singing of the Negroes must have made a mellow
background for life on his plantation.

In his *Notes on the State of Virginia* he says of the Negroes,
"The instrument proper to them is the Banjar which they brought
hither from Africa, and which is the original of the guitar; its
chords (i.e., strings) being precisely the four lower chords of the
guitar."

And he writes of the Negroes further, "They are more generally
gifted than the whites, with accurate ears for time and tune, and
they have been found capable of imagining a small catch [a
fragment of a round in one continuous melody]. Whether they

will be equal to the composition of a more extensive run of melody, or of complicated harmony is yet to be proved."

Though Jefferson had noticed that his slaves were musically gifted, no one paid much attention to his observation. It was not until the end of the nineteenth century that musicians began to realize that the Negroes were making a significant contribution to the music of the New World, and that their influence was to be stronger than that of any other of her people.

For Americans at first were concerned with settling a new land, with fighting to free themselves from England, with forming a new government. In fact, it was not until all these things had been done that they started to create music of their own. Then in William Billings of Boston, America found her first original and distinguished composer.

Billings was a tanner, blind in one eye, with one leg shorter than the other. He sang in a rasping voice as he went about tanning his hides, and sometimes paused to write his music down on one of them. He probably had no formal education. After he had become completely absorbed in his music he gave up tanning and, consequently, lived and died in poverty.

Billings led a church choir in Boston as well as a singing society. It was for them that he composed "fuguing pieces." These were not what we would understand as fugues. They were imitative vocal passages in which the parts came after each other with the same notes. When they were sung by large groups of powerful voices the floor trembled with the booming reverberations. "They are more than twenty times as powerful as the old slow tunes, each part striving for mastery and victory," it was said.

Billings' "fuguing pieces" revolutionized hymn singing in America. He wrote his own texts for them, and the words too were filled with passionate emotion. Harriet Beecher Stowe, who listened to one called "Old Majesty," wrote that there was in it "a grand, wild freedom, an energy of motion."

One of Billings' tunes, "Old Chester," became the marching

song for the Revolutionary soldiers, and the anthem "Be Glad Then, America" is filled with the joy and pride of the new nation.

2. The Middle Years

The middle years—the nineteenth century: the years when America was becoming a nation, the years when she was unsure of herself but sure of her strength; the years when many of her leaders leaned back on the culture of Europe, while, unheeded, a new music was developing among the people; the years when America was beginning to grow up.

The well-to-do and those who had the benefits of education considered music their special property in the early days of the republic. It was the rich who sat on the boards of directors of the orchestras and controlled the music of the concert stage. Prosperous merchants and their handsomely dressed wives made up the audience, and these powerful ones generally believed that only foreign performers were worth hearing. That was why in the first half of the nineteenth century a great many virtuosos crossed the ocean to perform for American audiences, and the patrons listened with the pride of exclusiveness. The Russian, Anton Rubinstein, who was the greatest pianist of his day, toured the United States with great success, and Ole Bull, who was Norway's famous violinist, performed before well-filled houses.

In 1850 Phineas T. Barnum, owner of the "greatest show on earth," saw a chance to outdo these performers by bringing Jenny Lind, the "Swedish nightingale," for an American concert tour. She sang with a voice of glorious sweetness, and Barnum enhanced her arrival by meeting her steamer and escorting her to her hotel in a coach drawn by four white horses.

But at the same time the well-dressed audiences were listening to concerts by European performers, another kind of music was growing, with its roots in the numerous singing societies that were so popular in America in those days.

There were singing groups among the people of every segment of society and in every part of the expanding country. In the cities like Milwaukee, Cleveland, Columbus, and Chicago, the citizens, many of them newly arrived from Europe, joined choral societies that performed Handel's oratorios and other classic works.

The rural folk of the South and West sang, too. There the "fuguing tunes" that Billings had made popular in Boston were worked into the hymn singing, and one little congregation after another welcomed the itinerant teacher who taught them to sing by what they called the "Fasola method." The teacher rode on horseback from one town to another, generally giving two lessons a week to each congregation before he rode on to the next. He was paid two dollars a night besides board and lodging for himself and his horse. He had no instrument save a pitch pipe or tuning fork, and he taught his pupils that there were but four notes—faw, sol, law, mi, and the scale ran: faw, sol, law, faw, sol, law, mi, faw.

A number of hymnbooks and songbooks used by the Fasola folk, as they were called, have been preserved. In them the notation is without staff lines or key signatures, and each of the four notes is represented by a character of a different shape, thus: faw, ◣ ; sol, ◗ ; law, ▮ ; mi, ◆ . The Fasola way of singing was therefore called singing by "shape notes." The *do, re, mi* system, newly brought over from the continent, was thought too elaborate and sophisticated for the rural folk. For a long time the "Fasola" and the "*do, re, mi*" systems of singing vied with one another, but "*do, re, mi*" finally won.

And now while the newly arrived immigrants sang the classic music they had brought to the New World with them and the traveling music masters taught them hymns by the Fasola method, a new kind of singing swept across the expanding country. This was the singing of the revival or camp meetings. The Reverend Francis Asbury, an itinerant Methodist minister, held the first revival meeting in 1800. After that he rode from place to place stirring the people to repentance until he had ridden 275,000 miles on horseback carrying out his enthusiastic work. Other ministers soon were riding back and forth across the frontier holding "revivals," and people from outlying districts traveled to the camping places to have their souls saved and to join in the singing. Sometimes they stayed several days, and the light of their campfires shone out through the dark at night.

It has been estimated that attendance at the revivals numbered anywhere from two thousand to twenty thousand people. Ministers of several different denominations preached, and Negroes as well as white people joined in. From Kentucky the movement spread to other places along the frontier, to the settlements beyond the Mississippi and back to New York, New Jersey, Connecticut, and Massachusetts.

As the ministers moved back and forth at these revival meetings exhorting the people to repent, a frenzy stirred the crowd, and they responded in song. Then the singers jerked and twitched and leaped into the air or sometimes fell fainting to the ground.

No instruments, not even tuning forks, were needed for the singing of the great revival hymns. The male voices carried the tune, their bass voices sounding a booming undertone, while the women sang an octave higher, sometimes reaching high C without realizing that this was any special feat.

> "O brethren will you meet me
> In Canaan's happy land?"

the minister would shout. And the crowd would answer with one voice,

> "By the grace of God, we'll meet you
> In Canaan's happy land!"

There was no thought of art in this singing; there was simply a rolling volume of sound, and the tunes—clear, stirring, and beautiful—have been woven into the fabric of America's music. The melody for "Mine eyes have seen the glory of the coming of the Lord" is one of these tunes.

One sect that joined in the revival meetings along the borders of Kentucky and Ohio were the Shakers, who called themselves "Believers in Christ's Second Appearing." They developed a large body of original, stirring, and sometimes gay tunes. One of them is "Simple Gifts," on which Aaron Copland, the twentieth-century composer, based part of the music for the ballet *Appalachian Spring*.

The Negroes joined in the great camp meetings with the white men and lifted their voices in the old revival hymns. But the Negroes knew a music of their own, and their gift was one of their contributions to the American culture, though apparently no one but Thomas Jefferson had noticed it.

The Negroes had brought their love of rhythm and melody with them from Africa. They had sung in all the misery of their passage on the slave ships, and had sung as slaves as they picked cotton or rowed the boats on the southern rivers.

> "Bendin' knees a-achin',
> Body racked with pain,
> I wish I was a child of God—"

they sang.

Not all the Negro songs were work songs; some of the finest ones were the religious "spirituals." Sometimes these spirituals were the background for a dance of religious ecstasy called a "shout." Then men, women, and children walked slowly, shuffling around in a circle one after another. And as they shuffled they sang the chorus of some spiritual, while a group of singers at the side of the room supplied the main body of the tune, slapping their hands on their knees to accent the rhythm. Sometimes European tunes or Methodist and Baptist hymns were used and slightly altered, and the singing generally had vocal effects that were hard to imitate. The rhythms were accented by stamping or clapping, or snapping of the fingers that brought a sound like an African gourd rattle.

As early as the 1830s white musicians and entertainers began to imitate the Negroes' music. They found no special beauty in it but thought it amusing. In 1830 the first minstrel show was held. Then Thomas Rice borrowed a Negro's clothes, blacked his face, and sang the "Jim Crow Song" in Pittsburgh, Pennsylvania. His performance was such a huge success that others were soon copying it.

In 1843, Dan Emmet started what he called the "Big Four Troupe of Minstrels" and went around from town to town giving shows. He had two "end men" and an interlocutor, all dressed in comic style with faces blackened with burnt cork, and they interspersed their songs with jokes. People looked forward to their coming to town and escorted them up from the railroad station in a grand procession with a brass band. It was Dan Emmet with a band of minstrels playing at Mechanics Hall in New York in 1859 who first sang "Dixie," that song that was to become so popular in the South though Dan Emmet, a Northerner, had written it.

The Negro minstrel songs were not really Negro songs at all. They were simply imitations of the Negro's way of singing, and they were sung in his happy, carefree style. Some of them were gay and lively, some sad, and always they were interspersed with jokes told in what purported to be Negro dialect.

Negro minstrel shows were the rage in the years before the Civil War, and a great many troupes toured the country. They might have been dismissed as simply an amusing and lively phase of America's life, had it not been for the fact that they helped to bring Stephen Foster into prominence. And Stephen Foster wrote songs of such sweetness and ingenuous simplicity that all Americans have loved them ever since. At the time he wrote them, however, Foster had to fight against middle-class respectability; it was not considered quite right to sing in the Negro dialect.

In some ways Stephen Foster's music was akin to Schubert's, for both men had a natural gift of melody. No one ever taught Foster music. Pittsburgh, where he grew up, was a frontier town; the river boatmen stopped there on their way down the Ohio River. There Stephen Foster's family were well-to-do; his father was mayor of Pittsburgh at one time. But they did not understand this son of theirs. They talked of his "idle, dreaming ways," and said he had a "strange talent for musicke." They wondered what they could do with him, and tried to get an appointment to West Point. A military career held no appeal for the youth, naturally; he drifted along until, in 1846, he went to Cincinnati where he worked as a bookkeeper.

All this time he was writing his unforgettable songs and publishing a few of them. Among his early ones were the familiar "Tioga Waltz," "Old Uncle Ned," and "Camptown Races."

The melodies for some of these songs were adapted from Irish folk tunes but many of them were his own. They were poignant, easy to understand and remember, and soon they were sung on every street corner. "Oh! Susanna" quickened the steps of the forty-niners as they pushed across the plains and the mountains to the west, and "Jeanie with the Light Brown Hair" was sung in numberless lamplighted parlors.

Many of Foster's songs were on Negro subjects, although up to the time "Old Folks at Home" was published he had never been south of the Ohio River. He had never seen the Suwannee River but like the sound of the name. He had gained whatever he knew of Negro music from church singing and minstrel shows.

All through the middle of the nineteenth century, while Americans were pushing toward the west, building up their cities and laying their railroads, the division continued between the classic tradition of Europe and the music the ordinary people enjoyed.

Americans seemed to be searching for a musical tradition of their own. There were a few serious composers but they were not generally encouraged. Take, for instance, Sidney Lanier of Georgia, a rare genius, a poet, and a talented flute player, the first flutist of the Peabody Symphony in Boston. He published several flute compositions and a number of songs, the words of many of which he wrote himself. When he died, at an early age, he left three unfinished symphonies, and most Americans had probably never even heard of him.

Louis Moreau Gottschalk of New Orleans, in whose veins flowed English, French, and noble Spanish blood, was much better known, for he was a polished and charming concert pianist, a friend of Berlioz and admired by Chopin. He wrote operas, symphonies, and oratorios that were quickly forgotten because they were imitations of European music. Much more significant were the piano piece *"La Bamboula"* and other compositions like it, based on the Negro dances and songs that he had heard as a boy on Congo Square in New Orleans. In spite of these he was not generally acclaimed as a composer of national reputation.

For in spite of the surge of popular singing by the Fasola folk, in spite of the rolling melodies of the camp meetings and the Negro rhythms, in spite of the gifts of Stephen Foster, America had no composer of national reputation; it appeared that she could not produce music of her own. Right into the middle of the nineteenth century, music for Americans was the music of Europe. It was on this premise that America founded her oratorio societies and her great symphony orchestras.

Her musical educators, too, believed that great music was necessarily European music. The orchestra leader Theodore Thomas gave the cities of the Middle West their first opportunity to hear chamber music and the playing of fine orchestras. He toured from city to city and was first to play Schumann, Brahms, and Wagner to American audiences.

Another conductor, Leopold Damrosch, came to this country from Germany in 1871, founded the Oratorio Society in 1873, and the New York Symphony Society in 1878. His orchestra was first to perform Berlioz' *Damnation of Faust* in America, and first to give a performance of Brahms' First Symphony. After 1882 when the Metropolitan Opera opened in New York City, and Damrosch was its first conductor, he introduced Wagnerian operas and brought a great many distinguished singers to this country to take part in them. His sons, Walter and Frank, also made valuable contributions to the education of Americans. And all this time Americans believed that Europeans had said the last word in music, that in a sense it was presumptuous to try to create anything different.

This was the belief of the group of musicians called the "Boston Classicists." Most of them had either studied in Germany or had German teachers, and the music they produced was both genteel and conventional. One of them, Daniel Gregory Mason, hailed their music as the "great classical revival in America."

John Knowles Paine, professor of music at Harvard, was one of the "Classicists," George Chadwick, director of the New England Conservatory of Music, another. Chadwick had been sent to Germany as a youth and had returned filled with enthusiasm for the laws of counterpoint and for the remote and legendary past. Arthur Foote, who was one of America's finest music teachers, was another of the Boston group. He wrote scholarly and beautiful chamber music, and Horatio Parker composed operas with choral music in contrapuntal style. Charles Martin Loeffler, a recluse and a mystic, was an authority on the Gregorian Chant and was interested in the old church modes of the Middle Ages, while Mrs. H. H. A. Beach, the first American woman to be a distinguished composer, wrote a Mass in E Flat for the Handel and Haydn Society, and so made the way easier for other American women composers of sound talent and training. Among them are

Mary Howe, Marion Bauer, and Gena Branscombe, as well as Ruth Crawford Seeger, who is an original and highly resourceful experimentalist.

All the members of the Boston group were scholarly and well trained, but their work did not contribute to the mainstream of American music. It might not be necessary to mention them at all, were it not for the fact that Edward MacDowell was for a time part of their group, and Americans at the end of the nineteenth century hailed Edward MacDowell as America's greatest composer.

MacDowell was in fact not considered by all to be a great composer, but he was the first composer to win nationwide and worldwide recognition for his "serious" compositions. He was born in New York City, the son of a prosperous businessman, and had been well educated so that at fifteen he was sent abroad to study music. He was taught in various places but found himself much at home in Germany.

He returned to America to marry Marion Nevins, who was also deeply interested in music, and with her he went abroad once more. Altogether he spent twelve years in Europe, most of them in Germany.

Back in Boston at thirty, he taught music and composed industriously so that his reputation grew. In 1896 he was invited to become head of the music department of Columbia University in New York. He filled this post for seven years, and resigned after a controversy with Nicholas Murray Butler, the University President. He conducted the Mendelssohn Glee Club for a while, but in 1905 his health failed.

MacDowell died in 1908 and his wife Marion, who lived until 1961, founded the MacDowell Colony in Peterboro, New Hampshire, where composers, artists, and writers may live and work in a congenial atmosphere. This is one of the leading colonies for creative workers in America. Other retreats of its kind are one at Tanglewood, Massachusetts; Yaddo at Saratoga Springs, New

York; and the Huntington Hartford Foundation in California.

MacDowell's piano compositions are his best known works. At first, perhaps because he had lived so long in Europe, they were patterned on European models. The titles of his four piano sonatas—*"Tragica," "Eroica," "Norse,"* and *"Keltic"*—reflect his interest in European mythology.

In time, however, though the style of his music did not change, it concerned itself with America. In 1891–92 he wrote his Second Orchestral Suite on American Indian themes. The tunes had been collected by Theodore Baker on American Indian reservations and published in his book *The Music of the North American Savages.* Other piano pieces that are well known today are his *Woodland Sketches,* his *Sea Pieces,* and his *Fireside Tales.*

But though MacDowell's eyes seemed to be turning toward America in this music, his work still reflected Grieg and Brahms. It was not until the beginning of the twentieth century that other composers began to create a truly American music. Strangely enough it was not an American but Antonín Dvořák, the Czech, who pointed the way.

3. New Music in a New World

In 1892 the eminent Czech conductor Antonín Dvořák was invited to be director of the National Conservatory of Music in New York. His coming was celebrated with a grand concert at which the Metropolitan Orchestra of eighty and a chorus of three hundred performed with several soloists. It was here that "America" was announced to be the national hymn and one of the patrons, Colonel T. W. Higginson, made an oration which had the grandiose title, *The New World of Columbus and the New World of Music.* The enormous audience greeted Dvořák enthusiastically; he was presented with a silver wreath.

Dvořák loved America. He spent hours at the Battery along New York Harbor watching the ocean steamers come and go, and he was fascinated with the railroad trains at the Grand Central station. He stayed in America three years, and while he was here he made what appeared to him an amazing discovery; he found that there was in America a rich treasure of music to which no one had paid any attention. He could not understand why American composers had not used American folk tunes for their themes, nor why they had not listened to the melodies the Negroes sang or to the rhythms of the Indians' music. Before he left America, Dvořák tried to express these ideas in what many believe to be his finest composition, the symphony *From the New World*. Its exquisite, full-bodied music is filled with awed wonder for the new land. He said he had not used Indian or Negro or other American themes in it. "I tried to write only in the spirit of those national American melodies," he said.

Dvořák's suggestion about national American melodies fell on responsive ears. When he left America at the end of the nineteenth century many Americans had an awareness that there was material for music in their own land. One of his most enthusiastic followers was Arthur Farwell.

Arthur Farwell was born in Minneapolis in 1872, had studied in Germany under the Humperdinck of Hansel and Gretel fame, and, returning to America, began to collect Indian tunes in the Southwest. He loved the exotic rhythm and color of this music, and wrote *Navajo War Dance for Chamber Orchestra, Impressions of the Wa-Wan [Omaha] Ceremony*, and other, similar compositions.

More important than Farwell's music, however, was his ability to spread his ideas. In 1901 he founded the Wa-Wan Press in Boston to encourage American composers and to foster distribution of their work. In 1905 he founded the American Music Society to promote American composition and to study the folk music of the Indian, the cowboy, and the Negro. Thirty-seven composers entered the Wa-Wan fold, and regional Wa-Wan centers sprang up across the country. Leaders of the group were

Henry Gilbert, Charles Wakefield Cadman, Cecil Burleigh, and Arthur Nevin.

The most distinguished member of the Wa-Wan group was Arthur Shepherd whose First Symphony, *Horizons*, reflects the size and breadth of the West. It was based in part on cowboy songs like "The Old Chisholm Trail," "The Dying Cowboy," "The Dogie Song," and on a Mormon hymn, "Horizons," and it was a landmark in American music.

The Wa-Wan Press lasted only until 1912 yet its influence cannot be overestimated.

Now interest in American music became more and more widespread. Carl Sandburg, the poet, traveled up and down the country collecting songs for his *American Song Bag* which he called a "rag bag of strips, stripes, and streaks of color from nearly all ends of the earth." Others were soon following Sandburg's example, collecting songs as one might collect postage stamps—recording, classifying, and discussing them, and just singing them for sheer enjoyment. Much of the material these men and women collected is now in the Library of Congress archives, where it has been made accessible to the country and to the world.

There were all sorts of songs in these collections. Among them were the songs the Negroes sang, some of them spirituals and "shouts," religious in character, some work songs and "blues."

Some collectors specialized in the songs the cowboys sang as they drove the cattle north over the long trail in the spring, or sang to quiet them when they were restless at night. John A. Lomax made a specialty of collecting these.

Others collected the songs of the lumberjacks in the woods of Michigan, Wisconsin, and Minnesota, and Maine. And some went to the New England coast to record the fishermen's songs. There were songs of an Irish flavor sung in New York and other big cities, and hobo songs, and railroad songs, and barber-shop quartets.

Up in the mountains of Kentucky, Tennessee, the Carolinas,

and Virginia, the collectors found songs that had been brought from England when those places were first settled in the seventeenth century. Civilization had made little impress on the people of those regions, and the changes that had come to America had not touched them. They were still singing the old English ballads as they had been sung since the days of Queen Elizabeth. Generally their singing was unaccompanied, but sometimes they had a fiddle or a guitar, and occasionally a dulcimer, which was a kind of elongated violin with three strings that are struck with hammers. Two of these strings were drones and the third carried the melody.

So, gradually, Americans discovered that their own land was overflowing with music; many composers began using American folk tunes in their music as Haydn had once used Slavonic folk tunes in his.

Perhaps the Negroes had more influence than any other folk on the New American music, for they developed ragtime which gradually evolved into that form for which New Orleans was to become famous: "jazz," a Creole word meaning to speed up.

In that city there were frequent parades, wedding processions, and funerals, which were always enlivened with band music. In time Negroes joined some of these bands, and in their hands the white men's instruments took on a different character. For the rhythms they played were the rhythms they had brought from Africa, the tunes of the cakewalks of the southern plantations, the syncopated piano playing, called "ragtime," so popular in the 1890s, which reached its peak between 1905 and 1910, the spirituals, "shouts," and "blues." All these were combined in the music they played on the white men's instruments. When finally they began to use this music in the New Orleans dance halls and when it was brought thence to Chicago and New York, jazz had been born. That was in 1915.

The Dixieland jazz bands were made up of three parts. There were the "brass" which included the trumpets and trombones;

the "reeds" which were the saxophones, clarinets, oboes, and flutes; and the "rhythm," or drums, piano, banjo, and string bass. Recently the harpsichord has often replaced the piano, and wood blocks, Chinese tom-toms, gongs, cymbals, anvils, castanets, xylophones, and glockenspiels have been used for percussion instruments. These do not necessarily improve on the playing of an inventive drummer who uses a bass drum, a snare drum, or an assortment of kitchen pans.

The craze for this music spread quickly. In the decade after the First World War people were dancing to it in widespread places—in Paris, London, Hong Kong, and Cairo. Composers in many countries were soon writing pieces that tried to catch its spirit. Ravel, Stravinsky, Milhaud, and Hindemith all used what was called in Europe *"le Jazz américain."*

But essentially jazz is more American than anything else. George Gershwin said of it, "Jazz is the result of the energy stored up in America. It is a very energetic kind of music." And he wrote, "Jazz I regard as an American folk music; not the only one, but a powerful one which is in the blood and feeling of the American people more than any other style of folk music. I believe that it can be made the basis of serious symphonic works of lasting value, in the hands of a composer with talent for both jazz and symphonic music."

George Gershwin, himself such a composer, was born in Brooklyn in 1898, studied harmony and composition under good teachers, and by the time he was fourteen had written his first popular song. At sixteen he was a "song plugger" for Remick, publisher of sheet music, but he was writing popular tunes on the side. At twenty-two he was commissioned to write a score for George White's *Scandals* and made a big hit with his song "Suwannee" which Al Jolson sang. After that one musical comedy followed another: *Lady Be Good* in 1924; *Funny Face* in 1927; *Girl Crazy* in 1930; and, topping these, in 1931 *Of Thee I Sing*, which won a Pulitzer Prize. Gershwin's musical comedies were an enormous success, and it looked as if writing them would be a successful career.

Then, in 1924, Paul Whiteman, the band leader, gave a concert at Aeolian Hall in New York and invited Gershwin to write a piece that embodied jazz elements in symphonic form. In three weeks he had completed the piano score for *Rhapsody in Blue*. It was orchestrated and performed February 12, 1924, with Whiteman conducting and Gershwin acting as piano soloist.

So Gershwin had become a composer of "serious music." He continued to compose songs for Tin Pan Alley but he wrote music also for Carnegie Hall. Sometimes he brought the two styles together in a way that had not been done before.

In 1925 Walter Damrosch, conductor of the New York Symphony, commissioned him to write a composition for his orchestra and he composed the Concerto in F for Piano and Orchestra. When this was performed December 3, 1925, Gershwin himself was the soloist, and he had done the orchestration.

An orchestral tone poem, "An American in Paris," followed. This is a gem. The wit and brilliance of the work, the score of which is equipped with Parisian taxicab horns, has made it a permanent number in the orchestral repertoire.

Gershwin wrote a film comedy called *Delicious*, in 1931, in which there was a sequence of New York street scenes. He used a theme which sounded like the beating down of rivets to express the restless energy of the city, and around this theme he composed a rhapsody for piano and orchestra. At first he called this "Rhapsody in Rivets" but later changed its title to the Second Rhapsody. It was performed by the Boston Symphony under the direction of Serge Koussevitsky.

The *Cuban Overture* of 1934 was Gershwin's last orchestral work, for now he turned to opera. The melodious, powerful *Porgy and Bess* tells the tragic story of Porgy, a crippled Negro who lives in Catfish Row on the Charleston, South Carolina, waterfront and whose woman Bess leaves him to go to New York with another man. The music, with its sultry harmonies, its bitter irony, and warm nostalgia, could not have been written by a European. It is completely American.

Gershwin's piano preludes are striking and full of personality. His music appeared to be at full tide; and who knows what other masterpieces he might have produced had he not died when he was only thirty-nine?

While George Gershwin was fascinating his audiences by his combination of jazz and serious music, another boy from Brooklyn was making his mark on the American scene. This was Aaron Copland, who was not only to become one of the most outstanding composers in America, but whose name was honored in Europe as well. He was to have a tremendous influence on American musical life.

Aaron Copland was born in 1900 on a side street in Brooklyn. "Music was the last thing anyone would have connected with it," he said of that street. His family were immigrant Russian Jews; his father was a tailor. But in spite of this, they managed to give the boy a good musical education. Rubin Goldmark, the composer, who was also Gershwin's teacher, encouraged Copland, and he was sent to the American School at Fontainebleau where he became the first pupil of Nadia Boulanger.

Nadia Boulanger was an inspiration to several American composers besides Copland. Among them were Roy Harris, Walter Piston, Douglas Moore, and Virgil Thomson. It was Nadia Boulanger who gave Copland his first real chance. She commissioned him to write a concerto for organ and orchestra which she was to conduct for the New York Philharmonic. He reworked this concerto later without the organ, making it into his first symphony. At twenty-nine he won the RCA prize of $5000 for his *Dance Symphony,* and his musical career was really under way.

At the same time Copland was winning this early recognition, he was doing many things to advance the cause of music in America. He soon became well known as a conductor, pianist, and speaker. He has been head of the composition department at Tanglewood's Music Festival in the Berkshires since 1940 when it was founded. He helped the cause of contemporary American music by founding the Copland-Sessions Concerts and the American Festival of Contemporary Music at Yaddo in Saratoga Springs. He was chairman of the League of Composers and founder of the American Composers Alliance.

Copland, the gifted musician, educator, and organizer, is also a talented writer. *What to Listen for in Music* is intended for laymen, *Our New Music* for students and musicians, while *Music and Imagination* is a collection of essays based on lectures he gave at Harvard while holding the Charles Eliot Norton chair.

But what of his music? It falls into two definite categories. There are his most serious works—the granite-hard Piano Variations, the tension-filled Statement for Orchestra, and the *Short Symphony*. Different from these are the works with a folk-song flavor that appeal more to the general public. These are statements in the simplest possible terms, employing with great skill, tenderness, and imagination the music and songs of the people. "El Salon, Mexico," is a colorful Mexican-inspired work which he wrote after a visit there; *Billy the Kid* and *Rodeo* are lively ballet scores, and *Appalachian Spring*, with the ballet score he wrote for Martha Graham, is based in part on the old Shaker song, "Simple Gifts."

In some later works Copland adopted the twelve-tone system, especially in Piano Quartet and Piano Fantasy and in *Twelve Poems of Emily Dickinson*. Yet his music is his own no matter what style he employs. Beautifully constructed, it pulses with life, rhythmic excitement, optimism, and big-heartedness. Rural life as well as big-city life are reflected in it.

Meantime Roy Harris came out of the West, thrilling those who were open-minded enough to listen to his sturdy music. He gloried in his American origins; his mother and father had been pioneers who traveled across the Kentucky border in an oxcart, while he himself was born, February 12, 1898, in a log cabin in Oklahoma.

He was still a boy when his family moved to California. There, when he was old enough, he spent four years driving a truck for a local dairy, but at the same time he was able to take a few piano lessons and to play the clarinet in the school band. Harris went to the Southern Branch of the University of California, and there he began to study harmony under Arthur Farwell. And later he went to Paris, where Nadia Boulanger taught him harmony.

After that when he was back in America Serge Koussevitsky became interested in his work and when his First Symphony was performed by the Boston Symphony Orchestra, with Koussevitsky himself conducting, Koussevitsky called this work, "the first truly tragic symphony by an American composer."

Harris explained the music thus: "In the first movement I tried to capture the mood of adventure and physical exuberance; in the second, of the pathos which seems to underlie all human existence; in the third the will to power and action."

Harris' Second and Third Symphonies were also performed by the Boston Symphony Orchestra, the Second in 1936 and the Third in 1939. The Third was a resounding success. The Boston Symphony gave ten performances of it within a year, and other American orchestras gave it thirty-three performances in 1941–42. There were also several performances by European orchestras and numerous recordings.

The Third Symphony has been called Roy Harris' finest work. It has canyon-long themes, desert-fresh harmonies and a rough-hewn counterpoint.

The *Folk Song Symphony*, as Symphony Number Four has been called, is intended to be performed by a high school chorus with professional orchestra in order, Harris said, "to bring about a cultural cooperation and understanding between the high school, college, and community choruses of our cities with their symphonic orchestras." The folk songs in it are taken from the collections of Carl Sandburg and John and Alan Lomax. There are songs of the Civil War time such as "When Johnny Comes Marching Home," songs of the Western plains—"Bury Me Not on the Lone Prairie," "As I Walked Out on the Streets of Laredo," the Mountaineer love song, "I'm Goin' Away for to Stay a Little While," and the camp meeting hymn, "De Trumpets Sounds It in My Soul." The chorus returns to a cowboy song in the finale with "The Gal I Left Behind Me" and a coda is added, "Good Night, Ladies."

"This music is nothing if not a hundred per cent United States of America," one critic wrote after he had heard it performed in Cleveland.

Roy Harris has written works for band, chorus, voice and piano, piano and orchestra, and various chamber music compositions. He has written seven symphonies, one of them based on Lincoln's Gettysburg Address. In all his music he seems obsessed with the idea of portraying the American character in music.

Our people . . . have qualities of heroic strength . . . determination . . . will to struggle . . . faith in our destiny. We are possessed of a fierce, driving power . . . optimistic, young, rough and ready . . . and I am convinced that our mechanistic age has not destroyed an appreciation of more tender moods. . . .

That is the kind of music Roy Harris has created—"a hundred per cent U.S.A."

There were, of course, many other composers whose music reflected their American background. There was the unpredictable Virgil Thomson, who liked to work with old American hymn tunes; and Douglas Moore, who wrote *Moby Dick* and *The Pageant of P. T. Barnum*, and other works, wanting, he said, to reflect in music "the exciting quality of life, tradition and country which I feel all about me." *The Ballad of Baby Doe* is one of his best recent works. It is an opera in two acts which tells the story of a silver miner in Leadville, Colorado, how he made a huge fortune, and was ruined when the United States adopted the gold standard.

Ernest Bloch writes music with a strongly Hebraic flavor; he has also written an epic rhapsody for chorus and orchestra called "America." Randall Thompson and Herbert Elwell belong with these: America inspired them too.

American patriotism, of course, was not confined to the United States. There were many composers south of the border who depended on the folk music of Latin America for their inspiration and who drew rich, exotic music from this source. One of these was Heitor Villa-Lobos. Villa-Lobos was a native of Rio de Janeiro, and he traveled through the Brazilian jungle to faraway villages and settlements to gather songs and legends from the Indian and African settlers. He studied for a time at the great musical centers of Europe but soon returned to Brazil. There he developed a new system of teaching music in the public schools and eventually became director of musical education. He was very active in promoting choral singing and music festivals in his country, and he was a tremendously fertile composer; he wrote over two thousand compositions. Almost all of these reflect his intense admiration for his native folk music. He combines impressionism with spontaneous vigor and tropical luxuriance, and often uses unusual native instruments.

His symphonic poem "Amazon" is one of his outstanding works. It tells the story of an Indian girl in a tropic wilderness.

His *Chôros*, which are orchestral compositions for different combinations of instruments, are rich with Brazilian Indian rhythms and atmosphere; while in *Bachianas Brasileiras* he pays homage to Johann Sebastian Bach by combining Bach's baroque style with Brazilian folk music.

Carlos Chávez of Mexico is another distinguished Latin American. He grew up during the stirring years of the Mexican Revolution and his awareness of the great Incan and Mayan civilizations prevented him from spineless imitation of European art. The paintings of Diego Rivera and José Orozco glorify the Indian and mestizo, and his music with its insistent rhythms and somber fiery tunes suggests their characters in a like way. His *Sinfonia*

India uses Mexican Indian song and dance tunes, while *Sinfonia Antigone,* though it is inspired by Jean Cocteau's version of Sophocles' *Antigone,* is Mexican in its feeling.

While love of country and for native folk music inspired many great American composers in the twentieth century, there were many who chose their own style of music. Their credo was summed up by Virgil Thomson, who said, "The way to write American music is simple. All you have to do is to be an American and then write any kind of music you wish."

So you could make a long list of other American composers who chose to work in their independent style and it would be hard not to omit some important names. But among them would certainly be Walter Piston, Charles Tomlinson Griffes, Lukas Foss, Peter Mennin, Norman Dello Joio, Howard Hanson, Roger Sessions, William Schumann, Gian-Carlo Menotti, Kurt Weill, Marc Blitzstein, Leonard Bernstein, and Samuel Barber—Samuel Barber is probably the finest lyric composer of his generation in America.

And there are also those who are followers of Schoenberg and are experimenters with the twelve-tone scale. They are Carl Ruggles, Elliot Carter, Wallingford Riegger, Gunther Schuller, Milton Babbit, Leon Kirchner, and many others.

One of the strongest and most original of all the twentieth-century composers in America, however, was the insurance man from Danbury, Connecticut, Charles Ives, whose work was unrecognized until near the end of his life.

Charles Ives' father was a band leader in Danbury and a violin teacher as well as an experimenter in the properties of sound. He made his son aware of the marvels of musical tone, of minute discriminations of pitch, of the accidental melodies of outdoors, of bells and bird cries. The youth himself studied acoustics at Yale and later was organist in various churches in Danbury, New Haven, and New York. One of his cardinal principles was that music should not be separated from life, but that a musician must take part in the life around him. He wrote as an afterword in one of his collections of songs, "An interest in any art-activity from poetry to baseball, is better, broadly speaking, if held as a part of life, or of a life . . ."

That was why he worked as a businessman by day, and wrote his music at night, trying to reflect the life he knew and remembered in his orchestral and chamber music, and in his songs.

His first published work, a piano sonata, bore the title, *Concord, Massachusetts, 1840–60*. It had four movements which he called "Emerson," "Hawthorne," "The Alcotts," and "Thoreau."

When this sonata was first published in 1919 musicians were terrified by its technical difficulty, so it was not performed until 1939 when it was played at the Town Hall in New York. Then Lawrence Gilman, writing in the *New York Herald Tribune,* paid it an extraordinary tribute. He wrote:

This sonata is exceptionally great music—it is, indeed, the greatest music composed by an American, and the most deeply and essentially American in impulse and implication. It has passion, tenderness, humor, simplicity, homeliness. It has imaginative and spiritual vastness. It has wisdom and beauty, and profundity, and a sense of the encompassing terror and splendor of human life and human destiny . . . a sense of those mysteries that are both human and divine.

In this piano sonata, as in all his music, Ives was a real experimenter. He used quarter-tones, jazz patterns, asymmetrical rhythms, wide melodic leaps, polytonality, intricate cross rhythms, and tone clusters made up of whole blocks of notes. When it suited him, he wrote his music without key signatures or bar lines. He was an amalgamator who fused the roots of American folklore with European traditions into music that was funny, powerful, virile, and wholly original.

Because he was a very proud man, he never made any effort to have his music performed, and the complexity of his symphonies made them difficult to perform. He was very successful in business, and after a hard day at his office he went back to his barn in Connecticut to write his music with the help and encouragement of his wife, but most musicians never heard what he wrote. He had some of his work printed privately and donated copies of it to friends or to libraries.

In 1951, the New York Philharmonic Symphony Orchestra performed his Second Symphony half a century after he had written it. Ives had not the courage to attend the performance for the emotional strain would have been too much for him, but he heard it with satisfaction on the radio.

Acknowledged after that as one of the greatest of American composers, he died in 1954 at the age of eighty. He had not composed any music since he was forty-five, but quietly, almost secretly, he had secured himself a place among the great.

Living as he did in seclusion Ives' experiments seemed to reach into the future. He was fascinated with all the technical experiments with which the most modern composers of the present day concern themselves. It is a pity that he had no opportunity to work with the electronic music which today is opening up a whole new world of sound.

CHAPTER THIRTY-FOUR

The Scientist Musicians

B E F O R E the twentieth century, musicians found their inspiration in the past. Some of them drew strength and confidence from the treasures of folk song; others depended on the
old masters of earlier centuries; and there were the disciples of
Schoenberg and Webern who worked with the twelve-tone scale.

But now, in the new age, a group of composers arose who
turned their backs on the past and looked toward the future. They
were influenced to some extent by the non-representational painters, the Cubists and Futurists. Revolutionists, they were bent on
breaking all the established musical rules, and wanted to do

281

away with all the old traditional forms and the familiar instrumental sounds.

This musical revolution started in Italy in the early years of the century. The Italians called it *Futurismo*. Instead of conventional instrumental sounds, the new Italian composers worked street sounds into their compositions, the shriek of factory whistles, the clanking of machinery, and all the strident noises of modern civilization.

Futurismo did not last long: it was forgotten in the suffering of the First World War. But it appeared again in France in the 1940s. There factory noises, machine sounds, the sounds of railroad locomotives, and of airplanes were woven into what the French called "concrete music."

But the twentieth century is an age of science. The musical experimenters were no longer content with trying to imitate modern sounds with old musical instruments. They began to work in laboratories with electrical devices.

They recorded the sounds they produced on tape and wove them into their compositions together with voices and conventional instruments. This was how the new "electronic music" was made.

The new electronic instruments were sometimes constructed like conventional instruments, but the sounds they made were altered and controlled by electricity. There were also specially developed new instruments. One of these was the therémin, an upright pole which produces sound by the movement of the hand near it. Another is the *"ondes martenot,"* a keyboard instrument whose notes, played one at a time, are said to resemble the sound of waves. Other new and ingenious instruments that produce strange new sounds are being constantly developed.

In the 1920s both the concrete and early electronic music had a great vogue among the avant-garde in New York. One of their chief advocates was Edgar Varèse.

Varèse had been born in France, but America was his adopted

country. At first he was interested in the music of Stravinsky, Schoenberg, and Bartók, but he rejected these, and gave his work new artistic form, using a new musical language. His compositions throb with the thousand noises of a big city. Gradually he stopped using conventional instruments altogether and worked with electronic instruments, for he said these were "the first step towards the liberation of music."

At first the public rejected Varèse's work but after the Second World War his genius was recognized, and now he is considered one of the outstanding musical experimentalists.

Varèse's longest work, *Ionization*, uses thirty-five different percussion instruments, including bongo drums, bells, chimes, piano, scrapers, anvils, high and low sirens, sleigh bells, and a lion's roar. This work has been called brilliant and original. Varèse's "*Poème Electronique*" was written in 1958 for the Brussels World's Fair. It lasts only eight minutes but was repeated over and over through four hundred loudspeakers that carried it to every part of the Fair grounds.

Varèse of course was only one of many who experimented with the new music. In America there was Henry Cowell, who got new effects on the piano by striking the keyboard with the forearm or the full hand; and John Cage of San Francisco who tries to create new sounds by using a "prepared piano" whose strings are studded here and there with wood blocks and clothes pins. Sometimes he employs two people, one to strike the keys, the other to pluck the strings. In this way he makes of the piano a percussion ensemble.

Milton Babbit, a professor of music at Princeton University, has delved into higher mathematics and into the complex permutations of Schoenberg's twelve-tone system. He has composed a number of musical works and written a number of articles on his theories. He is head of the Columbia-Princeton electronic laboratory where a good many of the new composers are working.

The experimentalists are not confined to America. In Germany

Karl Heinz Stockhausen tries for pure sounds and colors with electronic tape and "loose organization"; that is, there are no fixed beginnings, no fixed ends to his works. In France, Pierre Boulez, who is the pupil of Messiaen, has created a sensation with his strange work called *Le Marteau Sans Maître*. And George Antheil made a stir in Paris by writing *Ballet Méchanique* in which he uses automobile horns and hammers. "I scored a ballet for eight pianos, a pianola, and an airplane propeller," he said. The night the *Ballet Méchanique* was first performed in Paris was a rainy one. Most of the audience carried umbrellas, which they opened in the concert hall to ward off what they termed "the cacophony of modern music as created by this young genius."

All these experimentalists have one driving force. It is their desire for pure sound and new colors and combinations.

Is what they are composing really music at all? Are all these experiments pointing to unimaginable splendors of sound, as they claim? Who can say?

Most people hesitate to accept what is so new and strange. But this has always been true. We can hardly believe that the great classical masters once met with disapproval. Bach's *St. Matthew Passion* when it was performed at St. Thomas Church in Leipzig created a commotion unworthy of a church congregation. Many of Beethoven's symphonies were considered "barbaric." A contemporary connoisseur said of one of the most beautiful Mozart quartets that it was crude and had "no lasting value."

In the nineteenth century Brahms, Wagner, and Richard Strauss were often victims of newspaper slander. The riots caused by Stravinsky's *The Rite of Spring* in Paris and by Schoenberg's F Sharp Minor Quartet in Vienna are recent history.

Yet obviously Bach, Beethoven, and Mozart, as well as Brahms, Wagner, and Richard Strauss, now have their undisputed places, and Stravinsky, Bartók, and Schoenberg are becoming familiar figures; we can hear their music now without a tremor. For the human ear has an infinite capacity for adjustment, given time and opportunity. And future generations, undertaking their space travel, may find the music that startles us exhilarating.

Music needs constant renewal by interpreters, players and singers, for it exists only as they make it exist. Aaron Copland has written, "Music is in a continuous state of becoming."

Today music is flowing across America with a magnificent sweep. Here the high-school band blares out enthusiastic rhythms, there the suburban symphony plays with more enthusiasm still. There are bandstand concerts in many city parks, and young people with their guitars sing folk songs everywhere. The recording companies are turning out disks by the millions, and some of them are the music of Orlando di Lasso or of Mozart, but some are that of more ephemeral talents—Paul Anka or Connie Francis.

At Tanglewood, Massachusetts, on summer nights rapt audiences sit on the grass to listen while the Boston Symphony Orchestra performs classic music; in the darkness of the giant colosseum in New York, other music comes sweeping through the summer nights. *Birdland* on Broadway is the center for the latest experiments in creative jazz, and at the Lincoln Center for the Performing Arts the largest of the beautiful group of new buildings is the Philharmonic Hall, constructed according to the latest acoustical principles.

Composers, performers, conductors, and listeners—all are caught up and transported by the power of this music with its turbulence of styles. For this age is "one of the richest and most beautiful in musical history," the Belgian Paul Collaer has written. And lame William Billings' song is vibrant still—"Be Glad Then, America."

The Meaning of Some Musical Terms

Index

The Meaning of Some Musical Terms

Absolute music. This is music which does not depend on any literary, historical, or other extra-musical idea or suggestion. The classic instrumental music of the eighteenth and early nineteenth centuries is for the most part absolute music.

Allemande. French name for an early German dance. It is in 2/2 or 4/4 time, of moderate tempo, and generally in a pensive mood. Bach and others used it often for the opening section of an instrumental dance suite.

Antiphonal chant. This kind of chant was first practiced by the ancient Hebrews. It is the responsive singing of two or more choirs, one choir divided into two or more parts, or a soloist and a choir. In the seventeenth century at St. Mark's Cathedral in Venice these divided groups sang to each other across the nave.

Aria. Italian: air, melody. A type of song, artful in form, elaborate in execution, used in operas, oratorios, and cantatas. Handel's arias are often written in the style of *aria da capo;* that is, they consist of three sections: the first or opening section, followed by the second contrasting one, and then by a return of the first section, often with added flourishes. An aria by which a singer may demonstrate his versatility is often the emotional high point of an opera.

Atonal. Not in any key. The term is often applied to the twelve-tone system created mainly by Schoenberg (see page 235), which disregards tonal centers and the use of traditional harmonies.

Ballade. From Italian *ballare,* to dance. In ancient times a ballade was an air that accompanied dancing. Later a ballade developed into a narrative song of several verses, often commemorating a historical event. In recent times the term ballade has been used for instrumental compositions, either solo or orchestral, which suggest a narrative background. Chopin's four Ballades for the Piano are well known.

Ballet. A theatrical combination—music, dancing, and pantomime. where Lully wrote comedy-ballets in the sixteenth century. Later one The ballet was very popular as court entertainment especially in France, of the most popular ballets was Tchaikovsky's *Nutcracker Suite.* Among

289

the best-known modern ballets are Stravinsky's *The Firebird, Petrouchka,* and *The Rite of Spring.* Ravel and Prokofiev have also used this form successfully, and Aaron Copland, an American, has used it in *Billy the Kid, Rodeo,* and *Appalachian Spring.*

Brass. The collective name for instruments made of metal whose tones are produced by blowing through a cup or a funnel-shaped mouthpiece. Among the brasses, a symphony orchestra often contains horns, trumpets, trombones, and a tuba.

Canon. A form of polyphony in which a single voice or instrument is echoed by other voices or instruments according to strict rules. Bach employed this form with magnificent variety in such works as his "Musical Offering," and his "Goldberg Variations."

Cantata. From Italian *cantare,* to sing. A composition which is sung, as opposed to a *sonata,* a piece to be played. A cantata may be a large work for solo singers and chorus with orchestral accompaniment. Bach's cantatas are outstanding classic examples. Stravinsky, Bartók, and others have written compositions of this kind in the modern idiom.

Cantus firmus. Latin: fixed song. It is a melody, often plain song or some other religious tune, used as a basis around which other melodies wind in contrapuntal style. Many compositions built on this device were composed between the fourteenth and seventeenth centuries.

Capriccio. A short instrumental piece in a lively whimsical mood which has been called "fancy free." This form was very popular in the seventeenth and eighteenth centuries.

Catch. A short fragment which was originally a round, written as one continuous melody in which each succeeding singer "catches" up a part in turn with a lighthearted and jesting effect.

Chamber music. Intimate music designed to be performed in a room or small hall by a group of players or singers, all of them soloists. The literature of chamber music contains some of the most exquisite of masterworks.

This music was popular in the Middle Ages when lute, viol, and other contemporary instruments were used. The classical masters confined themselves to instruments used in symphony orchestras. Contemporary composers often delight in unconventional combinations. In America Gunther Schuller has achieved expressive originality in chamber music for brass ensemble.

Chorale. Catholic choral plain song or a metrical hymn of the Protestant Church intended to be sung by the congregation and favored in the sixteenth century by Martin Luther, who adapted it from plain song. Bach used chorales extensively in his arrangements, preludes, and large choral works.

Chord. Two or more tones sounded at the same moment. It usually refers, however, to a group of at least three tones.

Chromatic tone. A tone which does not belong to a given major or minor key, and is therefore an "outsider."

Coda. Italian: tail. It is a passage added after the formal completion of the work, like a last farewell. Beethoven enlarged the structure of his codas and often gave them climactic importance.

Concerto. A composition for instruments which features a solo part in contrast with an orchestra. Mozart helped to crystallize its classical form into three movements.

He wrote concertos for both violin and piano. Beethoven wrote five piano concertos and one concerto for violin which are very popular, while Tchaikovsky's Piano Concerto in B-Flat Minor is among his best works. Many contemporaries also have used this form. Among them are Shostakovich, Bartók, and Schoenberg. Among the American composers of concertos are Samuel Barber and Leon Kirchner with his Concerto for Piano.

Counterpoint. A style in which a given melody, called the *cantus firmus,* is countered by or poised against opposing melodies. Counterpoint reached its first climax in the Netherlands in the sixteenth century. Orlando di Lasso, Palestrina, Tomás Luis de Victoria and others composed immensely complicated counterpoint.

One of the first treatises on counterpoint was written by Johann Joseph Fux, who lived between 1660 and 1741. It is called *Gradus ad Parnassum.*

Courante. An ancient French dance of lively character which was later incorporated into the eighteenth-century dance suite.

Dissonance. Another word for discord. A cluster of tones that seem to jar—the opposite of a consonance or concord. However, the concept of jarring or restful harmonies has undergone a constant change from one century to another. In our times many new combinations of tones have been admitted to the legitimate family of "consonance." The twelve-tone music threatens a complete upheaval in this harmonic concept.

Folk song. A song which reflects the musical character and temperament of a nation or region, and whose author is not known. Transmitted from one singer to another, these songs may have many variants. Folk songs are often filled with melodic and rhythmic charm, and have been sources of inspiration to many composers. The full importance of folk songs has been realized only in modern times. Many important composers have collected and studied them. Foremost among these was Béla Bartók, who searched for them in three continents. In America

Arthur Farwell drew attention to the songs of the American Indians, while Carl Sandburg and many others collected songs, including those of the Negroes.

Fugue. A movement in which two or more "voices" combine in developing a single theme in a contrapuntal manner.

Gigue. A rapid, reeling country dance often in 6/8 or 6/4 time. The gigue was used as a last movement in many eighteenth-century dance suites.

Gregorian chant. See Plain song.

Harmony. The science of combining chords in a well-organized sequence. *Treatise on Harmony,* the first book on this subject, was written in the eighteenth century by the French composer Jean Philippe Rameau.

Homophony. A style of composition which employs a single melody accompanied by chords or broken chords. The term may be contrasted to polyphony, in which several melodies are woven together.

Impromptu. An instrumental composition in one movement without elaborate form or development. It may sound as if it had been conceived at the moment, or improvised. The Impromptus for the piano by Schubert and Chopin are well known.

Jazz. Music characterized by duple time, insistent syncopations, and great melodic suppleness. It originated in the improvisations of Negro musicians in New Orleans, and its African flavor has influenced many American and European composers. Blues, ragtime, and swing are varieties of jazz.

Key. The idea that a composition—or a section thereof—is built on a scale to which the first or *key*note gives its name.

Leitmotif. German: leading motive. It is a musical phrase of striking characterization used to describe and recall a character, idea, situation, or object such as a sword or a ring, and it is used recurringly. Richard Wagner employed many leitmotifs in his music-dramas.

Lied. German: song. It describes a type of concert song with which the German composers of the nineteenth and early twentieth centuries enriched the vocal musical literature.

Franz Schubert wrote over six hundred lieder, and Schumann, Brahms, and Hugo Wolf also wrote lieder of great beauty.

Madrigal. A lyric poem set to polyphonic music. It may employ from three to eight voices, usually unaccompanied, though sometimes instruments double the voice parts. The madrigal originated in Italy in the fourteenth century, but had another great period there and in England in the sixteenth.

Major and minor scales. The two principal groups of scales used in

Western music. All major scales and all minor scales of the same variety (there are two varieties of minor scale) are identical as to the intervals between the tones that make them up. But every major scale differs from every minor scale in the width of some of these intervals. This results in a very striking difference of mood between them, so that it is often said, "Majors are glad, minors are sad," though this is not always true.

Mass. The form of liturgy used in the Roman Catholic Church, celebrating and mystically repeating the sacrifice of Christ on the Cross. It is divided into varying parts (the Proper) and unvarying parts (the Ordinary). The sung parts of the Ordinary have been set to music by many of the great composers. Bach, Mozart, Schubert, and Beethoven wrote monumental Masses.

Melisma. A florid melodic ornament consisting of a group of notes sung on a single syllable.

Melody. A progression of single tones which differ in pitch and form a definite pattern.

Minuet. An ancient French country dance that in time became popular at the royal court. Bach and others incorporated it into dance suites. In the eighteenth century Haydn, Mozart, and Beethoven made it the third movement of their symphonies. Beethoven transformed it into the symphonic scherzo.

Mode. The term "mode" originally described scales originated by the ancient Greeks. These were named for the various Greek provinces —Phrygian, Ionian, Dorian, and so on. In the middle ages the Church adopted and altered these old Greek modes by pitching them a whole step down. Many folk songs are modal.

As time passed most of the old Greek and Church modes were dropped. By the sixteenth and seventeenth centuries only the major and minor modes remained. These are the modes in general use today. However, recent composers such as Mussorgsky, Satie, and Debussy have gone back to old modes for color effects.

Monochord. An ancient device with one string and a movable bridge which raised or lowered its pitch. It originated in ancient Egypt and was used by Pythagoras in Greece in his experiments in sound and musical theory.

Motet. In the middle ages a motet was a choral composition in elaborate contrapuntal style which combined two or more melodies with different texts, sometimes in different languages. In more recent times the motet has been a sacred choral composition on an anthem-like text.

Neumes. The signs used in early medieval musical notation.

Nocturne. A short instrumental composition in a pensive, romantic mood. The first piano nocturnes were written by the Irish composer John Field. Chopin took over the form and style in his book of nocturnes and so brought this form of composition to its full flowering.

Opera. A musical drama, with scenery and costumes, which combines voices and instruments and often includes dancing. The first opera was created in Italy about 1600 and was properly named *"dramma per la musica."*

Opera is now the national pastime in Italy. The most popular operas of our time are those by the Italians Verdi and Puccini, the operas of Richard Wagner, and the French opera *Carmen* by Bizet, as well as *Boris Godounov* by the Russian Moussorgsky.

Contemporary American composers have made notable contributions to the repertoire of operas.. Outstanding among these are George Gershwin's *Porgy and Bess,* Virgil Thomson's *Four Saints in Three Acts,* Samuel Barber's *Vanessa,* and Douglas Moore's *Ballad of Baby Doe.*

Opus. Latin: work. It is often used in the abbreviated form *op.* A composition or set of compositions is given an opus number (op 53, for example) to show its chronological place among a composer's published works.

Oratorio. A composition on a dramatic religious subject designed to be sung by a chorus and soloists and accompanied by an orchestra. It requires no action, scenery or costumes.

This form originated as early as the twelfth century, but this name did not appear until the sixteenth-century in Rome, where the followers of St. Philip Neri gathered in his chapel of the Oratory for informal devotions and religious singing.

Italian composers such as Carissimi and Scarlatti wrote music on Biblical texts to be used in this form. Gradually this music was transfered from the chapel to the nave of the church and later to large concert halls.

The oratorio reached its highest development in the magnificent works of Handel and Bach.

Mendelssohn's *Elijah* and Sir Edward Elgar's *Dream of Gerontius* are distinguished later oratorios. In the twentieth century Honneger's *King David* and Stravinsky's *Oedipus Rex,* which he calls an opera-oratorio, must be cited.

Orchestra. See Symphony Orchestra.

Overtones. The tones that accompany, more or less faintly, every tone produced by a string, pipe, or human voice. They add luster and richness to the sound. Sometimes they are called *partial* or *harmonic* tones.

Overture. An instrumental introduction to a play, opera, oratorio, and so on. It was highly developed by the Italian Lully in his French works. Mendelssohn established it as a separate one-movement concert number in sonata form, in his "Hebrides" or "Fingal's Cave" overture.

Percussion Instruments. The percussion instruments are those from which sound is obtained by striking them with the hand, a stick, or the like. Among them are kettledrums or tympani, snare drums, bass drums, cymbals, gongs, triangles, tambourines, castanets, xylophones, glockenspiels, and chimes.

Pitch. The place of a tone in the range of musical tones. Standard pitch has been established by a scientific determination of the frequency vibrations of the note called *á*—440 vibrations per second in the United States, 435 in Europe. The starting point of the tuning of an instrument or a whole orchestra is this *á*, the *a* above middle *c* on the piano keyboard.

Plain song. The earliest ritual music of the Western Christian church. It was sung in unison, unaccompanied, and in a free rhythm determined by the stress of the syllables of the text. The plain song still sung in the Roman Catholic Church is now usually called Gregorian Chant. (See page 26.)

Polonaise. A stately dance in 3/4 time which consists chiefly of a promenade of the dancers in couples. It was performed at formal feasts in Poland, where it originated in the sixteenth century, and later became popular in European courts, especially in France. Bach and many of his contemporaries used this form as a concert solo piece. Chopin wrote thirteen polonaises for the piano in which martial and lyric episodes alternate in a brilliant concert style.

Polyphony. Music which combines many melodies, weaving them together. It may be contrasted with *homophony*, which uses only one melody with accompanying chords or broken chords. Another name for polyphony is *counterpoint*.

Polyrhythm. The use of several contrasting rhythms at the same time. Stravinsky used polyrhythm in a striking manner in his "The Rite of Spring," and it has become a favorite device of many other modern composers.

Polytonality. The use of more than one key or tonality at the same time.

Prelude. A prelude may be an orchestral introduction to a play, drama, or opera; or be a solo composition; or it may precede a fugue; or be the opening number of a suite. Since the nineteenth century the prelude has attained independence as a self-contained composition, mostly for the piano. The best examples of this last sort of prelude are pieces by Chopin, Debussy, and Rachmaninoff.

Program Music. Descriptive music, based on a story, picture, character, or event, in contrast to absolute music which is detached from any non-musical subject.

The *Pastoral Symphony* by Beethoven and the symphonic poems of Liszt, Richard Strauss, and others, are good examples.

Recitative. A declamatory style of operatic singing in which the dramatic text suggests the line of the melody and rhythm. The Florentine Camerata (see page 58) first used it in the late sixteenth century. They called it *"stile rappresentativo."* Since the eighteenth century it has been used in opera to speed up the dramatic action.

Requiem Mass. The Roman Catholic Mass for the dead. Its first words, *"Requiescat in pace,"* mean "May he rest in peace."

Famous Requiem Masses were composed by Mozart, Berlioz, Verdi, and Gabriel Fauré. Brahms' German Requiem is not a true Requiem Mass, but in modern times Benjamin Britten and Delius have composed well-known Requiem Masses.

Rhapsody. An instrumental composition in one movement and in a very free style. It often employs folk melodies or national themes. Liszt popularized this form with his Hungarian Rhapsodies for the piano. Gershwin wrote his "Rhapsody in Blue" on jazz themes.

Rhythm. Everything that has to do with the duration and accenting of musical sounds.

Ritornelle. From Italian: *ritornello,* a little return. It may be a refrain, or a recurring instrumental interlude between verses of a song, or an interlude in a concerto, or a melody played between the scenes of an opera.

Rondo. A composition for a solo instrument or an orchestra whose first theme alternates with the second and third, thus reappearing unchanged several times. In the eighteenth century the rondo became a regular part of the sonata, concerto, symphony, and chamber works, often as the closing movement.

Round, or rota. A short vocal canon in which the singers begin the melody at different times. (See page 48). One of the finest rounds is the Reading Rota, "Sumer is I-Cumen In," which was written down in 1310 A.D. or earlier.

Sarabande. A slow, grave Spanish dance of Moorish origin. In the eighteenth-century dance suite it generally appeared with courtly dignity before the final gigue.

Scales. From Italian: *scala,* a ladder. The major and minor scales are "ladders" of seven steps between one tone and another one octave distant. (See Major and Minor Scales.)

Scherzo. Italian: sport or jest. A descendant of the minuet, this form developed as a symphonic movement until Beethoven discarded the name minuet and called it a scherzo. He speeded up its lively tempo and intensified its humorous character, filling it sometimes with sarcasm and merciless fury. Through this enrichment of its character the scherzo has also become an independent one-movement composition. Outstanding examples are the four scherzos of Chopin.

Serial Music. A twentieth-century technique developed mainly by Schoenberg, and employing the twelve-tone scale. It uses a chosen set or series of tones for its fundamental thematic material. This chosen series is strictly preserved in its rhythmic and melodic sequence though it may be inverted, diminished, or augmented in its time value, written backwards, or combined into chords.

Sonata. A composition for one or more instruments, usually composed of several movements of contrasting character. The word means a piece to be played, as opposed to *cantata,* which is a piece to be sung.

When a sonata is written for more than two instruments it takes on different names: trio for three instruments; quartet, for four instruments; quintet, for five instruments, and so on. A sonata for full orchestra became a symphony.

The form was highly developed in the eighteenth century by Carl Philipp Emmanuel Bach (a son of Johann Sebastian Bach), Haydn, Mozart, and Beethoven.

The characteristic musical pattern of the classical sonata consists of three sections: exposition, development, and recapitulation, sometimes with a coda. With Beethoven the development and coda sections took on increasing importance.

Among the best-known sonatas are Beethoven's "*Sonata Pathétique,*" "*Sonata Apassionata,*" Sonata for Violin and Piano (which is called the "Kreuzer Sonata"), and the Sonata in B-Flat Minor (which contains the familiar "Funeral March") and Liszt's sonata "After the Reading of Dante."

String quartet. 1) A group of four persons who perform on two violins, a viola, and a cello.

2) A composition for these four instruments, usually in sonata form.

This was a favorite form of Haydn, Mozart, and Beethoven. In modern times Bartók and Shostakovich have used it, as well as contemporary Americans such as Elliot Carter, Quincy Porter, and Roger Sessions.

Suite. An instrumental composition in several movements which is not a sonata or a symphony. Dance forms were organized into suites in the seventeenth and eighteenth centuries. These included allemandes, courantes, sarabandes, and gigues. Bach's French and English Suites are the best-known examples. The simple two-part form of these dances is an ancestor of the classic sonata form. In more recent times a suite often contains selections from an opera, ballet, or film score. Notable examples of modern suites are Grieg's *Peer Gynt Suite,* and Tchaikovsky's *Nutcracker Suite.* A suite is usually lighter by nature than a symphony or a sonata.

Symphony. A large composition for orchestra patterned on the sonata form. It usually has four movements, though these may be extended to five or six or welded into one continuous whole. It may be scored for chamber orchestra or for large orchestra.

The symphony was developed by Haydn, taken over by Mozart, and brought to a spectacular climax in Beethoven's Ninth Symphony. Well-known examples are Haydn's *Surprise Symphony,* Mozart's *Jupiter Symphony,* Beethoven's *Eroica, Pastorale,* and Ninth symphonies, four symphonies by Brahms, and Dvorak's *New World Symphony.* In America Charles Ives, Roy Harris, Peter Mennin, Roger Sessions, William Schumann, Leonard Bernstein, Howard Hanson, Walter Piston, Aaron Copland, and many others have written symphonies.

Symphony orchestra. One that is large enough and skilled enough to perform a symphony. It often has as many as a hundred players. These are divided into four groups or sections: strings, woodwinds, brasses, and the percussion instruments.

The symphony orchestra grew out of a small ensemble of which the first violinist or concert master was the leader. He indicated the start, tempo changes, and so on, by motions of his head and hand while he himself played.

Symphonic poem. Sometimes called a *tone poem,* it is a large orchestral work inspired by some extra-musical subject, such as a poem, a historical event, or a personality. It is akin to a symphony, but its combined sections flow in one uninterrupted stream. Franz Liszt's "*Les Preludes*" and Richard Strauss' "*Ein Heldenleben*" are good examples of symphonic poems.

Te Deum. A hymn of thanksgiving for which the Roman Catholics use a Latin text and the Protestant churches, texts in their own languages. Sometimes the Te Deum is set to a plain song melody. It was a favorite of Handel, who wrote it not only for church services, but also for ceremonies such as coronations.

Tetrachord. A ladder-like group of four tones in alphabetical sequence. It was first constructed by the ancient Greeks, who welded two tetrachords into an eight-tone scale or mode.

Theme. A musical idea, a group of tones that make a statement. In some compositions, like fugues, the theme is called a subject. When it is used as "theme and variations" the theme forms a complete musical sentence on which the variations are based.

Toccata. From Latin: *toccaro,* to touch. A lively display piece for a keyboard instrument (piano, organ, or harpsichord) in which polyphonic and free passages alternate in a rhapsodic manner. It is a virtuoso piece which invariably displays brilliant technique. Today the toccata may be written for any instrument or combination of instruments, as a movement of a symphony, concerto, suite, and so on.

Some of the best-known toccatas are those by Bach for the organ and harpsichord. Many twentieth-century composers—Debussy and Ravel, for example—have found the rapid motor-like character of the toccata appealing. Among contemporary toccatas is Louise Talma's Toccata for Orchestra.

Tonality. See Key.

Trio. The middle section of a minuet or scherzo in a classical sonata or symphony.

For instrumental trio, see sonata. A vocal trio is a composition sung by three independent voices.

Unison. When two or more voices sing the same melody in the same pitch they are said to be singing in unison. The term can be applied to a chorus of men and women. Then singing in unison means singing the same melody, but one or two octaves apart from one another.

Variations. Musical episodes that embroider a tune by means of melodic, harmonic, and rhythmic additions, changes, and enrichments.

There have been innumerable examples of variation in keyboard literature ever since the sixteenth century. Well known among these are Orchestra Variations on the "St. Anthony Chorale" by Brahms and Edward Elgar's "Enigma Variations." The American contemporary Elliot Carter has written Variations for Orchestra.

Well-tempered tuning. The system by which keyboard instruments (that is, piano, organ, and harpsichord) are tuned today. It is also called "equal-temperament tuning." This method of tuning equalizes the distances between any tone and the tones immediately next to it. It makes C-Sharp and D-Flat the same. This is in contrast to the acoustical mathematical calculation, in which some C-Sharps are higher in pitch by a few vibrations than some D-Flats.

Because well-tempered tuning was not practiced until the end of the seventeenth century, a retuning of the keyboard instrument for different keys was necessary up to that time.

Bach wrote the famous *Well-Tempered Clavier,* to demonstrate the versatility of an instrument tuned in this "equal-temperament" way.

Woodwinds. Woodwinds are a group of wooden or wood-and-metal instruments whose tones are produced by blowing into them (as with the clarinet) or across them (as with the flute). They include flutes and recorders, oboes, English horns, clarinets and bassoons. These form an important section of a symphony orchestra.

Index